Thomas Nugent, Eobald Toze

The Present State of Europe

Vol. 1

Thomas Nugent, Eobald Toze

The Present State of Europe
Vol. 1

ISBN/EAN: 9783337320157

Printed in Europe, USA, Canada, Australia, Japan

Cover: Foto ©Suzi / pixelio.de

More available books at **www.hansebooks.com**

THE

PRESENT STATE

OF

EUROPE:

Exhibiting a View of the

NATURAL AND CIVIL HISTORY

OF THE SEVERAL

COUNTRIES and KINGDOMS:

THEIR PRESENT

CONSTITUTION and FORM of GOVERNMENT; their CUSTOMS, MANNERS, LAWS, and RELIGION; their ARTS, SCIENCES, MANUFACTURES, and COMMERCE; their MILITARY ESTABLISHMENTS, PUBLIC TREATIES, and POLITICAL INTERESTS and CONNEXIONS.

To which is prefixed,
An INTRODUCTORY DISCOURSE on the Principles of POLITY and GOVERNMENT.

By M. E. TOTZE,

Late Secretary to the Univerfity of Gottingen, and now Profeffor of Hiftory in the Univerfity of Butzow, and Duchy of Mecklenburg.

Tranflated from the GERMAN

By THOMAS NUGENT, LL.D.
And Fellow of the Society of Antiquaries.

VOL. I.

LONDON,
Printed for J. NOURSE, Bookfeller to HIS MAJESTY.
MDCCLXX.

TO HER

SERENE HIGHNESS

ULRICA,

PRINCESS OF MECKLENBURG.

MADAM,

THE following Work having been firſt publiſhed in your native tongue, under the auſpices of that excellent Prince, the Duke, your brother, may, with ſome propriety

A 2 claim

claim the patronage of your Highnefs, when cloathed in a language for which you have conceived fo extraordinary a predilection. It is indeed a circumftance highly glorious to the literature of this nation, that a Princefs of fuch amiable accomplifhments, fhould dedicate her leifure hours, which too many of her fex are apt to wafte in trifling amufements, to the ftudy of our language, fo as to delight in the beft Englifh authors, and to read them with a true tafte for their beauties. The fubject of this performance may alfo render it not unworthy of your notice, fince you have been ever ready to improve your mind, not only with the perufal of works of polite literature, but likewife

DEDICATION.

wife with the nobler studies of religion, history, and politics. I am too sensible of your delicacy to indulge a vein of panegyric on this occasion, by enumerating the many virtues which have rendered your Highness the delight and ornament of a court, renowned for its urbanity, and the generous encouragement of true piety and learning. History may afford a better field for so pleasing a topic; here I am confined, and cannot praise without offending. I shall, therefore, content myself, at present, with declaring, how happy I am to have this opportunity of paying a distant homage to your princely perfections, and of publicly testifying the pro-

found

found respect and esteem with which I have the honour to subscribe myself,

MADAM,

Your HIGHNESS's

Most obliged, most devoted,

And most humble Servant,

THOMAS NUGENT.

THE

AUTHOR's PREFACE.

THE advantages of political knowledge having been so well explained by many able pens, I may save myself and the reader the trouble of repeating what has been already said upon that subject; I shall therefore be satisfied with laying before him a succinct account of the method and scope of this work.

Besides the introductory principles, in which the plan of the whole performance is stated, and the maxims and technical terms of the science are explained, I have prefixed a short dissertation on Europe in general, as well to assist the reader in forming a clear idea of the present state of our quarter of the world, as to give a connected view of several necessary and useful observations relative to this subject, which must have been otherwise totally omitted, or scattered up and down with less method and congruity. I am nevertheless apprehensive left this precaution may have occasioned another inconveniency, namely, that of some repetitions. Care, however, has been taken, that these should be as few as possible, and for these few I entreat the reader's indulgence.

In the description of each state, I have made use of the most authentic writers and informations that I could possibly procure, and these I have punctually quoted, not only as vouchers for what I advance, but for the conveniency of such as may be desirous of a more circumstantial acquaintance with the matter in question.

The

THE AUTHOR's PREFACE.

The objects deserving notice are, in every state, so numerous, that I could only sketch the outlines of them. In some, however, and especially the forms of government, I have been more explicit; and together with their constitution, I have given an account of their principal revolutions, and shewn how the present system came to be established. This to me appeared the more necessary, as in all European states, and even those where the form of government has lately undergone a total change, some practices and usages still obtain, the cause and origin of which are to be found only in the antient polity. The knowledge of them will contribute to a better understanding of historians, particularly in points relating to reasons of state; as those especially of the middle ages, for the greater part, contain only jejune narratives of transactions, without one word concerning the caufes. This will fufficiently evince, that politics and hiftory mutually tend to illuftrate each other.

As I have been circumftantial on the antient forms of government, fo in the article of monies I propofed to fhew their former ftandard and value. The writers of all nations, and efpecially thofe of the middle ages, mention feveral kinds of money now no longer current, but without fpecifying their value. I took fome pains with regard to this article, in order to remove the uncertainty in which it leaves many curious readers; but, for want of proper information and helps, I have not been able to accomplifh my defire. Hiftories of antient times likewife mention monies in their modern names, as Reals and Maravedis in Spain, and in France Livres, Sols, and Deniers, but with an infinite difference in value from that which they bear at prefent; another
fource

source of perplexity to readers, as not acquainted with the proportion between the antient and the prefent coins. I could, on this account, have wifhed myfelf in a capacity to have indicated the gradual alteration of the ftandard in every ftate, as then the reader might have eafily compared the value of the old monies with that of the prefent, and thus calculate the amount of whatever fums occur in hiftories and records. But this, from the caufe abovementioned, I have not been able to compafs, except in the French, Englifh, and Swedifh coins, and thefe, I own, but very imperfectly.

At the end of every chapter I have enumerated the feveral treaties concluded between the refpective powers, at one view pointing out both the mutual relation between different ftates with regard to certain rights and obligations, and at the fame time their greater or leffer fhare in the general tranfactions.

One

THE AUTHOR's PREFACE.

One apology I have ſtill to make, and that is concerning the title of this work, as promiſing a deſcription of all the ſeveral ſtates of Europe: whereas for want of information adequate to that extent, I am obliged to confine my plan to thoſe ſtates, which have a confiderable influence in the general affairs of this part of the globe. However, to complete my plan, I propoſe, if this Eſſay be approved, to publiſh the State of Germany, with the addition of a brief account of the temporal and ſpiritual monarchy of the fee of Rome, as having always acted a leading part in every important tranſaction in the ſeveral governments of that communion.

THE

THE

TRANSLATOR's PREFACE.

*T*HE *following work was originally written by that learned Profeſſor Mr.* Edward Totze, *a name well known to many* Engliſh *gentlemen, who have travelled in* Germany. *The polite behaviour, exemplary morals, and extenſive erudition of this judicious author, render him ſo deſervedly the object of public notice, that it is proper I ſhould give ſome account of him, for the information of ſuch gentlemen as have not been abroad. Such a precaution, indeed, appears in ſome meaſure neceſſary with reſpect to readers of every claſs, ſince, according to the obſervation of a celebrated writer, men ſeldom peruſe a book with pleaſure, till they have ſome knowledge of the character and perſonal qualities of the writer.*

Mr. Edward Totze, *the ornament of* Germany, *which gave him birth, was led by his*

early

The TRANSLATOR's PREFACE.

early inclinations to the study of the law, which he pursued with the most assiduous application at Jena, Helmsted *and* Halle: *but he had a particular taste for the nobler parts of jurisprudence, the law of nature and nations, the study of politics and history. In order to increase the inlets to knowledge, by the perusal of the best books published in foreign countries, he was at the pains of learning most of the modern* European *languages. He at last settled at* Gottingen, *where he translated several* English *books into* German, *among others* Lord Anson's *Voyage round the World, and the learned Dr.* Campbell's *Lives of the* English *Admirals. In the year* 1755, *he was chosen secretary to the university of* Gottingen; *and in* 1761, *he was invited by the duke of* Mecklenburg Schwerin *to fill the place of Professor of History in the university of* Butzow, *founded by his serene highness in the year* 1760. *There he distinguished himself by his great assiduity and care in his public department, and employed his leisure hours in completing the present work, which had been the chief object of his attention during a considerable number of years. It was published at length in* 1767, *and soon met with the universal approbation of the literati of* Germany. *The preceding year, viz.* 1766, *I had the honour of getting acquainted with the learned author in my tour through*

The TRANSLATOR's PREFACE.

through Mecklenburgh, *and have ever since thought myself happy in cultivating his friendship. This gave occasion to his sending me a copy of the present work; and, upon an accurate perusal of it, I thought I should do a considerable service to this kingdom by translating it into* English.

Amongst other circumstances, which concur to render this a valuable performance, there is one that cannot fail to recommend it to the curious. Mr. Totze *has been at the utmost pains and expence in procuring a true state of facts from every government in* Europe; *so that the accounts of the several military and civil departments may be depended upon. The list of the military forces of* Russia *he received from the learned Mr.* Busching, *who lived several years at* Petersburg, *and is well acquainted with the state of the* Russian *empire. With regard to the affairs of* Denmark, *it will be proper to mention, that at the author's request I had the honour of waiting upon that worthy minister Baron* Dieden, *envoy extraordinary from the court of* Copenhagen; *this visit procured me those remarks which occur at the end of the chapter of* Denmark, *and were written by the learned and very ingenious Mr.* H———. *The notes interspersed throughout the work, were designed for the use of those who may happen to be desirous of a more cri-*

tical

tical knowledge of the subject; and some were added by the translator, to rectify a few errors that have escaped the pen of our learned professor. Besides these instances of the author's care to render his performance every way worthy of the public esteem and approbation, he has favoured me with several corrections and additions down to the present year, which must greatly contribute to enhance the value of the present edition. It has also another advantage, that of a complete Table of the most interesting particulars contained in the whole Work: such tables are usually placed at the conclusion of a book, but I thought it no impropriety to invert that position, in order to preserve an equality in the size of the volumes.

INTRODUCTORY PRINCIPLES

OF

POLITY AND GOVERNMENT.

SECT. I.

THE earlieſt ſtates fell very ſhort of their preſent perfection. They who firſt united into large civil ſocieties, had no other view than ſecurity againſt foreign and domeſtic violence; which, indeed, was ſufficient for their original ſimplicity and rudeneſs: but the gradual invention of Arts and Sciences introducing a more refined manner of living, and at the ſame time more wants, they enlarged their firſt ſimple plan; and not contented with bare ſafety, affected conveniency, elegance, and pleaſure; the combination of which conſtitutes what we call public welfare. Thus it was that ſtates, in procefs of time, attained to that perfection which they at preſent enjoy, eſpecially in our part of the world: ſo that a ſtate, conſidered according to its preſent nature and conſtitution, conſiſts of a large ſociety

States at firſt not ſo perfect as at preſent.

Definition of a ſtate.

society of men, united under one government, for the maintenance and advancement of their common security and welfare.

SECT. II.

End of society. Thus the end of a state is the security and welfare of all its members; the prospect of this happy situation having been the principal motive for uniting into one body: a natural consequence of which is, that they must live together, and be possessed of a certain part of the earth. This is called the State's *The state's territory.* *Territory*; and the body of the inhabitants *The people.* are the People. The land is the property of the people, if constantly inhabited by them; for the roving savages of the northern parts of Asia and America, cannot be said to have any certain property: as they stay only for a time, their property necessarily ceases on their removing from the country.

SECT. III.

The right of ordaining and transacting whatever is necessary for the safety and welfare *Sovereignty.* of the state, is called the Sovereignty. *Administration.* The exercise of this sovereignty is the Administration; and the person who exercises it is distinguished by the title of Sovereign. He has, consequently, a power of directing the conduct of all the other members of the state.

OF POLITY AND GOVERNMENT.

state, in a manner correspondent to that end of society; or, which is the same thing, of prescribing laws to them; and they, being obliged to pay obedience to such laws, are named *Subjects*.

Subjects.

SECT. IV.

The form of government is the stated manner according to which the sovereignty is to be exercised. This is various; either by one single person, or by a select number of the better sort, or, in fine, by the body of the people. A state under the first form is a Monarchy; under the second, an Aristocracy; under the third, a Democracy. When one of these three forms obtains alone, the government is called Simple; and when two, or all three are united, it is denominated a Mixed Government. The question which of these three several forms is the best, has been concisely and energetically decided by an English poet:

Form of government.

Monarchy.
Aristocracy.
Democracy.
Simple, or

mixed government.

> For forms of government let fools contest,
> Whate'er is best administer'd is best. (*a*)

SECT. V.

Those states in which aristocracy and democracy obtain, are generally called Free States, or Republics; the former, very im-

Free states.

(*a*) Pope's Essay on Man, Epist. ii. v. 304.

B 2 properly;

properly; for, in an ariſtocracy, the nobility are juſt what the monarch is in a monarchy; and as little liberty is left to the other members of the ſtate as in the latter (*b*). The name of a free ſtate properly belongs only to a democracy, the whole body of the people having then a ſhare of the government, and conſequently a public freedom (*c*).

SECT. VI.

Monarchy, the moſt antient form of government.
The monarchical form is indiſputably the moſt antient (*d*), being derived from that of the father of a family, who was in ſome meaſure ſovereign of his own houſe: and as they had ſuch a government daily before their eyes, it was perfectly natural that, at the firſt inſtitution of ſtates, one perſon ſhould be inveſted with the ſupreme power (*e*).

Riſe of free States.
But the free ſtates, or republics, are moſtly derived from monarchies; the abuſe of which form of government ſtimulated the oppreſſed people to ſhake off the yoke; and this, as ſufficiently appears from the hiſtory of all ages, gave riſe to moſt republics (*f*), both antient and modern.

(*b*) See Mr. Juſti's Nature of States, ſect. 74, 76.
(*c*) Wolf. Inſtit. Juris Nat. et Gentium, ſect. 990.
(*d*) Juſtin. lib. 1. c. 1.
(*e*) Science du Gouvernement par M. de Real, Part. I. Tom. I. p. 73.
(*f*) Ibid. p. 75.

SECT.

OF POLITY AND GOVERNMENT.

SECT. VII.

What is meant by United States. Several states have sometimes, in support of their common safety, entered into a perpetual alliance. These are called United States *, signal instances of which we find in ancient and modern history; as in the Greek (*i*) and the Achaian Republics (*k*); in the Swifs Cantons, and the States of the United Provinces. The nature of such United States renders certain assemblies necessary for deliberating on the public concerns, and resolving on the measures suitable to critical conjunctures (*l*).

SECT. VIII.

In the general consideration of a state, we meet with four essential objects. 1. The territory or country. 2. The inhabitants or people. 3. The government. 4. The end of government, or state-interest. But in the consideration of any single state, these objects have their particular contingencies, *Contingencies of a state.* which distinguish it from every other sove-

---

* Syftema Civitatum.
(*i*) Potter's Antiquities of Greece, Vol. I. Book I. Chap. xvi. p. 89. Histoire des Anciens Traités, par M. Barbeyrac, Part I. p. 1, 2.
(*k*) Ubbonis Emmii vet. Græc. Tom. III. p. 274, &c. Mart. Schokii Refp. Achæor. et Vejent. p. 6.
(*l*) Puffendorffii Differt. de Syftem. Civit. §. 17 in ejus Analectis Polit. p. 312, 313.

reignty.

reignty. Thefe contingencies form what we call the ſtate or condition of a country.

SECT. IX.

Politics in general.
European politicks.

The knowledge of the ſtate or condition of countries is, in a general fenfe, called *Politics:* but when limited to Europe and the prefent time, no more is underſtood by it than an authentic account of the prefent condition of the European ſtates.

SECT. X.

Objects to be treated of in it.

As the particular contingencies of a country, relatively to its territory, its people, its government, and its intereſt, conſtitute its ſtate or condition; fo are thefe four capital objects to be treated of, and illuſtrated in the defcription of each particular country.

SECT. XI.

The prefent ſtate of a country not to be well known without a knowledge of the paſt.

The prefent ſtate of a country arifes from the paſt, and a true knowledge of the former requires a thorough acquaintance with the latter. This we draw from hiſtory, which informs us of the origin of ſtates, with their great events and revolutions. Thefe relate either to the territory of the ſtate, as having either enlarged or curtailed it; or to the form of government; or to the reigning family. All thefe varieties and revolutions

OF POLITY AND GOVERNMENT.

lutions have their particular confequences, and thus are objects of politics.

SECT. XII.

The firſt object to be confidered in a ſtate, is its territory; and in this, 1. Situation. 2. Extent. 3. Natural quality. And 4. Political quality. *[margin: Wherein the territory of a ſtate ought to be confidered.]*

SECT. XIII.

The fituation of a country either relates to the degree of longitude and latitude between which it is included, or more particularly to the contiguous countries, or ſea, with which it is either wholly, or partly, furrounded. The fituation is found in maps, and thefe were known to antiquity*; but *[margin: Situation.]*

---

* The art of delineating countries, or even the whole earth, was known in the moſt antient times. Ariſtagoras, chief of the republic of Miletum, applying to the Lacedemonians for their affiſtance againſt Darius Hyſtaſpis, king of Perſia, brought with him to Lacedemon a brazen table, on which were engraved the whole earth, the ocean, and all the rivers; and by this reprefentation he ſhewed what large and opulent countries the Lacedemonians might conquer, if they would fide with the Milefians. Herodot. lib. V. c. xlv. Alcibiades, valuing himfelf extravagantly on his many eſtates, Socrates took him to a place where hung a table containing the draught of the earth; in order to let him fee how infignificant his boaſted eſtates were in comparifon of the globe he lived on. Elian. Var. Hiſt. lib. III. cap. xxviii. Anaximander of Miletus, is fuppofed to be the firſt inventor of fuch a table, or map. Jo. Scheffer. ad Ælian. l. c.

in

in modern times have received great improvements.

SECT. XIV.

Extent. The extent of a country confists in its length and breadth, but thefe can fcarce be precifely determined; moft countries being of fuch an irregular figure as to caufe a great difparity between its dimenfions in different parts. To this muft likewife be added, that miles are far from being equal in all countries *. In order to come at the moft exact dimenfions of a ftate, recourfe muft be had to a good map, and then bring the country into one or more fquares, meafuring it by geographical miles; and thus giving the whole fuperficial contents † in fquare miles. The boundaries of a ftate are either placed by nature itfelf, as mountains, rivers, and fea; or are fettled between neighbouring ftates by exprefs, or tacit conventions; the

---

* A juft comparifon of the miles in different countries is that in Bufching's Geography, viz. one degree on the equator is equal to ten Swedifh miles and a half; thirteen Hungarian miles and a half; fifteen common German, or geographical miles; feven Silefian; feventeen and a half Spanifh; twenty fea leagues; twenty-five common French; fixty common Italian; fixty-fix one and a half Turkifh; feventy Englifh; an hundred and four Rufian miles, or werfts.

† See Bufching's Introduction to the Knowledge of the Nature and Conftitution of the European States. Templeman's New Survey of the Globe. Likewife, the Rev. Mr. Sufmilche's Book on the Divine Œconomy in the Viciffitudes of the Human Species.

former

OF POLITY AND GOVERNMENT.

former are called natural, the latter political limits.

SECT. XV.

In the natural quality of a country are to be confidered its good and bad natural properties; as its air and weather; whether it be level or hilly, well-watered or dry, fruitful or fterile. *Natural quality; in which is to be confidered, its*

The air and temperature is very different on fome parts of the earth; and the latter, fometimes, is partly owing to the climate: for the nearer the equator, the greater generally is the heat; and confequently, the farther from it, and the nearer to the poles, the more intenfe the cold. The fituation, however, does not abfolutely determine the heat and cold, it being manifeft from undoubted experience, that the moft eaftern and weftern countries are much colder than thofe which lie between thofe extremities *. In mountainous places, likewife, the air is colder than in flat countries, but on that account the pureft; along the fea-coaft it is foul, and very variable (*l*). *air and temperature;*

* Ruffia is a proof of the feverity of the cold in the more eaftern countries. See Bufching's Geography, Vol I. See the like obfervation concerning the weftern countries. See alfo Anfon's Voyage, Book II. ch. v. and Mr. Ellis's Voyage to Hudfon's Bay.
(*l*) Bufching's Introduction, fect. 18.

Hills

INTRODUCTORY PRINCIPLES

hilly or level;

Hills are computed by some to take up the tenth part of the continent (*m*); the highest are under the equator, and towards the south pole (*n*). Hills, in some respects, as on account of the woods with which they are covered, the waters issuing from them, and the minerals in their bowels, are of an advantage to a country; not to mention the salubrity of air.

Lofty and steep hills, however, and especially of a considerable extent, are great inconveniencies. They deprive the country of too much ground, as being fit neither for tillage nor habitation; likewise, volcanos are often found among the vast chains of mountains; and what terrible neighbours these are, the histories of all ages afford deplorable instances: for not to mention their eruptions, the adjacent countries are subject to earthquakes, by which whole cities have been destroyed and swallowed up (*o*). Thus flat countries, being secure from such dangers, have great advantages over the mountainous; and as they are fitter for agriculture, they can maintain more inhabitants.

watery or dry;

Lands destitute of water must necessarily lie waste, as neither men nor cattle can live

(*m*) Burnet's Theory of the Earth, Vol. I. c. xi.
(*n*) Lehmanni Specimen Orographiæ generalis, (Petrop.)
(*o*) Whiston's New Theory of the Earth, Book II. Hypoth. 3. p. 84.

in

OF POLITY AND GOVERNMENT.

in them; whereas rivers and waters not only promote fertility, but likewife, when navigable, are a great conveniency to inland trade; and for the laft purpofe, where there is a want of them, art affifts nature with canals.

A country is fruitful when it brings forth plentifully whatever the fupport, the wants, and the conveniency of the inhabitants require; and when deficient in thefe, it may be faid to be barren. Fertility includes the feveral productions of the animal, vegetable, and foffile kingdoms *. The former contains the quadrupeds (1), the birds (2), infects (3), and fifhes (4); but of all thefe, fuch

fruitful, or unfruitful.

---

* *Animalia* funt corpora organifata et viva et fentientia, fponteque fe moventia. *Vegetabilia* funt corpora organifata et viva non fentientia. *Lapides* funt corpora congefta nec viva nec fentientia. C. Linnæus in Syftem. Nat. Tom. I. p. 6.

(1.) Among the tame beafts, the principal, by reafon of their ufe, are, the horfe, afs, mule, horned cattle, fheep, and goat; and among the wild, the ftag, deer, and hare: the bear, wolf, and fox, though detrimental as beafts of prey, yet, like the otter and beaver, are in fome meafure ufeful on account of their fkins. Some beafts, as the fable, black fox, ermine, hyena, and fome kinds of fquirrels, afford fuch fine furs, that their fkins fetch a very high price. See Bufching's Introduction.

(2.) Birds may in general be divided into land, water, and fhore-birds; and are ferviceable to mankind by their flefh, eggs, and feathers. Bufching, fect. 56. The cider-duck is particularly remarkable for its incomparable down. Concerning it, fee Mr. Anderfon's Account of Iceland, Greenland, and Davis's Streights.

(3.) Of thofe, the moft beneficial are the bee and filk-worm. Penfylvania has a fpecies of caterpillar which delights in one particular tree, and fpinning filk not inferior to that of the

fpe-

ſpecies only come within the verge of politics, as are of domeſtic or commercial uſe. This is likewiſe applicable to the productions of the vegetable kingdom, to which belong all trees (5), ſhrubs (6), grain, plants, and fruits (7). The foſſile kingdom contains the greateſt treaſures of the earth; thoſe noble metals gold (8) and ſilver, by which the value of all things is regulated; cop-

---

ſilk-worm. Commentar. de Reb. in Scient. Nat. & Medicina Geſtis. Vol. I. p. iii. p. 483. where this is cited from the Philoſophical Tranſactions, Vol. LI. Part I. p. 54.

(4.) The largeſt of theſe is the whale, which moſt abounds in the North Seas, where a great number of ſhips of all nations are annually employed in that fiſhery. With regard to the ſeveral kinds of whales, ſee Anderſon. The other ſpecies of fiſhes which come under obſervation, are, the ſalmon, cod, tuſk, ling, herring, pilchard, and tunny; being articles of conſiderable trade. See Buſching's Introduction. Among ſhell-fiſh, the moſt noted are the lobſters, crabs, oyſters, and muſcles; the moſt valuable of the laſt are the pearl muſcles. The great Linnæus has found the ſecret of multiplying pearls by art. Concerning this, ſee Profeſſor Schreber's Diſſertation in the Mecklenburgh Gazette for the year 1763, N° 5 and 6.

(5.) Among the trees are chiefly to be conſidered thoſe which yield timber, fuel, and likewiſe wood for handicrafts, together with fruit-trees.

(6.) Beſides the ſpice-trees and ſhrubs, are farther to be noticed in the vegetable kingdom, the vine, the ſugar-cane, the cotton-tree, indigo, woad, ſaffron, kali. Buſching, ibid.

(7.) Hemp, flax, grain of ſeveral kinds, tobacco. Concerning the laſt, which is of American origin, ſome curious particulars are to be found in the Chevalier d'Oliveyra's Memoirs of Portugal, Tom. II. p. 275.

(8.) Gold is not only eminently uſeful, as it can be coined and worked various ways, but as in the hands of chymiſts it affords many excellent medicines. Lewis Siries, a French cutler, has diſcovered a method for giving ſuch a temper to gold, that any cutting inſtrument may be made of it. Hamburg Literary Gazette for 1762, N°. 25.

per,

OF POLITY AND GOVERNMENT. 13

per, iron, tin, lead, and the femi-metals (9); likewife gems (10), and other valuable (11) or ufeful ftones (12); befides thofe ufed by the ftatuaries and architects (13). To the foffile kingdom, likewife, belong clays (14), dies, coals, falts (15.) and mineral waters.

SECT. XVI.

Next to the natural is to be confidered the political ftate of a country: this comprifes the improvements it has received from the government. All ftates had not originally their prefent extent, having gradually acquired more lands, partly by inheritance and efcheats, and partly by conquefts. This aggrandizement produced the divifion into provinces or diftricts, with their cities, towns

Political nature; in which is to be confidered

the divifion into provinces, and thefe into cities, towns, and villages.

(9.) Quickfilver, antimony, cadmia, zink, bifmuth, cobalt.
(10.) Thefe are the diamond, topaz, chryfolite, hyacinth, ruby, garnet, amethyft, fapphire, opal, beryl, and emerald. See Bufching's Introduction. The names, properties, and country of gems, together with inftructions for ufing them in drefs with tafte and propriety, are to be found in Mr. Pouget's Treatife on Jewels, and the way of ufing them in Paris, 1762. Quarto.
(11.) Cornelian, agate, jafper.
(12.) Among thefe may be juftly claffed the magnet, a black and unfightly ftone, which attracts iron, and has been greatly conducive to the improvement of navigation fince the year 1300, when Flavio Gifia, an Italian of the country of Amalfi, difcovered the ufe of the magnetic needle.
(13.) Porphyry, marble, alabafter.
(14.) Porcelane, fuller's earth, terra figillata.
(15.) Of thefe there are three kinds, rock, fpring, and fea-falt.

and

and villages, which owe their being to the several occupations and ways of living of the inhabitants: according to the rules of good policy, cities should be appropriated to trade, manufactures, arts, and handicrafts; towns only to such shops and handicrafts as are of absolute necessity, with a little farming; and the villages intirely to agriculture, grasiery, and farming (*p*).

SECT. XVII.

Into the mother-country and dependencies. When lands are acquired, whether by arms or otherwise, instead of their being immediately incorporated with the state, such are more generally accounted dependent provinces, subject to its sovereignty, and treated accordingly. That country which is the main part of the state, and the seat of government, is termed the mother-country; while the acquisitions are called dependencies. These, consequently, are not on a footing with the mother-country, but must content themselves with the stipulations entered into at their subjection, or surrender. The distinction between the mother-country and the dependencies, shews itself most in free-states; for whereas part of the inhabitants, as

(*p*) Busching's Introduction.

OF POLITY AND GOVERNMENT.

in an ariſtocracy, or all, as in a democracy, have a ſhare in the government; the people of theſe dependencies are mere ſubjects, and totally excluded from every ſuch privilege: ſuch, for inſtance, were the Corſicans in reſpect to the Republic of Genoa. Dependencies, however, ſo far from being a conſtant advantage to a ſtate, ſometimes bring it into great inconveniencies; as, when lying at a great diſtance, and convenient for a powerful neighbour, ſo that it is difficult to defend them: ſuch was formerly the caſe of the Spaniſh Netherlands, very remote from Spain and contiguous to France.

SECT. XVIII.

The ſecond capital object relating to a ſtate is, the people, or inhabitants. Thoſe have either founded the ſtate originally, or, as foreign invaders, have maſtered it by force. The latter event has chiefly been occaſioned by wars and migrations. There are, indeed, few ſtates in the univerſe who can boaſt of the former circumſtance, and prove an uninterrupted ſettlement in their preſent territories; for the more ancient a nation is, or pretends to be, the more uncertain is its origin, and that of the ſtates founded by it, and the deeper it lies involved in fable and obſcurity.

The inhabitants.

It

INTRODUCTORY PRINCIPLES

It is the fame with the names of people and ftates, which have undergone different mutations at diftances of time. Moft countries in Europe, Afia, and Africa, which were fubject to the Roman empire, on its overthrow came to be called by new names. The names of fome modern ftates are derived from foreigners who conquered them. Thus, for inftance, France received its denomination from the Franks; England from the Angles; Scotland, from the Scots; Hungary from the Huns. Some people, on the other hand, are called by the antient and modern name of their countries; as the prefent Spaniards from Spain, the Portuguefe from Portugal. Sometimes the capital has given its name to the ftate, as Naples to the kingdom fo called; and the Ruffian empire, for a very long time, bore the name of Mufcovy from its chief city.

SECT. XIX.

What to be confidered in them. On the people depend the ftrength and power of a ftate, and no lefs its weaknefs and impotency; therefore the qualities both of their bodies and minds, their virtues and vices, number, language, different degrees, and parties, are to be confidered.

SECT.

SECT. XX.

To the bodily qualities belong large- *Influence of the climate* neſs and beauty, and the oppoſite defects. *on the body.* There is in general a very great difference in the bodies and faces of men, according to the nature of the country. This is not purely owing to the heat or cold of the ſeveral climates, but to the grains, vegetables, and other aliments, which they produce, and are uſed by the inhabitants for food. A certain writer has remarked, that the human ſpecies towards the north-pole, are brown; from thence to the ſixtieth degree, red; from thence to the forty-fifth, fair; from thence to the thirtieth, yellow; afterwards greeniſh, then ſwarthy, and laſtly, under the tropics, black (*q*): that the northern people are large, fair-complexioned, with lank red hair, blue eyes, ſanguine, and their blood thick; the ſouthern, of a middling ſtature, brown complexion, black and curled hair, black eyes, their blood thin, and in no great quantity (*r*). Another learned perſon di-

(*q*) Spirit of Nations, lib. I. c. vi. p. 34. Linnæus in Syſt. Nat. p. 3. makes the following diſtinction of the complexions of men according to the four parts of the world: the European, white; the American, reddiſh; the Aſiatic, tawny; the African, black.
(*r*) Spirit of Nations, p. 36.

Vᴏʟ. I. C vides

vides the whole human race into three nations, alike in ſtature, ſhape, and features. The firſt are known by a hideous countenance, ſwarthy ſkin, large jaw-bones, ſmall flat noſe, ſmall hollow eyes, little or no beard, black hair, and jolt heads. Among theſe he claſſes the Calmucs, Mungals, Oſtiacs, and other people of Siberia; the Samojedes, Greenlanders, Chineſe, Japaneſe, Americans, Indians, and Africans. The ſecond nation have handſome faces; and this claſs he makes to conſiſt of Jews, Turks, Perſians, Armenians, and Georgians. The third nation are the Europeans and Tartars; and theſe he accounts the founders of the north-weſt people of Europe (*s*). But the difference of the bodies and faces of people in different countries is ſcarcely greater than that of their ideas of beauty. Thus the Moors place it in the blackneſs of their faces; the Chineſe and Calmucs in a flat viſage; nay, the Omaguas, a people of South-America, preſs the foreheads of their new-born children between two boards, in order more effectually to give them that odd figure (*t*).

(*s*) P. V. Havens nye og verbedrede Efterratninger om der Ruſſiſke Rige, 11 Deel, cap. v. p. 101, &c.

(*t*) Condamine's Travels into the inward parts of South-America, Vol. II.

Th'

OF POLITY AND GOVERNMENT. 19

Health. The different situation and quality of countries have an influence on the health of the inhabitants. Accordingly, different nations have their peculiar distempers; such as the leprosy and pestilence, in the eastern and southern countries. The venereal distemper is said to have been first known in the islands of the New World, when discovered by Columbus, and to have been brought into Europe by the Spaniards (*u*) : of this, however, some make a question (*w*).

SECT. XXI.

Mental qualities. As the climate has an influence on the body, it cannot be denied to affect the mind; whose dispositions depend not a little on the nature of the body. The effect of the different climates herein is manifest from the corresponding nature both of the country and inhabitants (*x*). Experience shews a temperate climate to be the best adapted to the human understanding; and in antient and modern ages,

---

(*u*) Guicciardini's History of Italy, lib. II.
(*w*) Schreiber in Observationibus de pestilentia quæ annis 1737, 1738, in Ucrania grassata est. Petropoli 1750. Sanchez, in the Journal de Medec. Tom. XI. p. 372.
(*x*) Florus, lib. III. c. iv. sect. 2. says of the Allobrogians, or Savoyards, " Atrox cœlum, perinde ingenia ;" and cap. iv. sect. 4. of the Thracians, " Sylvarum et montium situs cum ingenio consentiebant." The like is applicable to the savages of North America.

C 2 such

such has been the seat of arts and sciences: whereas the very hot or very cold countries never produced many great geniuses, or great scholars. The like difference between men living in different climates, appears in certain virtues and vices. The northern people, their bodies being steeled by the sharpness of the weather, are less inclined to a soft way of life, and sensual gratifications, than the southern, with whom voluptuousness is the predominant vice (*y*). They likewise can bear labour and hardships: thence their fitness for war, and their intrepidity in danger, which the luxurious people of the south and east dare not face.

> Omnis in Arctois populus quicunque pruinis
> Nascitur, indomitu bellis et Martis amator.
> Quidquid ad Eoos tractus mundique teporem
> Labitur, emollit gentes clementia cœli (*z*).
>
> In cold laborious climes, the wintry north
> Brings her undaunted hardy warriors forth;
> In body and in mind untaught to yield,
> Stubborn of each, and steady in the field;
> While Asia's softer climate form'd to please,
> Dissolves her sons in indolence and ease.

This truth, which was known even to remote antiquity, is perfectly confirmed by history; the northern nations having generally vanquished the southern; and the

---

(*y*) See Spirit of Nations, book I. ch. vii.
(*z*) Lucan. lib. viii. 353.

OF POLITY AND GOVERNMENT. 21

greateſt and moſt remarkable conqueſts having been carried on from the north ſouthwards (*a*). The northern people have always been fond of liberty, and eſtabliſhed it in all their colonies; whereas the ſouthern have ſubmitted to deſpotic governments, being little better than ſlaves to their princes (*b*). The north has always been famous for fidelity and probity; whereas the ſouth lies under the imputation of treachery, craft, and deceit (*c*).

SECT. XXII.

The effect of the climate is alſo obſerved in the languages *, the number of which is infinite †; and that occaſions another diverſity among people. At firſt there was no ſuch variety of languages, but many are derived from the intermixture of nations, occaſioned by migrations and conqueſts ‡.

The language.

(*a*) Spirit of Laws, l. XVII. c. iv. Spirit of Nations, l. I. c. vii. p. 45.
(*b*) Ibid. c. ii. & iv.
(*c*) Concerning the difference of men in different climates, ſee a Diſſertation written in German, On the Climate, and its Influence on the Human Mind.
* At leaſt in the pronunciation. Spirit of Nations, B. I. c. xlvii. &c.
† This is particularly ſeen among the multitudes of ſmall tribes of ſavages in America; all ſpeaking different dialects. The Spaniards once took twenty Indians priſoners, ſeven or whom were found to ſpeak quite different languages. Vita e lettere di Americo Veſpucci.
‡ The Jews boaſt that God, at the building of the tower of Babel, altered the univerſal language, but left it to

Lan-

Languages may be divided into original or dialects: the former have no affinity with any other; the latter in some measure correspond with one or more. From the multiplicity of languages are derived the many differences in writing and letters: of these the Chinese characters are the most numerous, the most difficult, and the strangest *.

Language deserves a place in a political consideration, no farther than as well framed and improved to a certain degree of ornament and perfection: for some nations affect a preference of language for euphony, copiousness, and force; as antiently the Greeks and Romans, and at present the French. 'A language chiefly recommends itself to foreign nations, by the useful and entertaining books which it has produced. On this account it is that we learn several living and dead languages.

SECT. XXIII.

Number of inhabitants. The strength of a state is estimated by the number of its inhabitants: the

---

be used by them as his own peculiar people; and that therefore the Hebrew is the most antient tongue. Univ. Hist. Vol. I. p. 356.

* The Chinese, instead of an alphabet, have as many characters as words, to the amount of eighty thousand; consequently scarce possible to be learned. Du Halde's China, Vol. II.

greater

OF POLITY AND GOVERNMENT. 23

greater the increafe of people, and the more they excel in bodily and mental qualities, in ingenuity and wealth, the greater the power of the ftate. It is not extent of territory alone that makes a ftate powerful, it muft be fuitably inhabited; and a government fhould by all means promote population. There are few ftates in the world which could not admit of more inhabitants than they actually poffefs (*e*). The whole earth, according to fome computations, would contain fourteen thoufand millions; whereas the aggregate number of its inhabitants does not exceed a thoufand or eleven hundred millions; and the people in many countries are ftill in a lefs proportion to the number which could fubfift there (*f*). The chief impediments to population are famine, war, and peftilence, or epidemical contagions; otherwife the inhabitants of fome countries would, in a certain number of years, be doubled (*g*). But from the preceding, and other caufes, connected with the internal arrangement of a ftate, this cannot come to pafs; fo that the whole body of human fpecies, confidered in general, and one country compared with ano-

(*e*) See M. Sufmilch. Vol. II. c. xx. fect. 378, and 395.
(*f*) Ibid. fect. 375, 405.
(*g*) Ibid. Vol. I. c. viii. fect. 152, 153.

C 4 ther,

ther, continues without any confiderable alteration of number. It is, indeed, manifeft, that fingle diftricts and towns fometimes increafe very faft from particular caufes; but this increafe, inftead of continuing in the like extraordinary proportion, has a certain term, where it ceafes. Inftances of this are, Paris, London, and Amfterdam, where the inhabitants have, for a long time, known no confiderable increafe (*b*).

SECT. XXIV.

Different degrees.

The citizens of a ftate are not all on a level; the laws, or cuftoms, giving to fome perfons or families a dignity, accompanied with privileges; and fuch pre-eminence

---

(*b*) Sir William Petty has, from a comparifon of the burials in a courfe of years, fhewn, that fince the year 1565, the inhabitants of London have been doubled every forty years; and accounts, that fuch duplication will continue till about the year 1800, and then ceafe. The number of the inhabitants in the faid year 1565, he ftates at 77040; and in the year 1682, when the duplication muft have come about near three times, he makes them 669930. From the year 1682 to 1722, he computes another duplication; and from the latter to the year 1762, ftill another. Thus the number of inhabitants of London muft, in the year 1722, have amounted to 1,339,860; and in 1762, to 2,679,920. Sir William Petty's Effays on Political Arithmetic, p. 7—17. But experience has already confuted this calculation; for London, fince the year 1730, when it might have had fomething above the number Petty gives it in the year 1682, has rather decreafed in inhabitants. See Sufmilch, Vol. II. c. xxv. Thus London, in all appearance, will never attain to the grandeur and populoufnefs which Sir William affigns to it in the year 1802, viz. 5,339,440 fouls.

confti-

OF POLITY AND GOVERNMENT.

conſtitutes Nobility. This dignity either ceaſes with the life of the perſon, or deſcends to his heirs: the firſt is called *perſonal*, the other *hereditary nobility*, which obtains in all the Chriſtian parts of Europe; whereas in China (*i*) and Turkey (*k*), and other deſpotic governments, only perſonal nobility takes place.

As the nobility are diſtinguiſhed from the other inhabitants of the ſtate by their privileges; there is, likewiſe, a difference between the latter, owing to their office and manner of living, or occupation, either in the towns or in the country: hence ariſe ſeveral degrees among the inhabitants; and theſe conſtitute different ſtates or conditions in the political body.

SECT. XXV.

In large and popular ſtates, it is no uncommon caſe for ſome men to entertain relatively to certain objects different thoughts and diſpoſitions from their fellow-citizens. An open declaration of theſe their thoughts and diſpoſitions, and as open an oppoſition to them, eſpecially if carried to violence, are productive of parties; and theſe affect

Parties in a ſtate.

(*i*) Du Halde, Vol. II.
(*k*) Buſbequ. Epiſt. I. p. 40, 100. Beeman. in Hiſt. Orb. Terr. Geogr. et Civ. P. II. c. x. ſect. 16.

their

their reciprocal intercourfe. This divifion is either in matters of belief or in politics; and thus the parties are called either Religious or Political. Such parties are particularly owing to the internal defects and diftempers of republics, and ftates of a mixed government; and are of fuch dangerous confequence, that it greatly concerns the fupreme powers to apply efficacious remedies againft this evil before it grows to a head; as, befides its other various inconveniences, it may break out into tumults and civil wars.

SECT. XXVI.

Government; what to be confidered in it. The exercife of the fupreme power makes the third capital object in the confideration of a ftate. In this are included, 1. The conftitution, or fyftem of laws; and 2. The departments of the feveral offices of the adminiftration.

SECT. XXVII.

The form of government in a ftate is known by its fundamental laws, to which the adminiftering power is obliged to conform. Thefe fundamentals are very different in all ftates, feveral of them depending on the original eftablifhments made by the

OF POLITY AND GOVERNMENT.

the people, or introduced by subsequent revolutions.

In some states they are many, in others few; in some they are committed to writing, and in others only traditional. The contents of the fundamental laws are called the Constitution, or Legal System. Now amidst such a difference in the fundamental laws of states, the constitution must also differ; and in proportion to the greater number of fundamental laws, its legal system must be more widely extended.

SECT. XXVIII.

When the sovereign of a monarchy is, in certain cases specified by the fundamental laws, bound to exercise the supreme power according to the opinion of the nobility, or the body of the people, such a monarchy is said to be *limited*. This makes the mixed form of government, in the first case, *monarchical* and *aristocratical*; and in the latter, *monarchical, aristocratical,* and *democratical.* The view of such a mixed arrangement is, that the regal prerogative being limited, the liberty of the subject may in some measure be maintained: but this is scarce reconcileable with the first of these governments; for it has all the inconveniencies of aristocracy; and the people

being

A limited monarchy.

INTRODUCTORY PRINCIPLES

being excluded from all share in the government, instead of enjoying any freedom are generally oppressed. In the second, however, where the power of the prince, of the nobility, and the people, is tempered by a proper distribution, freedom extends itself to every individual of the state; and this form of government has manifest advantages over the other two. When the power however of the three governing states is not justly distributed, so as to form an equipoize, but one of the three preponderates, intestine disturbances and civil wars, and even a total subversion and change of the former government may be apprehended. This is what befel England under Charles I. The democracy having gained the upperhand, the House of Commons raised itself on the ruin of monarchy and aristocracy. The consequence was a bloody intestine war, and the subversion of the form of government, which afterwards, from being first an anarchy, became a democracy; and lastly, was modelled almost into an unlimited monarchy. The like baneful consequences will certainly shew themselves in such a mixed form of government, when the aristocracy, instead of being duly balanced, infringes on the monarchical and demo-

OF POLITY AND GOVERNMENT.

democratical power, even so as to abolish them.

SECT. XXIX.

Persons, or assemblies, to whose opinion the monarch is to refer in the exercise of the sovereignty, are called States of the kingdom. These in an aristocratical monarchy are only the Great, or the Nobility. Such was the original constitution of all the monarchies founded by the German and Northern nations, and still subsisting in Poland (*m*); whereas in monarchies mixed with aristocracy and democracy, besides the nobility, the People form one of the states. At particular conjunctures, when, by the constitution, the king cannot decide of himself, the States of the kingdom are to be assembled; and such assembly is called the *diet*. The resolutions of their assemblies are generally regulated by a majority of votes, a perfect unanimity being scarce possible among such numbers: accordingly, where such unanimity is required, it is very seldom that an affair is carried into execution. The power of kings and states, with regard to affairs brought before the diets, and the resolutions taken concerning them,

States, or diets.

(*m*) Justi's Nature and Essence of States, §. 75.

are

are to be regulated by the constitutional laws. In some states, the prince may refuse his assent to resolutions which the other two States have agreed to; and there are states where he is absolutely obliged to acquiesce in such resolutions.

SECT. XXX.

An unlimited monarchy. If the government of the state is lodged intirely in the monarch's pleasure, this constitutes an unlimited monarchy. Here the prince exercises the sovereignty in an arbitrary manner, according to his own sentiments, and uncontrouled by any of those limitations, with which the prerogative is tempered in mixed monarchies; *Regis in unius concedunt omnia legem.* An unlimited monarch, however, is not to be looked on as raised above all human laws, and so as to have a power of making his own pleasure the rule of government; for even an unlimited monarchy is not without certain tacit fundamental laws, which it behoves the prince to observe (*n*).

SECT. XXXI.

A despotic state. If the sovereign, besides his unlimited prerogative, be invested with the power of

(*n*) Ibid. p. 67.

a lord

OF POLITY AND GOVERNMENT. 31

a lord over his slaves, such a state is called a despotic government; and the sovereign a despot. Now as a lord makes the most he can of his slaves, so in a despotic government, both the persons and substance of the subjects are devoted to the avidity and passions of the despots; consequently their welfare, in his eye, is a meer collateral concern (o). But as such servitude is diametrically contrary to the end of society, a despotic sovereignty is, with very good reason, not classed among the particular forms of government, but considered as a corruption and abuse of monarchy (p). The despot, however, being not only regent, but likewise lord of his subjects, the government is absolutely subordinate to his will. Yet there are, even in despotic kingdoms, some ancient fundamentals, which the sovereign himself is not to violate; such as the established religion, and the succession to the throne. Were the Grand Seignor himself, with all his unbounded sway, to attempt any alteration in either of those two articles, it would, very probably, cost him both his throne and his life.

(o) Wolfe's Institut. Jur. Nat. et Gent. §. 997.
(p) See M. Justi's Nature and Constitution of States. sect. 65. The Greeks looked on despotism as a medium between monarchy and tyranny. Vid. Jo. Nic. Hertii Elem. Prudentiæ Civilis, P. I. sect. ii. §. 5.

SECT.

SECT. XXXII.

The system of laws in a limited monarchy, is of a wide extent; in the unlimited, short; and in despotic states, the shortest of all. Where the fundamental laws are many, the system of laws is extensive; and where few, it is concise. Now a limited monarchy having most fundamental laws, the legal system must of course be multifarious. The unlimited monarchies having but few, and despotic still fewer, the system of laws in the former is but short, and in the latter still more compendious; therefore it may well be said, that the will of an unlimited monarch, and much more of a despot, constitutes the substance of the legal system.

SECT. XXXIII.

A kingdom, or monarchy defined. A monarchy, whether limited or unlimited, is called an empire, or kingdom; and the sovereigns of them emperors, or kings.

SECT. XXXIV.

Hereditary and elective kingdoms. The sovereignty may be conferred on the sovereign, either for his own person, or at the same time for his heirs. In the first case, the kingdom is called *elective*; in the second, *hereditary*. If in the latter the hereditary succession be limited to the male *Male, and mixed, succession.* line alone, this is termed a *male succession*; but

but where females likewife are admitted to the fucceffion, this is called a *mixed fucceffion* (*q*).

SECT. XXXV.

Election-compact.

Some nations prefer election to hereditary fucceffion, as better calculated for fecuring their rights and privileges, and keeping the monarchical prerogative within falutary limits. For this purpofe, they lay before the new-elected fovereign certain conditions, which in his future government he muft promife, upon oath, moft punctually to obferve. Thefe conditions thus propofed, and by the prince folemnly agreed to, is called the election-compact. This is fometimes accompanied with a declaration, that if the elected prince acts contrary to them, he thereby forfeits his dignity; or that whatever he does contrary to that compact, fhall be of no force. Such declaration in the firft cafe is termed *lex commiſſoria*; in the fecond, *lex caſſatoria* (*r*). The election-compacts are the primary and chief fundamental laws of a ftate; as thofe of ancient date are fometimes explained or al-

---

(*q*) See Kahrel's Law of Nature, Part IV. chap. vii. fect. 14.
(*r*) Everard Otto in notit. rerump. proleg. fect. L. (5).

tered by others more recent. But the people, even in hereditary ſtates, having a right, on the extinction of the reigning family, to elect a new ſovereign; may, likewiſe, lay down to him certain conditions as a rule of government, and by the two laws abovementioned, bind him and his deſcendants to the punctual obſervance of the compact.

SECT. XXXVI.

An hereditary kingdom may become an elective, and vice verſa.
The ſupreme power in hereditary ſtates reverting to the people, on the failure of the reigning family, they may alter the form of government as they think fit, and turn an hereditary into an elective ſtate; as, on the other hand, the ſtates of an elective kingdom are at liberty to make the throne hereditary.

SECT. XXXVII.

Ceſſation of the government.
The government, or regency, ceaſes by the death, reſignation, or depoſition of the ſovereign.

SECT. XXXVIII.

Guardians requiſite in an elective kingdom;
The throne in elective kingdoms becoming vacant by the demiſe of the ſovereign, guardians of the kingdom are to be appointed for conducting the government till the election of

OF POLITY AND GOVERNMENT.

of a new sovereign, unless he has been chosen whilst his predecessor was still living; for, in such a case, he immediately takes possession of the throne (*s*).

SECT. XXXIX.

In hereditary kingdoms, the throne, in-*and sometimes even* stead of being vacant by the demise of the *in heredi-* sovereign, immediately devolves to the law-*tary kingdoms.* ful successor: but in case of his being a minor, tutors or guardians are appointed for his person, and a regency for managing the affairs of the kingdom. The latter must likewise be instituted when the monarch, by reason of other impediments, cannot take the reins of government into his hands.

SECT. XL.

That a sovereign may resign the supreme *A sovereign* power, unless the fundamental laws, or *may resign the sove-* election-compact, have enacted otherwise, is *reignty.* unquestionable; but whether he can be deposed, is a more difficult and important question. The case mostly occurs in limited kingdoms, and especially if he has subjected

---

(*s*) Of this Germany affords many instances, which have given rise to the proverbial saying, "When the emperor dies, the king seats himself in the saddle." See M. Eissenhart's Maxims of the German Law in Adages, p. 559.

him-

himself to the law of forfeiture (*t*). In elective kingdoms, the consequence of such deposition is the choice of a new sovereign; in hereditary kingdoms, the investiture of the next heir: but when the deposition is attended with a total change of the form of government, the royal family is likewise excluded from the succession.

SECT. XLI.

Title and arms. States have their particular arms and titles, which are borne by the sovereign. The title consists in the enumeration of the dignities belonging to him, on account of the kingdom and its dependencies. Titles differ not a little, according to the different usages of nations; but those assumed by the Eastern and other barbarian monarchs, are the most singular and extravagant (*u*). The arms of a state are emblems of the dignity and the possession of its territories, or of its right to them; for sometimes the state bears both the title and arms of countries which it is not in possession of. This

---

(*t*) Huber de Jure Civit. Lib. I. Sect. ix. cap. vi §. 17, 25.
(*u*) Ammian Marcellinus, lib. XVII. p. 103, mentions a letter from Sapor, king of Persia, to the emperor Constantius, with this preamble; " Sapor, king of kings, prince of the stars, brother to the sun and moon, &c." The causes of this turgid title are specified by that writer, l.b. XXIII. More instances of strange titles assumed by the Asiatic and African kings, may be found in Becman's Synt. Dignit. Illustr. Dissert. III.

is

OF POLITY AND GOVERNMENT.   37
is partly to keep up a claim to them, and partly in memorial of former poſſeſſion.

SECT. XLII.

On the acceſſion of a ſovereign, there are certain ceremonies performed both in elective and hereditary kingdoms; they are proclaimed, crowned, and receive homage. {Solemnities on a ſovereign's acceſſion.}

The coronation is a ſolemn act in which, the ſovereign being anointed, the crown put on his head, and the regalia delivered to him, he is publickly inaugurated. Not that this formality is of abſolute neceſſity: for in certain circumſtances it may be omitted (w). Homage chiefly conſiſts in the ſubjects taking an oath of fidelity and allegiance to their ſovereign. {Coronation.} {Homage.}

SECT. XLIII.

The ſovereign's reſidence is generally in the capital city: his palaces, and other remarkable particulars of the metropolis, are not to be paſſed over unnoticed. The numerous retinue of domeſtics and ſervants of various degrees form his houſehold, and impart a ſplendor and air of grandeur to the court. {Sovereign's reſidence.}

(w) Nettelbladt Diſſert. de Coronatione ejuſque effectu inter gentes, cap. III.

SECT. XLIV.

Sovereigns remarkable above others. The sovereign being the principal person in the state, the welfare of which greatly depends on him, particular notice is to be taken of princes, who, by their virtues or vices, their good or bad government, have promoted the welfare and aggrandizement of the state, or injured its prosperity: it is especially proper to get a knowledge of the reigning prince's character.

SECT. XLV.

Observation on the names of sovereigns. The christian names of sovereigns seem quite a matter of indifference; yet have some names been remarked as fortunate in some kingdoms, and unfortunate in others. Ferdinand was formerly accounted a very auspicious name among the Spaniards; and that of Lewis is still beloved and honoured among the French; whereas the name of Henry they look on as ominous; and the Scots have no better opinion of that of James.

> Il ne faut plus nommer Henrys les Rois de France,
> La mort par deux couteauz et un eclat de lance
> A tués trois Henrys: l'un joutant à cheval,
> L'autre en son cabinet, le tiers en son carosse.
> Cirq Rois du nom de Jaques ont fait croire à l'Ecosse,
> Qu'il y a dans le nom quelque secret fatal (*y*).

(*y*) Bierlingii Differt. de eo quod divinum est in historia civili, c. II.

SECT.

SECT. XLVI.

Their families. The like obfervation has been made on fome royal families. That of Capet in France, and that of Oldenburg in Denmark, have been very fortunate; whereas the Merovingians and Carlovingians in France, and the Stuarts in Scotland and England, make a difmal figure in the hiftories of thofe countries.

SECT. XLVII.

Department of the feveral ftate officers. Next to the fyftem of laws come the departments of the feveral officers of the adminiftration. Of thefe are to be confidered, 1. Thofe which relate to the internal conftitution of the ftate; and 2. Thofe which regard foreign affairs.

SECT. XLVIII.

Affairs relating to the internal conftitution of the ftate. To the former belong, 1. The ftate of religion and the churches, together with univerfities, colleges and fchools; likewife, arts and fciences. 2. The laws and courts of juftice. 3. The military eftablifhment. 4. The revenue and commerce.

SECT. XLIX.

Religion. Religion confifts in the articles of belief and mode of doctrine appointed for the worfhip of God. This appointment being various, there are various religions; and thefe, according to the different ideas entertained of the Supreme Being, are principally four; the *Chriftian*, the *Jewifh*, the *Mahometan*, and *Pagan*; all which are fubdivided into many fects. The two laft prevail over the greater part of the earth. Mahometanifm comprehends Turkey, Perfia, the Mogul country, feveral of the Tartar nations, and all the northern part of Africa. Paganifm reigns in China, Japan, Siam, and many other Afiatic countries and iflands: likewife, in a large part of Africa, and a multitude of nations in America. Chriftianity is chiefly feated in Europe, from whence it has been propagated into the three other parts of the world by European colonies. Judaifm confifts of communities difperfed in all the quarters of the earth, and efpecially in trading places.

Difference between the eftablifhed and tolerated religions. A religion introduced and confirmed by a law of the ftate, fo that they who profefs it enjoy all the privileges and advantages appertaining to citizens, is termed the *eftablifhed*, or predominant *religion*.

Sub-

Subordinate to this are the *tolerated* religions, the free exercise of which is matter of favour, and with limitations of privileges to the professors of such sects. According to this division, religion comes within a political consideration only so far as it has an influence on government, and the welfare of the state. It is an observation of baron Montesquieu (*y*), that Christianity is highly advantageous, and productive of the greatest benefits to a state; for as its doctrines chiefly turn on purity and gentleness of manners, with the strongest exhortations to forbearance and brotherly love, it perfectly corresponds with a limited government; and as far remote is it from despotism, which seems, indeed, peculiar to Mahometanism. To the Christian religion mankind is indebted for a certain political system in the government, and for a certain law of nations in war, by which the fury of the conqueror is restrained, and the conquered are protected from extirpation and extreme oppression. But unhappily the same celebrated writer brings in a charge against the Christian religion, that by prohibiting divorces, and by the celibacy of the clergy, and the cloisteral life, it injures popula-

Advantages of Christianity.

(*y*) Spirit of Laws, book XXIV. c. iii.

tion (z). The first accusation rests on the groundless opinion, that were divorces allowed of at will, the number of births would be greatly increased; the second does not affect the Christian religion universally, but only the Romish, and partly the Greek church (a).

SECT. L.

The church is subject to the state.

A number of persons professing a religion, and meeting for the exercise of it, form a society which is called the Church. This being within the state, must necessarily acknowledge its supremacy and laws; and thus, together with all its members, is dependent on the state. The sovereign has a right to keep such an eye over it, that it may not form, or take in hand, any thing contrary to the end of government; but in all things act with temper, and agreeably to the laws of the state: this is the foundation of the State's *spiritual power* *.

Spiritual power.

If a congregation, or church, withdraws itself from the supremacy of the civil government, and sets up an independency, it is said to make a *state in a state*.

(z) Persian Letters, 110, 111, 112.
(a) These erroneous positions are unanswerably confuted by the Rev. Mr. Susmilche, in his Display of the Divine Oeconomy, Vol. II. cap. 18.
* Jus circa sacra.

As

OF POLITY AND GOVERNMENT. 43

As this of courſe muſt be extremely detrimental to the public, the government has a right to prevent it. But as, on one ſide, it is impowered to keep the church in a dependency on the ſtate; ſo, on the other hand, it is not to interfere in the eccleſiaſtical œconomy, or impoſe ceremonies, or articles of belief, as this would be aſſuming a dominion over conſcience, a prerogative to which no mortal is intitled.

SECT. LI.

The ſciences have a near affinity with religion; for the former, by enlightening the underſtanding, promote a convictive acknowledgment of the truths of the latter, the happy conſequence of which is a rectitude of the will : religion, on the other hand, preſents motives for applying the ſciences to a ſalutary uſe, and ſuch as anſwers the end of government. Religion makes good citizens; the ſciences render them capable, ingenious, and uſeful; bringing not only gain and wealth to a ſtate, but conſideration and honour to the whole people. The ſciences are divided into the high and the liberal. In the former are included divinity, law, phyſic, and mathematics; the latter are, hiſtory, philology, oratory, poetry, and muſic.

Advantages of the ſciences.

High and liberal ſciences.

music. These all have their advantages; so that it is the concern of a wise government not to let them want encouragement.

SECT. LII.

Universities, and inferior seminaries. The advancement of sciences requires schools of higher and lower ranks. In the former, called Universities, are taught all the sciences, both the liberal and the higher;* in the latter, youth are only instructed in the liberal sciences, or go no farther than writing, casting accompts, Latin and Greek, and the rudiments of religion. Besides the universities and lower schools, there are some of an intermediate class, known by the name of Academies; where young gentlemen learn the exercises, languages, sciences, and arts becoming their station.

* Though music be reckoned among the fine arts, yet it is very seldom taught by appointed professors: this, however, obtained anciently, and even in some measure still subsists. Alphonso X. king of Castile, in the year 1254, founded in the university of Salamanca a professorship of music, with a salary of fifty maravedis a year. See Ferrera's History of Spain, book IV. §. 461. p. 477. Music has likewise a professorship at Coimbra. Noticias de Portugal por Manoel Saverin de Faria, Discurso V. §. iii. p. 207.
There is likewise a professor of Music at Oxford; and at the English universities, even Doctors of Music are created. See Alberti's Letters on the State of Religion and Learning in Great Britain, Letter XLVIII. and L.

SECT.

OF POLITY AND GOVERNMENT.

SECT. LIII.

The difference betwixt sciences and arts is, that the former consists in a readiness to perceive and illustrate certain truths; the latter, in a facility of performing any thing according to certain rules. The one employs only the intellect: the other, though not exclusively of the mind, depends chiefly on manual skill. The rules in some arts are very simple, so as to be learned by mere practice; in others they are more complex, and deduced from the liberal, or even from some parts of the higher sciences. The former are called common, or mechanical arts, and include all kinds of handicrafts; the latter are stiled the fine arts, of which the principal are painting, sculpture, engraving, and architecture.

Difference betwixt Sciences and Arts.

Betwixt the mechanical and fine arts.

SECT. LIV.

The improvement and increase of sciences are owing to nothing more than to Academies and Scientifical Societies. The discovery of new truths being their professed study, the members of them should be persons of eminent talents. Academies and societies are usually divided into three classes, the mathematical, the physiological,

Advantage of Academies and Scientifical Societies.

logical, and the philological; each with their particular director, and a prefident over all. In imitation of the Scientifical Academies and Societies, have likewife been inftituted Academies of the Fine Arts, as painting, fculpture, and architecture, which by thefe inftitutions have been brought to perfection. With the fame view of promoting the arts in general, great applaufe is due to the Royal Schools as they are called; where youth, befides what is taught in common feminaries, are inftructed in the fundamentals of the fine and mechanical arts.

Academies of the Fine Arts.

Royal Schools.

SECT. LV.

Printing. In the progrefs of the fciences and of literature, Printing has been a main inftrument; manufcripts, or written books, having been formerly fo dear, that none but the rich could purchafe them (*a*). This fcarcity has been removed by the ineftimable invention of the typographical art, which the Dutch afcribe to their countryman Laurence Cof-

---

(*a*) It is related of the famous Anthony Beccatelli, commonly called Panormita, that he fold a parcel of land to purchafe a copy of Livy. In the eleventh century, Gracia, countefs of Anjou, gave for a collection of homilies, 200 fheep, a meafure of wheat, a like quantity of rye, and a like quantity of millet, together with a number of marten fkins. Henault Abregé Chronologique, or Abridgement of the Hiftory of France, Tom. I. p. 154.

ter,

OF POLITY AND GOVERNMENT.

ter, of Haarlem (b); but it is now sufficiently proved, that John Guttenberg, of Strasburg, found out the real printing of books; that is, the art of printing with single moveable types *.

From printing sprung Bookselling, which Bookselling is of such vast benefit to the republic of letters; the writings of the learned being now easily conveyed from one country to another.

SECT. LVI.

The advancement of the sciences shews Laws, the great care of government for the honour and benefit of the state; as good laws are a proof of its wisdom. Laws are rules prescribed by the supreme powers for the behaviour of the subject. A celebrated civilian observes, that nothing is more difficult than to make laws; for to invent and properly express rules in an infinite number of procedures, in an infinite number of cases,

---

(b) See General History of the United Netherlands, Vol. II. p. 112, 113.

* John Guttenberg was born at Mentz, of a noble family, and lived at Strasburg from 1430 to 1445. He afterwards went into partnership with Faustus of Mentz; but a dispute between them producing a law-suit, he was cast, and thereby lost his printing-house. Faustus then entered into connections with Peter Schoiffer, who, between 1450 and 1455, invented the cast types. All this has been sufficiently proved by counsellor Schopflin, in his Vindiciæ Typographicæ. Argentor. 1760. 4. See Leipsic Gazette, N° 18. 1760.

is

is certainly of all things nearest to the Divine wisdom and foresight (*d*). The more the actions of men are directed towards the end of government, that is, towards the general safety and welfare, the better and more compleat are its laws. A perfect code of laws, says a great legislator, would be the masterpiece of the human understanding (*e*): but, adds he, perfection is beyond the reach of human nature. There are innumerable kinds of laws; but here it is sufficient to observe, that they, in general, relate to cases occurring in civil life, or to the public and private safety; forbidding, under proportionate penalties, the doing any injury to another in his property, character, and person: the former are termed *civil*, the other *penal*.

SECT. LVII.

Courts of justice.

The guardians of the laws are the judges, or persons nominated by the government for deciding processes according to the laws of the land, and for punishing malefactors. When several are appointed as one society for this end, it is called a *court of justice*. These courts, before which a cause is brought, are

(*d*) Huber de Jure Civit. lib. II. Sect. I. cap. i. §. 21.
(*e*) Dissertation on the Reasons for confirming or abrogating the Laws. By the author of the Memoirs of Brandenbourg.

stiled

OF POLITY AND GOVERNMENT. 49

ftiled *lower courts*; and thofe to which a cauſe is carried by a ſecond or a third appeal, are diſtinguiſhed by the appellation of *higher juriſdictions*. The capital virtue of higher juriſdictions, judges and courts, is impartiality and diſpatch. Lower Courts.

SECT. LVIII.

The laws and courts of juſtice, however, are not always capable of preſerving the tranquillity of a ſtate, but loſe their ſtrength amidſt the violence and tumult of popular commotions. Now, in order to quell theſe, and likewiſe for the ſecurity of the ſtate againſt the attacks of foreign enemies, a competent body of armed men, from thence called an army, muſt always be kept on foot. This is the leſs to be avoided, war being a common, if not a neceſſary evil in the world; neither religion, nor enlightened reaſon, nor the gradual introduction of refinements in life, having been able to eradicate this ſcourge. Hence a large military force ſeems neceſſary to a ſtate for its own defence; but at the ſame time is a heavy load; as, beſides draining a country of the flower of its men, it brings on enormous charges for the ſeveral branches of liſting, cloathing, and maintaining a Military eſtabliſhments. Army.

VOL. I.   E   large

INTRODUCTORY PRINCIPLES

large body of horse and foot (*f*); for the support of fortifications, magazines, arms, artillery, and an infinite number of other military implements.

SECT. LIX.

Marine. Maritime countries, or islands, being liable to be attacked by sea, farther require a considerable naval force; which is, *To what states necessary.* likewise, indispensibly necessary to a state possessed of dependencies and colonies in the other remote parts of the world, or engaged in an extensive trade to foreign parts; for it is by a naval force both the one and the other must be protected. This is the grand use of a marine. But to a state not so circumstanced, which has neither distant territories nor colonies, nor any considerable foreign trade, a marine is a mere show and parade. For a foreign trade and naval force are intimately connected; so that the latter cannot subsist without the former; it being a nursery for multitudes of seamen, who, upon an emergency, may be removed on board the men of war; an advantage which an uncommercial state cannot possess. Thus the naval power of states which are masters of a considerable foreign trade,

(*f*) Busching's Introduction, §. III.

OF POLITY AND GOVERNMENT.

trade, is natural; whereas that of others is only forced, and sometimes may be baffled, or ruined, by one unfortunate accident.

A marine is infinitely more expensive than a land force; the building and equipment of men of war requiring stupendous quantities of timber, tar, pitch, cordage, iron-work, guns, and other stores and tackling*.

Expence of a marine.

Ships of war are divided according to the largeness of their cannon, and the number of their men; and thus are called a first, second, or third rate ship. Those from the

Difference of ships of war.

---

* In England, about forty years ago, a ship of 100 guns } cost per Sterling.

Guns	£.
100	35553
90	29886
80	23638
70	17785
60	14197
50	10606
40	7858
30	5846
20	3710

Burchet's Compleat History of the most remarkable Transactions at Sea, in the Preface. From this, Lediard, in the Introduction to his Naval History of Great Britain, p. 12, computes the charge of the whole navy of Great Britain, in the year 1734, when it consisted of two hundred and nine ships, great and small, and makes it amount to 2,591337 l. exclusive of rigging, ammunition, provisions, and men. See Lives of the British Admirals, Vol. I. Introduction, p. 14, 15.

The fitting out a sixty-gun ship in Spain for six months, costs, including the pay of the officers, 84000 Escudos de Vellon, about 56,000 dollars. See Theory and Practice of Trade and the Marine, by Don Geronimo de Uflariz, chap. lxxi. p. 266.

E 2   first

INTRODUCTORY PRINCIPLES

first to the fourth *, are stiled Ships of the Line, from their being placed in the line; ships being generally drawn up in a line, when they happen to engage. Those of the fifth and sixth rates are commonly called Frigates (g).

Fleet.   A certain number of ships of war, at least above ten, are called a Fleet; fewer Squadron. make only a Squadron. The commanders of the fleet are an admiral, vice-admiral, and rear-admiral.

Single ships of war are commanded by sea-captains, who, on board their vessels, are as a colonel to a regiment.

SECT. LX.

Revenue.   The support of the sovereign and his houshold, the payment of the several degrees of civil officers, and the military establishment, require vast sums. The state, however, must indispensably have a revenue answerable to such disbursements. The monies and incomes of the state, together with every thing appertaining to the administration of them, are included under the general name of Finances.

---

* For the different rates of the English ships of war, see Chambers's Cyclopedia, or Dictionary of Arts and Sciences, Article RATE.

(g) Campbell's Life and Actions of the British Admirals, p. 14.

SECT.

SECT. LXI.

Money is the common measure of the value of things and labour. Gold and silver having from the most remote times been used for such measure, pieces of these noble metals were marked with the stamp of the state, to ascertain their value. These are called Coins, and have an intrinsic and extrinsic value. The former is the fineness and weight of the metal itself; the latter it receives from an ordinance of the government, which likewise may alter it; whereas the former admits of no change.

Money.

Coins.

The proportion appointed by the laws between the intrinsic and extrinsic value of coins, is termed the standard. The nearer the intrinsic and extrinsic value, the better are the coins; and of course the worse, where the difference is greater.

In the gold and silver for coining money, a great deal depends on the reciprocal proportion of these metals. But this having in all times been so very different, and still continuing so in most countries, nothing positive can be said upon the subject.

Proportion between gold and silver.

SECT. LXII.

The state's revenues arise either from its own property, or from that of the people. Among

The state's revenues.

Among the former are, firſt, the crown-lands, or Demeſnes: theſe are properly aſſigned to the ſupport of the ſovereign, on which account they are inalienable.

Demeſnes.

SECT. LXIII.

From the regalia.

There are alſo certain things and rights, in the uſe and benefit of which the primitive natural freedom of the inhabitants has been taken away, or at leaſt limited: theſe are accounted as the ſtate's property, and bring in certain revenues. Among theſe are, 1. Seas, lakes, and rivers. 2. Highways. 3. Foreſts. 4. Wild beaſts. 5. Mines. 6. Salts. 7. Coinage. From theſe ariſe, 1. The water-royalties; containing harbour and anchorage, bridge, paſſage, and mill-tolls. 2. Paſſports, dues, land-tolls, poſtage. 3. Foreſtagium. 4. Hunting. 5. Working of mines. 6. Salt and coinage. But here it muſt be obſerved, that different ſtates have different royalties; what is a royalty in one country, not being ſo in another (*b*).

Upon certain incomes.

There are farther ſome uncertain and caſual incomes, which are likewiſe reckoned among the royalties; as fines, confiſcations,

(*b*) Vid. Bockmeri Introd. in Jus Publ. Univerſ. Lib. I. cap. iv. §. 10.

inhe-

OF POLITY AND GOVERNMENT.

inheritances of aliens, or thofe who have no heirs, treafures found, and things forfaken (*i*).

SECT. LXIV.

The greater part of the ftate's revenues arife from the property of the people, under the general name of taxes, rates, and duties. Thefe are fo many, and fo various in their nature, as fcarcely to be enumerated in regular claffes. The moft cuftomary are the taxes on land; next, thofe laid on the very perfons of the fubjects, or on their trade, or their fubftance: others, again, on provifions, and other kinds of things for confumption; fuch are head-money, cuftoms, and excife. To thefe may be added, duties on articles of fhew and conveniency, as coaches, chairs, &c. and a multitude of other expedients, by which no fmall part of the cafh of individuals is brought into the exchequer, or public treafury.

Taxes and impofts payable by the people.

In cafes of neceffity the former taxes are augmented, or others impofed; fuch as the twentieth or fifteenth penny, free gifts, loans, &c. Expert financiers, in urgent exigencies, have recourfe to other expedients for raifing confiderable fums; as lot-

(*i*) Huber de Jure Civit. Lib. I. Sect. III. c. vi. §. 40, 41, &c.

teries,

teries, annuities (*k*). But to have always a large fund of ready money at hand, is infinitely the best and most effectual expedient.

SECT. LXV.

How to increase the state's revenue.

The wealth of the subjects being the main source of the state's revenue, every lawful measure should be taken for encreasing the former. The most natural way for this is the improvement of the land and its products; so that all the inhabitants, according to their several degrees and callings, may be employed in a manner beneficial to the state; and thus not only earn a subsistence, but lay up money, or purchase lands.

SECT. LXVI.

Agriculture.

The chief property of the state is its land, which is the more industriously and carefully to be tilled, as from thence must come the primary and most indispensable necessaries; so that the very subsistence of the inhabitants, in a great measure, depends on its products. The great necessity and importance of agriculture is too evident to be enlarged on; and graziery is

(*k*) Concerning these and the advantageous use of them, see Mr. Susmilch, Vol. II. cap. xxiii. §. 507.

OF POLITY AND GOVERNMENT.

so connected with it, that one can scarce subsist without the other.

If a land be so fruitful, that the three kingdoms of nature, or one or other of them, afford a surplus beyond what is necessary for home consumption, this is to be exported abroad, and made a profitable article of trade. But the profit will be much greater, if the natural and raw materials which admit of preparation, be turned into manufactures and fabrics*, before they are carried to a foreign market. Another great advantage of manufactures and fabrics, is, that they procure subsistence to multitudes; and consequently, encrease the number of the inhabitants, and thereby the national strength. *Manufactures and fabrics.*

SECT. LXVII.

Trade consists in the disposing of goods for money, or other goods; that is, in buying or bartering: and it is carried on either among the inhabitants, or with foreigners. The former is called *home*, the latter *foreign* commerce. Goods are ex- *Trade, Home and foreign trade.*

---

* By manufactures are understood such kinds of works, either of raw, or partly prepared materials, in which neither fire or hammer are required; whereas those works which are done by fire and forges, go by the name of fabrics. See Mr. Justi's Grundsatza Der Policey Wissenschaft, §. 150.

ported either by land or water; but the trade carried on beyond sea by ships, is the most considerable, and by which whole nations have become opulent and powerful.

SECT. LXVIII.

Equilibrium of trade. If two nations only barter goods for goods, the trade between them is in equilibrio, to their reciprocal advantage. But where one adds money to make up the deficiency of its goods, the equilibrium no longer subsists; and the sale turns in favour of that which receives the money (*l*).

SECT. LXIX.

Exchange. Trade becoming more general and extensive, many schemes have been invented for its greater exactness and facility; such as exchange and banks. By means of the former, large sums are sent from one country to another in written draughts*: this class of merchants are termed bankers. The main article in banking is the proportion between the specie of one country and that of another; and this is very variable. In the

---

(*l*) Progrès du Commerce, p. 207.

* This invention is attributed to the Jews, who, when driven out of England and France, lodged their money in the hands of certain persons, on whom they afterwards gave draughts to others. See Spirit of Laws, Lib. XXI. cap. xvi.

settle-

OF POLITY AND GOVERNMENT.

settlement of this proportion, the several states must in general regulate themselves by that which has the most ready cash (*m*).

Banks are publick societies, instituted with the consent and guaranty of the state, for receiving money in trust; so that the disposal of it remains with the proprietors, who may transfer it to others. Such banks are particularly called *banks of exchange* (*n*), by way of distinction from *loan banks*, which lend money on interest. Some are of a complex constitution, being both exchange and loan banks (*o*).

Commerce, and particularly the foreign and maritime, is greatly promoted by trading companies. These are under the protection of the state by charter; and the members contribute a large capital, in order for their jointly carrying on some very considerable branch of trade. This capital is divided into a great number of shares (*p*); and according to the amount of them, every proprietor receives his portion of the profits, which is called a Dividend.

Banks.
Trading companies.
Shares.
Dividend.

(*m*) Spirit of Laws, Lib. XXII. c. x.
(*n*) Franck. Institut. Jur. Camb. Lib. I. Sect. III. Tit. xi. §. 1, 2.
(*o*) Progrès du Commerce, p. 167, &c.
(*p*) Ibid. p. 191, 192, &c.

SECT.

SECT. LXX.

Foreign affairs.

The objects of government hitherto considered lie within the inward constitution of the state; we now proceed to foreign affairs. These comprehend every thing relating to war and peace, negotiations, embassies, treaties, alliances with foreign states. The more considerable and powerful a state is, the busier the part it acts on the theatre of the world, and the more various and important must the affairs likewise be, which occur between such a state and foreign powers.

SECT. LXXI.

Administration of government affairs.

The government of a state comprehending so many and such important objects, which the sovereign himself cannot personally conduct; certain persons, or even boards and councils, are appointed, especially in large and monarchical states, for administering the affairs of government, immediately under the prince's inspection, and to transact whatever is necessary therein. These are called the Cabinet, or the Privy-council; and the members of these assemblies are stiled, Privy-counsellors, Cabinet-counsellors, or Ministers of State. Sometimes a Prime Minister is appointed, who,

OF POLITY AND GOVERNMENT.

in some measure, represents the sovereign. The variety of government affairs necessarily causing various departments in it, as those of the church, the law, army, marine, finances, trade, and foreign affairs, &c. each of those is conducted by one or more ministers of state, forming a college or board.

Its several departments.

SECT. LXXII.

The particular provinces and dependencies are governed by an officer, who sometimes, if the country be a kingdom, is stiled viceroy, and generally has a council. Cities and towns have their own magistracy, either of the sovereign's nomination, or chosen by themselves. Villages are subject to the jurisdiction of the prince's officers, and the lord of the manor.

Government of particular provinces and dependencies.

Cities and towns.

Villages.

SECT. LXXIII.

The fourth object of politicks is the ultimate end of the institution of a state, which consists in its security and welfare. As this end presupposes certain means for the attainment of it, the most prudent and mature deliberation is to be used in the choice and execution of such means. This is the business of policy, which lays down rules, by which they who sit at the helm

helm may effectually maintain and promote the safety and welfare of the state. The spirit of these political rules is stiled State-Interest *. In this respect states are to be considered, 1. According to their internal constitution and form of government; and, 2. According to their situation and relation one to another. Thus every state has one set of political rules with regard to its domestic concerns and government, and another for its conduct towards other states. This constitutes a Domestic and Foreign State-Interest.

marginal notes: State-interest. Domestic and foreign.

SECT. LXXIV.

marginal note: Domestic interest of the state.

The domestic includes all lawful means for making the state wealthy, respectable, and powerful; as improving the arts, sciences, manufactures, trade, and navigation; peopling and cultivating the country, and keeping on foot a numerous military force. These are common to all states; but the difference of the forms of government suggests to the sovereign, or members of the government, more particular rules for their conduct in the administration of affairs. Hence arises that particular state-interest which is very different in all governments.

* The Italians term it, *Ragione di Stato*, or, **Reason of State.**

OF POLITY AND GOVERNMENT.

In an unlimited monarchy, the sovereign makes it one of his chief concerns that his power suffer no diminution. Thus it is his state-interest not to allow any order of men, and particularly the great, to become over-powerful; as, in such a case, the unlimited may be reduced to a limited sovereignty. *In an unlimited*

In the latter, the sovereign and the states of the kingdom have an eye upon each other, so that the several orders keep within the limits of the constitution. The first sees, that neither the great nor the commonalty extend their immunities too far, so as to turn the state into an aristocracy or democracy; and the others watch against any stretches of the prerogative, which may prelude to the establishment of arbitrary power. *and a limited monarchy.*

In an aristocracy, the state-interest is to exclude the commonalty from any share of government, and keep them in subjection, that they may not attempt to erect a democracy. On the other hand, it behoves the nobility in the administration to see, that no particular person affect a superiority over others, by which an aristocracy may easily degenerate into a monarchy. *Aristocracy.*

In

Democracy. In a democracy the state-interest is, that an equality be maintained among the citizens, and no extraordinary power or superiority be allowed to one or more over the rest of the body, as such pre-eminence may lead to the establishing of monarchy, or aristocracy.

In a body of united people. In a political body of united nations the capital concern is, that the union be punctually observed: and the object of their chief attention must be, that none of the united members deviate from its obligations, or in the general consultations obtrude its opinions on the others; for this tends, in process of time, to make the others dependent, and the encroaching member becomes a kind of sovereign.

SECT. LXXV.

Foreign state-interest variable and uncertain. Foreign state-interest is, by its nature, not only very different, but likewise extremely variable; for as it relates to the situation, and the proportion of states in regard to one another, that is, the strength and weakness of one in comparison of the other, which in all times and places is not alike; so nothing fixed and certain can be laid down for their conduct towards one another. All that can be said, is, that a state having cause to fear from the power of its neighbours, is to lay hold of every juftifiable opportunity of curtailing it, and be as alert in augmenting its own ftrength and power.

SECT. LXXVI.

This enlargement of dominion, and augmentation of power, has, both in ancient and modern times, been the particular fcope of many nations. Some have placed their profperity in wealth: fome have held war and conquefts to be moft fuitable to their interefts; others an extenfive trade and marine: and others in fine have comprehended in their views both the commercial and military objects.

[margin: Power, or opul-nce, or both jointly, the fcope of many nations.]

SECT. LXXVII.

As individuals, either from a want of underftanding, or from deftructive paffions, do not always make their real welfare the rule of their meafures, the like is not feldom feen in governments. Many ftatefmen are fo fwayed by felf-intereft and other paffions, as to facrifice both the ftate and the people; and in their refolutions and undertakings, turn the deaf ear to juft politics: this is called acting on a falfe ftate-intereft.

[margin: Falfe ftate-intereft.]

Vol. I.   F   SECT.

SECT. LXXVIII.

Reciprocal claims and obligations of states. The behaviour obferved by nations towards one another from ftate-intereft, depends on the rules of policy, and is regulated by the circumftances of the times, which may give them an opportunity of advantaging themfelves: but with legal claims which ftates or their fovereigns have on one another, or with ftipulated obligations, the cafe is very different; thefe being grounded either on exprefs conventions, or public laws, which muft neceffarily be complied with.

SECT. LXXIX.

Obfervation on great ftatefmen and warriors. Great ftatefmen and warriors have often been the chief inftruments of the profperity and glory of nations. The virtues and eminent qualities of fuch deferving perfonages,

Quorum fama inclyta longo
Tempore poft cineres populorum in pectore vivit (*q*),

deferve honourable commemoration in politicks; and as little are the vices and failings of perfidious and weak ftatefmen or commanders, to be paffed over in filence: the examples of both fhould be held out to pofterity; the former for imitation, the latter for admonition.

(*q*) Marcell. Palingenius in Zodiac. Vit. P. M. 119.

of POLITY AND GOVERNMENT. 67

SECT. LXXX.

This is a short sketch of the objects to *Advantages and necessity of politics* be treated of in Politics; and the knowledge of them necessarily recommends itself both to the learned by profession, and to statesmen; to the latter, indeed, they are of indispensable necessity (*r*). The ever-shifting variety of objects is a matter of no small entertainment (*s*): but the knowledge of these requires helps of many kinds, borrowed partly from other sciences, as geography, natural, civil, and literary history; *in general.* together with travels and accounts of countries, state-papers, public records, conventions, treaties of peace, negociations, ambassadors letters, and other state documents; lives of celebrated princes, statesmen, naval and land commanders. (*t*) To these helps, at present, the learned have free access; an advantage to which politics owe their being taught in universities like other sciences (*u*).

(*r*) Vid. 10. Andr. Bosii Introd. General. in Notitiam Rer. pub. cap. IX. et X. §. 2, 3, 4. Everardi Ottonis Notit. Rer. publ.
(*s*) Bosius et Otto, II. cit.
(*t*) Vid. Bosius, cap. IV. V. VI. Otto in Prolegom. §. 68.
(*u*) Vid. III. Achenwallii Dissert. de Notitia Rerum publicarum Academiis vindicata. Goettinge, 1748. 4.

F 2 THE

THE PRESENT STATE OF EUROPE.

CHAP. I.

Of EUROPE in General.

SECT. I.

EUROPA, daughter to Agenor king of the Phenicians, a beauty so accomplished that Jupiter himself became enamoured of her, was by the Antients thought to have given name to our part of the world (*a*). But this derivation being grounded on a manifest fable, or, at least, on very uncertain accounts, a celebrated modern wri-

---

(*a*) Herodot. lib. IV. cap. xlv. Nicol. Gurtlerus in Originib. Mundi, lib. I. cap. iii. cites the following passage from Festus: "It is certain that Europe, the third part of the world, was so called from Europa, daughter to Agenor; but some talk of Jupiter's being in love with her, and carrying her away into that country in the shape of a bull: others, that she was carried off by pirates in a ship which had the figure of a bull in its prow. Some relate that Agenor, with his Phenicians, taken with the beauty of the country, made himself master of it, under colour of his daughter's having been carried away thither.

ter has found the origin of the name in the Phenician words *ur-appa*, White-face; he therefore thinks the Phenicians to have been the firſt who gave that appellation to the Europeans, on account of their fair complexions (*b*), in which they far exceed the ſwarthy Africans.

SECT. II.

Extent and limits.

Europe reaches from the 36th to the 71ſt degree of northern latitude; and thus, a ſmall part excepted, lies in the temperate zone. Its length is uſually reckoned nine hundred geographical miles, from Cape St. Vincent in Portugal, to the mouth of the river Obi in Ruſſia; and its breadth five hundred and fifty ſuch miles, from the North-Cape in Norway, to Cape Matapan in Morea. It is by much the ſmalleſt of the four parts of the world; for were our globe divided into three hundred parts, Aſia would contain 101, America 90, Africa 82, and Europe only 27 (*c*). Europe, on the ſouth, is bounded by the Mediterranean ſea; weſtward, by the Atlantic ocean; northward, it confines on the North and Frozen Seas; and its

(*b*) Bochart Phaleg. lib. IV. cap. xxxiii. p. 337.
(*c*) Preſent State of Europe, Chap. II. p. 113.

eaſtern

PRESENT STATE OF EUROPE.

eastern limits are the Hellespont and the Black-Sea. Farther eastward, it joins to Asia; and the Antients made the river Tanais, or Don, the boundary of these two parts of the world, as the Poet introduces it:

> (*d*) ——————— Tanais diversa nomina mundi
> Impofuit ripis, Afiæque et terminus idem
> Europæ, mediæ dirimens confinia terræ,
> Nunc hunc, nunc illam, qua flectitur, ampliat orbem.
> Luc. l. iii. v. 273, 276.

> With Tanaïs falling from Riphean snows,
> Who forms the world's division as he goes,
> With noblest names his rising banks are crown'd,
> This stands for Europe's, that for Asia's bound.

Modern geographers extend this boundary to the Volga, and others still farther, even to the Obi (*e*): but according to a just observation of Strahlenberg, the Riphean mountains, by the Russians called Kamenoi, or Wellichi Poyas, that is, the Stony, or Great Rocky Girdle, running southward from the 70th to the 54th degree, form the most natural boundary between Europe and Asia; there being on both sides of this enormous chain, a very great difference in the countries, in the animals, and in the

---

(*d*) Lucan. lib. III.
(*e*) Cluverius Introduction to Geography, B. I. c. xiv. Beeman in Hist. Orb. Terr. Geog. et Civ. P. I. cap. iv. §. 5.

products (*f*). By this limitation, however, Europe loses no inconsiderable part of its above mentioned length.

SECT. III.

Mountains. The many mountains in Europe are, by some, reckoned to occupy the tenth part of its continent (*g*). The highest are the Alps, one arm of which runs through France to the Pyrenees, and under that name farther on to the ocean. A second extends itself through Syria, Hungary, Dalmatia, as far as Thrace, and the Black Sea. A third chain takes its course southward through Italy, where it is called the Appennine. The Sudet Mountain, between Bohemia and Silesia; the Hartz in Germany; the Carpathian mountains, which separate Hungary from Poland; are also connected with the Alps. In Scotland, Norway, and Sweden, are likewise several high ridges; and Europe cannot in general be said to contain many tracts quite level.

SECT. IV.

Waters. The greatest part of Europe being environed by the sea, it may be properly called

---

(*f*) Strahlenberg's Northern and Eastern part of Europe and Asia, in the Introduct. Sect. VI. §. 15—19.
(*g*) Burnet's Theory of the Earth, Book I. c. ii.

a large

PRESENT STATE OF EUROPE. 73

a large peninfula; but many of the European countries, inftead of being contiguous to others, are feparated by feveral waters, as France from Great Britain by the Channel; as the latter is from the Netherlands, Germany, Denmark, and Norway, by the German ocean. Between North Jutland, the iflands of Funen and Zealand, and the coaft of Sweden and Norway, is an arm of the North Sea, called the Kattegat, and Skagerrack (1), through which is an inlet into the Eaft Sea (2), or Baltic. This is a very large gulph between Denmark, Sweden, Finland, Ingermania, Eftonia, Livonia, Courland, Pruffia, and Germany. An arm of the Baltic runs northward into Sweden, and another eaftward between Finland, Ingermania, and Eftonia. The former is called the Gulph of Bothnia, the latter that of Finland : farther north towards Archangel, the northern ocean forms a gulph known by the name of the White Sea. The Black Sea feparates Europe from Africa, and through the Streights of Caffa (3) communicates with that of Azoph; (4)

(1) Sinus Codanus.
(2) This name was given it by the Hollanders, who likewife called the Hans-towns Eafterlings, and Eaftern Staples, by reafon of their eaftern fituation.
(3) Bofphorus Cimmerius.
(4) Palus Mæotis.

and

and through the Streights of Conftantinople (5), and the Mar di Marmora (6), with the Egean fea, as this with the Mediterranean: the latter fpreads itfelf into a gulph between the coafts of Dalmatia, Iftria, and Italy, which is called the Adriatic Sea.

The great foreign trade carried on by means of thefe waters, has occafioned moft of the European ftates to become maritime powers.

SECT. V.

Fertility — Though Europe, by reafon of the different quality of the climate and countries, is not every where equally fruitful; yet it produces a fufficiency for the neceffities, conveniencies, and pleafure of its inhabitants, and of many things even a fuperabundance. What little is wanting, or rather the articles of luxury, are imported from the other three parts of the world.

in the animal kingdom. — Of the animal kingdom Europe has the beft and moft ufeful kinds, both of tame and wild beafts and fowls, as likewife of fifhes; though as to fifheries, fome European nations, on account of trade, carry them on to the north and weftward, at a great diftance from the limits of Europe.

(5) Bofphorus Thracicus.
(6) Propontis.

That beneficial infect the filk-worm, which for a long time was a ftranger in Europe*, is now bred in moft European countries.

In the vegetable kingdom, Europe in- *Vegetable kingdom.* deed muft yield to the other parts of the globe, which have a greater number and more valuable fpecies of trees, herbs, and plants. Our principal fruit-trees are likewife of exotic origin †.

The vine, which thrives beft in the fouth part of Europe ‡, is, unqueftionably, a

---

* The Romans had their firft filk ftuffs from Perfia; and it was not till the time of the emperor Juftinian the Great that filk was woven at Conftantinople. He procured filk-worms eggs from India by means of two monks, who taught the people of Conftantinople the method of breeding filk-worms, and making filk. Zonaras Annal. Tome III. in Corp. Hift. Byzantin. fol. 130. Under the emperor Conrad III. Roger king of Sicily having, in his Grecian wars, made fome filk-weavers prifoners, brought them away with him to Palermo, and by thefe was the firft culture and weaving of filk propagated throughout all Sicily and Calabria. Fazellus de Rebus Sicul. Dec. I. Lib. I. in Scriptorib. Rer. Sicul. p. 16, 17.

† Lemons and oranges came from Media and Perfia; cherries from Cerefunt in Pontus; peaches from Perfia; plums from Armenia and Syria; figs and pomegranates from Carthage; and china-oranges from China. Bufching's Introduction, §. 26.

‡ The beft wine in Europe grows beneath the 50th degree of north latitude, and becomes both the more palatable and ftronger, the farther a country lies to the fouthward. Of all the European wines, the Greek are the ftrongeft. The perfon who firft introduced the ufe of Greek wine into Naples, was murdered by his drunken guefts, from a conceit that he had given them a kind of poifon to drink. This fingular adventure is painted as a document on the wall of St. Januarius's church in that city. Pauli Hentzneri Itinerar. p. 313.

a na-a native of Asia; and tobacco, of which at present such quantities are grown in most parts of Europe, we owe to the New World.

In the fossile kingdom.

The fossile kingdom in Europe is not inconsiderable, but we have very little of the noblest metals, gold and silver, comparatively to the other parts of the globe: and tho' several kinds of gems are found in some European countries, yet, like pearls, they do not come up to the Oriental.

SECT. VI.

Division of its countries.

There are in Europe twenty-three independent states, viz. three empires, 1. the German, 2. the Russian, 3. and the Turkish; eleven kingdoms, 4. Portugal, 5. Spain, 6. France, 7. Great Britain, 8. Denmark, 9. Sweden, 10. Poland, 11. Hungary, 12. Prussia, 13. Sardinia, 14. The Two Sicilies; seven free states or republics; 15. The United Provinces, 16. The Helvetic Body, 17. Venice, 18. Genoa, 19. Lucca, 20. Ragusa, 21. San Marino. And lastly, among the independent powers of Europe may be classed, 22. the pope, on account of the ecclesiastical state; 23. and the Knights of St. John, on account of the island of Malta. But the difference between the power and extent of these several states is

very

PRESENT STATE OF EUROPE.

very great; and the republic of San Marino, which the Italians nick-name *La Republichetta*, or the Petty Republic, is to Ruffia fcarce as one to three hundred thoufand.

SECT. VII.

What Europe wants in extent, is abundantly compenfated by the large poffeffions of fome European ftates in the other parts of the world. The greateft, and likewife the beft part of America is under Spain, France, Great Britain, and Portugal. To thofe crowns likewife belong confiderable tracts and places in Africa and Afia; and the poffeffions of the Dutch Eaft-India Company in thofe parts are not lefs valuable: befides, the whole northern part of Afia is fubject to Ruffia. All thefe dependencies taken jointly, are of a much larger extent than Europe itfelf; and this muft create a very high idea of the grandeur and power of the European nations, which muft farther be much heightened by confidering the numberlefs quantities of gold and filver, of gems, and other coftly commodities, with which it is furnifhed by thofe remote countries.

Dependencies.

SECT.

SECT. VIII.

Revolutions in Europe. Europe, in the times of remote antiquity, was inhabited by a multitude of smaller nations independent of one another. Among these, the Greeks and Romans became the most celebrated, by reason of their superior skill in the arts of peace and war, and their extensive conquests. The former erected, under Alexander the Great, an empire of a prodigious extent both in Europe and Asia; but it was of a short duration. The latter, whose whole domain was at first confined to their small town, began with making themselves masters of the several nations of Italy, and afterwards by their victorious arms, extended their dominion in all the three known parts of the globe; so that, according to a poet's expression, the whole universe was subject to the Romans.

> Jupiter arce sua totum cum spectet in orbem,
> Nil nisi Romanum, quod tueatur, habet.
> Ovid. Fast. l. I. v. 85.

This extensive and celebrated monarchy, which amidst many intestine wars and commotions, supported itself for ages, at length became divided into the Eastern and Western empire. The latter was soon overthrown by the irruptions of the Germans and

and northern nations; and from its ruins are risen most of the European states. Among these the French monarchy, by the conquests of Charles the Great, acquired an eminent superiority; to which the revival 800. of the dignity of Western emperor in his person, added a farther lustre: and had his successors equalled him in valour and prudence, it is not improbable that they would have united under their sceptre all the European possessions of the Romans. But by their divisions and misconduct, this monarchy fell into several pieces, of which were formed three kingdoms, Italy, France, and 843. Germany; and at length the Roman western empire was inseparably annexed to the latter.

Christianity coming in time to spread 964. over Europe, brought all the states of this part of the world into a kind of community and union; so that in the opinion of some, the whole European Christendom made but one political body, with the pope for its spiritual, and the emperor for its temporal head (*i*). But this absolutely contradicts the common ideas of the freedom and independency of states. The formality of rank alone excepted,

---

(*i*) Furstenerius (Georg. Guil. Leibnitius) de jure suprematus ac Legationis Principum Germaniæ in præf. et ejusd. Cod. Jur. gent. Diplom. in præf.

the

the emperor has no real dignity above a king; and much less has he been invested with any authority over them. The case, however, has been very different relatively to the spiritual power assumed by the See of Rome. The popes maintained that they are the supreme head, and that the temporal powers are absolutely subordinate to them (*k*). They arrogated to themselves the right of making laws, and issuing orders, leaving to the emperor and kings the honour of obedience. A consequence of this papal ambition were the croisades. By their frantic and turbulent practices all Europe rose up in arms, to wrest Palestine out of the hands of the Saracens, and to restore Christianity in the East by the sword. Their view was to set up a new monarchy in that part of the world; and as all the princes and people vied with each other who should be most forward in sacrificing their blood and treasure in this enterprize, to augment and strengthen the dominion which the popes had already acquired in Europe, the latter in a great measure compassed their design. The emperors of the house of Suabia, who, after the division of the empire of the

---

(*k*) C. I. Extravag. comm. de majorit. et Obed.

Franks,

Franks, became the greatest potentates in Europe, set themselves against the ambition of the popes with great spirit and perseverance; but the latter allowed themselves no rest till they had totally ruined and extirpated so dangerous a family.

Since that time all the European powers have been in a state of mediocrity; for the conquests of Edward III. and Henry V. in France, were of short duration. Likewise the monarchy of the three kingdoms, Denmark, Norway, and Sweden, set up by the renowned queen Margaret, soon saw its period; and the consequences of that union were continual quarrels and wars between those northern nations.

The Eastern empire, which was continually distracted by intestine commotions, and from which the Saracens and Turks had gradually wrested its best territories, was at length reduced to so narrow a compass, as to consist of little more than the capital Constantinople. Of this sultan Mahomet II. made himself master in the year 1443; and he and his successors have ever since bore the title of emperors. Thus sprung up in Europe a new Mahometan state, which has long been formidable to the neighbouring kingdoms of Hungary and Poland, and even to the German empire.

1469.
 The sixteenth century saw a great revolution both in the temporal and spiritual state of Europe. Spain had before been divided into several kingdoms; but the marriage of Ferdinand of Arragon with Isabella of Castile, united most of the Spanish territories under one sovereignty. Soon

1491.
after was discovered the New World, and the Spaniards reduced the greatest and best part of it; so that since these conquests, whole fleets go annually from Spain, and return with immense quantities of gold and

1496.
silver. By the marriage between archduke Philip and the infanta Joan, the Spanish monarchy came to the House of Austria, with the addition of the hereditary states of Burgundy, among which were the greatest part of the Low-Countries, at that time very wealthy. Charles V. who was a fruit

1519.
of this marriage, united in his person the dignities of Roman emperor and King of Spain, being thus the most powerful monarch whom Europe had ever known since the time of Charles the Great.

 France about the same period, received a very considerable aggrandizement in the resumption of all the feudal principalities, and annexing them to the crown: Spain, however, was yet too strong for her. It was this superiority which first put other powers on the scheme of preserving a balance between the two crowns; and Henry VIII. king of England, made it his boast, that he held this balance in his hands (*l*); though in the wars between Charles V. and Francis I. he gave himself little concern about keeping it. Thus the former retained his overpoise with a singular constancy of good fortune till the latter end of his reign, losing it when he was least apprehensive of a reverse. The Reformation, which began 1517. in Germany, brought about a very important alteration of affairs, and very much to the detriment of the see of Rome. Its sovereignty was greatly curtailed in regard both to the arrogance with which it had been exercised, and to its extent. Europe became divided into two religious parties; one adhering to the pope, the other separating from him. The latter he looked on as so many heretics and rebels, whom he was for reducing to obedience by the sword; and particularly he instigated the emperor to take this good work in hand. This prince intended at the same time to execute a grand scheme which he had formed against the liberties of Germany,

---

(*l*) Science du Gouvernem. de M. de Real, vi. partie. p. 446.

1546.
and accordingly was the first European prince who appeared in arms against those who had separated from the Romish church. But the issue of this undertaking fell so short of his expectation, that it put him out of conceit both of the sovereignty and the world.

1556.
He, however, left to his son Philip II. a very large and powerful monarchy; containing Spain, Naples, Sicily, Sardinia, Milan, the county of Burgundy, all the Netherlands, the gold and silver kingdoms of Mexico and Peru, together with other large possessions in the New World. To

1580.
this formidable power Philip added Portugal, and its settlements in the East and West-Indies; so that never was a prince known with dominions of such an extent, having possessions in all the four parts of the globe. But this prince's reign was the period of Spanish grandeur: his continual wars, and those of his successors, extremely impaired the monarchy. They had, indeed, great designs in view: they were for enlarging their dominions, reducing nations who had shaken off their yoke, and assisting Ferdinand II. to extinguish Protestantism, and bring the German princes under subjection. But in every article they miscarried,

carried, and especially in the latter, which France and Sweden frustrated; the trea- 1635. ties of Munster and of Osnabrug put a check on the emperor's power, and secured 1648. the freedom of Germany and the Protestant religion. By those treaties, Europe likewise acquired two new free states: the Swiss cantons, and the republic of the United Netherlands. To the former, the oppressions of the Austrian governors gave rise: the latter was owing to the spiritual and temporal tyranny of the Spaniards: both are memorials of the decline of the Austrian, German, and Spanish power.

From this time, and still more since the 1659. treaty of the Pyrenees, France gained the ascendency. Lewis XIV. grew to be what Charles V. and Philip II. had been: and as all nations had formerly united against Spain for preserving the ballance, so now from the like view, a general alliance was formed against France; and as Charles V. and Philip II. were said to have aimed at the universal monarchy of Europe, so, with like reason, was the same charge brought against Lewis XIV.

This prince enlarged France by many considerable acquisitions in war; which, at the treaties of Munster, the Pyrenees, Aix-

Aix-la-Chapelle, and Nimeguen, were formally ceded to him by Spain and the empire; and in the following war, which was terminated by the peace of Ryſwick, he withſtood half Europe leagued againſt him.

Soon after this he had the ſatisfaction to ſee his grandſon on the Spaniſh throne; but to maintain him in poſſeſſion of it he was obliged to enter on a new and very burthenſome war, in which the confederates had ſo far the advantage, that he was near loſing all the fruits of his fifty years victories. But the queen of Great Britain helped him out of this adverſity by the peace of Utrecht, which was no leſs glorious than advantageous to him; having fully obtained the capital end for which he had embarked in the war, and wreſted Spain and India from the Houſe of Auſtria, though the latter had a much better right to thoſe poſſeſſions.

France, however, had been extremely weakened by this long and bloody war; but Great Britain was rather become more powerful. This crown, beſides obtaining great advantages for itſelf from France and Spain, preſcribed the articles of the peace; by which, among other particulars, Naples, the Milaneſe, and Sardinia, with the Spaniſh Netherlands, were given to the emperor Charles

Charles VI. who made over Sicily to Victor Amadeus Duke of Savoy.

Thus the peace of Utrecht gave to Europe another crowned head, a King of Sicily, who within a few years was obliged to exchange it for Sardinia. 1717.

Before the great war which was carried on in the fouth and weſt part of Europe for the Spaniſh fucceſſion, another had broke out in the north, which laſted much longer, 1700. and occaſioned great revolutions. Sweden, which in the laſt century had been the moſt confiderable power in the north, loſt in this war the greater part of its dependencies, and was reduced to the loweſt ebb. Ruſſia, which before had very little interfered in the concerns of Europe, aggrandized itſelf by its conqueſts, and ſtill more by ſetting up a military force, intirely in the European diſcipline, and by the introduction of arts and fciences, with which, till then, Ruſſia had been totally unacquainted. The ſovereign of this vaſt monarchy, Peter I. heightened its dignity by aſſuming the title of emperor, which, in time, all the European powers 1722. fucceſſively acknowledged.

At the fame period roſe in the north of Europe another confiderable ſtate. Frederic III. elector of Brandenburgh had in the beginning of the prefent century taken on him the 1701.

the title of King of Pruffia, without gaining thereby the leaft increafe of territory; but his two fucceffors, by improvements in the conftitution and police of the country, by good regulations in the finances, by an increafe of the revenue confequential to thofe regulations; and particularly by keeping on foot a numerous and well difciplined army, and by the conquefts which that army has atchieved; has raifed its power to fuch a pitch, that the crown of Pruffia is of confiderable weight, not only in the affairs of the North, but likewife in the general concerns of Europe.

The peace of Utrecht had not totally extinguifhed the conteft for the Spanifh momarchy between the emperor Charles VI. and king Philip V. They came to a frefh

1717.
war in Italy, which, by the powerful intervention of France and Great Britain,
1718.
was firft terminated preliminarily, and afterwards very fecretly at Vienna, by a decifive treaty of peace and friendfhip between the Imperial and Spanifh courts. This clofe alliance, in which the then queen of Spain, Eliza-
1725.
beth of Parma, chiefly aimed at a marriage between her eldeft fon Don Carlos, and the eldeft of the emperor's daughters, Maria Therefa, the prefent emprefs-dowager (*m*), oc-

(*m*) Memoires de Montgon. Tom. 1. p. 149. et fuiv.

cafioned

casioned the treaty of Hanover between 1716. France, Great Britain, and Prussia. Both parties endeavoured to strengthen their alliances, and the principal powers of Europe sided with one or the other. The two branches of the house of Bourbon were now separated, and at open variance; but the Spanish court seeing itself defeated in its capital design, viz. the Austrian marriage, things soon returned into their natural situation. Spain again united itself with France; and the effects of this appeared not long after, in an alliance which they both en- 1733. tered into against the emperor, on his opposition to the French designs in the election of a king of Poland. In this war the emperor had the disadvantage, relinquishing at the peace the kingdoms of Naples and Sicily to Don Carlos of Spain, who thus again encreased the number of sovereigns in Europe. The king of France, to whom this peace gave certain expectations of annexing the Dutchy of Lorrain to his domains, in consideration of such accession, took on himself the guaranty of the emperor's pragmatic sanction, for securing the succession in his dominions; and some years before, Great Britain and the United Provinces had laid themselves under the like obligation. But that monarch dy- 1737.
ing

ing after a very unfortunate war, which, pursuant to his alliance with Ruffia, he had entered into againſt the Turks; France, ſo far from making good the ſaid guaranty, ſupported Bavaria in its claim to the Auſtrian ſucceſſion. The two maritime powers, however, acted up to their obligations with great firmneſs, ſo as to aſſiſt the emperor's heireſs with ſuccours of men and money, and to procure the Imperial dignity for her huſband Francis-Stephen, Grand-duke of Tuſcany. To them, in ſhort, it was owing that, of her father's hereditary dominions, ſhe loſt only Sileſia, Parma, and Placentia. The peace of Aix-la-Chapelle put an end to this war. Europe now found itſelf divided into two great parties, which, by the equality of the forces they could oppoſe to each other, kept the balance in an equipoiſe. On one ſide was Great Britain, Auſtria, Ruſſia, the United Provinces, and the king of Sardinia; the other was compoſed of the three Bourbon branches, the kings of France, of Spain, and of the Two Sicilies, together with Pruſſia and Sweden.

But this ſyſtem was of no long duration. A new war in the mean time breaking out between Great Britain and France about the limits of their American countries, the former entered into an alliance with Pruſſia,

and

and the latter with Austria. To this last alliance acceded Russia, Sweden, and the greater part of the German empire; and at length it came to be farther strengthened by Spain; so that the parties seemed very unequal, and the former by much the weakest; yet at the upshot it proved the strongest. In this war, which was carried on with more animosity and more armies than were ever known in Europe, Great Britain exerted itself to that degree, and with such fortunate consequences, that the united French and Spaniards were obliged to accept of such articles as this power prescribed to them. Thus a comparison of former and present events shews, that as Spain was the first European power in the sixteenth century, and France in the seventeenth, Great Britain may be deemed such in the present century; so uncertain and mutable is the grandeur of states.

1757.
1762.
1763.

———————— Sic robora verti
Cernimus, atque illas assumere pondera gentes,
Concidere has (*n*).

SECT. IX.

Character of the Europeans.

The European nations are of various origin, which, with other natural and moral

(*n*) Ovid. Metam. lib. xv. v. 420.

causes,

causes, makes a visible difference in their qualities and manners; so that no general portraiture can be drawn of them. Compared, however, with the inhabitants of the other parts of the world, they may be affirmed infinitely to surpass them in all sciences and arts, and especially those of government and war, navigation and commerce. Aristotle gives this character of the Europeans, that they are brave and zealous assertors of their liberties, but something deficient in capacity, either to govern their own states, or rule over others (*o*). But this exception, together with the arrogant saying of the Chinese, " that they " have two eyes, and the Europeans but " one;" (*p*) is fully refuted by present experience.

SECT. X.

European languages. The various origin of the European nations has necessarily occasioned a great difference in their languages. The European original languages may be divided into the greater and the lesser. The former are three, the Latin, German and Sclavonian. The first spread itself throughout all the Roman conquests, but has been long since confounded

(*o*) Aristotle's Polit. lib. VII.
(*p*) Petr. Maffeii Hist. Ind. lib. VI. p. 275.

amidst

amidst national emigrations, and preserved only by the learned, whose peculiar language it continues in every part of Europe. It has farther the pre-eminence of being used in the Romish church for divine worship, in the pope's secretary's office, and may be called the European State Language (*q*); all treaties of peace, and other conventions, between the powers of this part of the world being usually drawn up in it; altho' its daughter, the French, has for some time past begun to supplant it; * and is at present grown into such favour, as to be used in the several courts of Germany, and all over the North. The other languages derived from the Latin are the Wallachian, Spanish, Portuguese, and Italian: the last may be called the speech of European music.

The German language is, besides Germany, spoken in part of Swisserland and Lorrain, in Royal and Ducal Prussia; in the towns and among the gentry in Courland, Livonia, and Esthonia; likewise in some particular parts of Poland, Hungary, and Transilvania; and the northern powers of-

(*q*) Gorg. Wilh. Overkampi Commentatio de Ratione Status Curiæ Romanæ circa usum Latinæ Linguæ in sacris cultuque publico. (Jenæ 1732. 8.) shewing the origin and reasons of this custom.

* The rights of the Latin language, however, are secured by a declaration, that the use of the French shall not be of any prejudice to it.

ten

ten make use of it in state instruments. Akin to it are the Danish, Norwegian, the Swedish, the Dutch, and, in some measure, the English.

The Sclavonian language comprehends the third part of Europe, and, according to some, is spoken by sixty different nations (r). From the Sclavonian are derived the Russian, Bohemian, and Moravian; it is likewise used, though with different dialects, in Hungary, Stiria, the Ukrain, and Lusatia.

The lesser original languages are, 1. The Greek; but this has undergone such alterations by the Turks subduing the Eastern empire, that the language now spoken in Greece is called the *new Greek*; the old language being used only by the learned. The others are, 2. The Cantabrian, used in Biscay and part of Navarre. 3. The Cambrian in the principality of Wales and Lower Brittany. 4. The Irish in Ireland and the Highlands of Scotland*. 5. The Islandic

---

(r) Becman Hist. Orb. Terr. Geogr. et Civil. Part. I. c. ix. §. 5.

* This and the two former are supposed to be the offspring of the old Celtic; the great extent and nature of which is treated of at large in the following work; Memoires sur la Langue Celtique, contenant 1. L'Histoire de cette Langue. 2. Une Description Etymologique des villes, rivieres, montagnes, forets, &c. des Gauls, de la meilleure partie de l'Espagne, de l'Italie, de la Grande Bretagne 3. Un Dictionnaire Celtique, par M. Bullet, à Besancon, 1754. 3 Tomes, fol.

in

in Iceland and some parishes of Dalecarlia. 6. The Finnish in Finland, Esthonia, and Lapland. 7. The Lithuanian in Livonia, Courland, a part of Lithuania, and in Prussian Lithuania. 8. The Turkish in Turkey and Crim Tartary (*s*).

SECT. XI.

All countries in Europe are not equally populous, which is partly owing to their different situation, and the greater or less fertility; partly also to the manners and qualities of the people, their religion and form of government. Europe, considering its extent, might contain near five hundred and fifty millions of inhabitants (*t*); yet the highest computation makes them only a hundred and fifty millions. *This number

Number of its inhabitants.

(*s*) Becman, p. I. c. iii. §. 3. Busching's Introduction.
(*t*) Susmilch, Vol. II. c. 20.

* Baron Bielfeld computes in Portugal and Spain	10 Millions.
France	20
Italy, and its Islands	8
Great Britain	8
Germany, the Low Countries, Swisserland	30
Denmark, Norway, Sweden	6
Russia, with all its conquests	18
Poland, Bohemia, Hungary, and Turkey in Europe	50
	150 Millions.

See his Institutions Politiques, Tom. II. c. xiv.

is hindered from encreasing, as under certain circumstances it probably would, first, by the many wars in which the greater part of Europe is frequently involved; secondly by the numerous armies kept on foot even in the times of peace, and of whom the greatest part

According to M. Busching's computation,

Russia in Europe contains	20 Millions.
Germany	24
Poland, with its dependencies	20
France	17
Turkey	14
Hungary	10
Great Britain and Ireland	8
Italy	9
Spain	7 $\frac{1}{2}$
The Low Countries, and Swisserland	6
Denmark and Norway	2
Sweden	2
Portugal	2
Royal Prussia	$\frac{3}{5}$
	142 $\frac{1}{10}$

See his Introduction, §. 63.

According to Mr. Susmilch, Vol. II. cap. 20. there are

In Portugal and Spain	10 Millions.
France	17
Great Britain	8
All the Netherlands	5
Swisserland	1
Italy, and the Islands	10
Denmark	2 $\frac{1}{2}$
Sweden	2 $\frac{1}{4}$
Russia	24
Livonia, and Courland	2
Poland	12
Hungary	6
Turkey in Europe	8
Germany	24
	130

die

PRESENT STATE of EUROPE.

die unmarried; the various and extenfive fettlements of the Europeans in the other parts of the world, and to which great numbers remove every year to make their fortunes; and laftly, the fea-fervice, and naval trade, in which many meet with an untimely death. Thefe feveral caufes muft neceffarily diminifh the number of inhabitants in Europe; and the more, as the lofs is not recruited by any emigrants from other parts of the world.

SECT. XII.

Difference of ranks in the European ftates.

The inhabitants of the European ftates are divided into four principal claffes or orders; the nobility, the clergy, the citizens, and the peafantry. In the Roman Catholic countries, the clergy conftitute the firft order; but in the Proteftant, it is the nobility. In all Chriftian ftates in Europe, nobility is hereditary; and with this advantageous pre-eminence, that the great employments, ecclefiaftical, civil, and military, are filled out of this body. Nobility is founded either on the antient and immemorial poffeffion of anceftors, or on records, by which fome families, not noble, obtain a patent for nobility (*u*).

(*u*) Hertii Elem. Doctr. Civil. Part I. Sect. 5. Parag. 12.

The antient European nobility, in general, owe their origin to war. Fighting was the only bufinefs with which the German nations, who founded moft of the ftates in this part of the world, were acquainted. This was the only road to glory and nobility; and to this day, the military nobility in France ftand in a much higher rank of efteem than thofe who belong to the law (*x*).

——————— Mavortia
Nobilitas fpoliis armifque exultat avitis (*y*).

Superior and Inferior nobility. The high pofts with which the nobility were invefted, and which afterwards became hereditary in their families, have, in length of time, introduced fuch a difparity between them, as to be divided into Superior and Inferior nobility, which obtains in moft parts of Europe. The former are diftinguifhed by certain titles, with great privileges annexed to them. The titles of the fuperior nobility are, 1. in German, Hertzog (*z*); in Latin, Dux; French, Duc; Italian, Duca; Spanifh, Duque; Englifh, Duke. 2. German, Markgraf (*a*); Latin, Marchio; French and Englifh, Marquis;

(*x*) Spirit of Nations, B. II. ch. vi. p. 132, 133.
(*y*) Claudian. in Epithal. Pallad. et Celer. v. 70.
(*z*) Bechmani. Synt. Dignit. Illuftr. Differtat. X. cap. 2. §. 1.
(*a*) Id. Differtat. XII. cap. xi. §. 6, 7.

Italian, Marchese; Spanish, Marques †. 3. German, Graf (*b*); Lat. Comes; French, Comte; Italian, Conte; Spanish, Conde; English, Earl *. 4. Viconte (*c*), a French title; in Latin, Vicecomes, or Vicarius Comitis; Italian, Viscomte; Spanish, Vizconde; and English, Viscount †. 5. Baron (*d*).

Besides these several classes of the superior nobility, Germany has another, bearing the title of Fursts (*e*), which ranks between the duke and marquis and the count. In England and France, it is only the males of the royal family who are stiled Fursten, or princes; except that in the latter, a few eminent families likewise partake of this honour. This title in Spain and Portugal

† Though the titles of duke and marquis are used in Germany, Italy, Great Britain, France, Spain, and Portugal; yet the reigning dukes in Germany, and some such there are in Italy, are far superior to those in the other said kingdoms, having the titles of sovereigns of the country, and almost all the prerogatives. The like difference is there between the German Markgrave, and the French and other Marquisses. Germany, besides Markgraves, has likewise Landgraves, and both are on a level with Dukes.

(*b*) Ibid. Differt. XII. cap. i. §. 1, 2, &c.
* So the English call their own Graves; but the foreign they distinguish by the title of Count.
(*c*) Becmani Differt. XII. cap. iii. §. 11.
† This title is not used in Germany. Some compare the Viscount with the German Burgraves; (see Becman. Differt. XII. cap. iii. §. 11.) which will by no means answer in general; some Burgraves are equal to princes, and precede Graves. Becm. Diert. XII. c. ii. §. 11.
(*d*) Loccenius in Antiquit. Sueco-Goth. Lib. II. c. x. p. 62. Becmani Differt. XI. c. 1. §. 1, 2, 3.
(*e*) Becman. Differt. XI. cap. i. §. 1, 2, 3.

is very rare, but Italy has abundance of princes. In Ruſſia the Kneze are reckoned on a footing with princes.

The lower nobility are ſuch who, without any of the above titles, have certain privileges, and particularly bear a coat of arms.

In the northern kingdoms, it is only of late that there has been any diſtinction of nobility. Counts and barons were firſt introduced into Sweden by Eric XIV. and into Denmark by Chriſtian V.

Poland, to this day, has but one kind of nobility; for though ſome families bear the title of prince, or count, yet having been moſtly conferred by foreign potentates, it does not give them the leaſt ſuperiority in the public aſſemblies, or diſtinction above the other nobility or gentry.

Chivalry. The nobility gave riſe to chivalry, ſo famous in the middle ages (*f*); being an engagement of perſons by a ſolemn vow, at their own charge and peril, to protect and defend religion, widows, and orphans, and all helpleſs perſons in diſtreſs (*g*). Another capital duty in chivalry was, to defend the fair-ſex, when in any danger of

(*f*) Boulainvilliers dans l'Abregé Chronol. de l'Hiſt. de France, Tom. I. p. 325, 326. where he mentions a ſingular cauſe of chivalry being inſtituted.
(*g*) Velly Hiſt. de France, Tom. IV. p. 414.

their

their life or virtue *. On thefe accounts, the nobility who had fo engaged were held in great honour, and enjoyed diftinguifhed privileges (*b*); and chivalry was in fuch confideration, that kings themfelves became members of that glorious body, and were dubbed knights †.

From this chivalry, which was general, and not confined to one nation, and had its beginning in the eleventh century, are derived all the celebrated orders, fpiritual and temporal, now exifting in Europe. The former were chiefly inftituted for the defence of the Chriftian religion, and making war on the Infidels, as well as for other devout purpofes; fuch were the Knights of Malta, the Templars, the Teutonic Knights, &c. The latter are either military or honorary. The firft are given to land or fea-

---

* The Portuguefe Academy of Hiftory tells us, that fome knights of their nation, or Caftilians, refcued the virgins, whom, by treaty between Aurelius king of Afturias and Abderama king of the Moors, the former was annually to deliver up to the latter, in lieu of a tribute. Colleccam dos Documentos e Memorias da Academia Real da Hiftoria Portugueza, de 1722. Na Conferencia do 2 Janeiro. Thefe expeditions undertaken in behalf of fuch diftreffed damfels, probably gave rife to the Spanifh knight-errantry.

(*b*) Velly, Hift. de France, Tom. IV. p. 18, 21.

† The French kings were formerly dubbed knights before their coronation. Francis I. received that honour from the renowned knight Bayard; and Henry II. from Marfhal du Biez. Ceremonial de France, ap. Becman. Differt. XIX. cap. 1. §. 1.

officers,

officers, as an incentive to valour, or recompence of good services; the second are conferred as marks of particular honour on principal officers, civil and military.

SECT. XIV.

<small>Form of government in European states.</small> The most ancient European nations accounted liberty the supreme good: it was the soul of their political constitution; and, according to a great philosopher, it was by this attachment to liberty, that they distinguished themselves from the Asiatics, who were always slaves to their rulers (*i*). In the monarchies erected after the downfall of the Roman empire, liberty was connected with sovereignty, the nobility being a check against the excesses of prerogative. They were originally the only state of the realm; but the clergy growing rich and powerful, gained admittance into the public consultations; and in process of time the more wealthy cities and towns came to make a branch of the legislature. This compound of monarchy, aristocracy, and democracy, was in the middle ages almost the universal form of government in Europe. But in the sixteenth and seventeenth centuries it became, in most states, purely monarchical; the sovereigns finding means

(*i*) Aristoteles Polit. Lib. VII. cap. vii.

PRESENT STATE OF EUROPE.

gradually to exclude the states from the government, and get all the power into their own hands. Accordingly, there are now in Europe the following unlimited monarchies: 1. Portugal. 2. Spain. 3. France. 4. Denmark. 5. Russia. 6. Prussia. 7. Sardinia. 8. The Two Sicilies. 9. The Pope is likewise unlimited in the Ecclesiastical State. 10. And the Grand Master of the order of St. John within the Isle of Malta. But the only despotic state in Europe is Turkey.

The European mixed states are, 1. Germany. 2. Great Britain. 3. Sweden. 4. Poland: and 5. Hungary; yet with considerable differences; for in Great Britain and Hungary, monarchy has the ascendant; in Sweden and Poland, aristocracy; and the Germanic constitution, in many things, resembles a body of united nations.

Among Europe's free states are four aristocracies. 1. Venice. 2. Genoa. 3. Lucca. 4. Ragusa: one aristo-democratical republic, San Marino: and two states of united people. 1. The United Netherlands. 2. The Swiss Cantons.

SECT. XV.

Fundamental laws in unlimited monarchies. All European kingdoms have their fundamental laws, which the sovereigns are bound to observe; even those states where the prerogative is unlimited, are not without such securities. For most, if not all the present absolute monarchies having been limited governments, some institutions were left standing at the change of form; and their authority gathering strength by prescription, they are held sacred as the bases of the state. Among these must indisputably be reckoned, 1. That the monarch cannot make any alteration in the established religion of the state, neither with regard to himself nor his subjects. 2. Likewise he is not to alter the legal succession to the throne, nor invest improper or disqualified persons with a pretension to it. 3. That he shall administer justice according to the laws; consequently, he cannot decide any cause arbitrarily. 4. He must maintain the hereditary rights and liberties of the people. And it being a maxim generally received in Christendom, that only the administration of the state, with proper rights and honours, is committed to the sovereign, and that it is by no means his property; another fundamental law consequential to this is, that the

the domain, or crown-lands fhall not be alienated. Thus the fovereign is not allowed to parcel out the fame or difpofe of them at his will*.

SECT. XVI.

Exclufive of thefe fundamental laws, an unlimited monarch has the government in his own hands; whereas in limited monarchies the cafe is very different, thefe having many more fundamental laws, by which the prince is, in the exercife of his fovereignty, bound in many cafes to have the confent of the ftates of the realm. Thefe cafes, indeed, are not totally alike in all limited kingdoms: but in moft they relate to, 1. Making laws. 2. Impofing taxes. 3. Entering into alliances, making peace and war. When a refolution is to be taken concerning one or other of thefe objects, it muft undergo a deliberation in the affembly of the ftates. Thefe in moft countries confift of the nobility, the clergy, and the towns. In England the people are reprefented in par-

marginalia: Particular fundamental laws in limited monarchies.

---

* In the oath of the former kings of France was this claufe: "Superioritatem, jura et nobilitatis coronæ Franciæ inviolabiliter cuftodiam, et illa nec tranfportabo nec alienabo;" but fince the coronation of Charles VIII. this has been omitted, being but a neceffary confequence of the king's other promifes. Ceremonial de France dans le ceremonial diplomatique des cours de l'Europe, par M. Rouffet, Tom. I. p. 234.

liament

liament by the house of commons; and in Sweden the free, or crown peasants, as they are called, have a seat in the diet. In Poland it is only the nobility and the higher clergy who compose the states; and all resolutions in their diets must be unanimous, whereas in the other parts of Europe only a majority of votes suffices.

SECT. XVII.

Nature of the succession.

In most European nations, no succession to the throne was at first absolutely hereditary; for though the son usually succeeded the father, yet was not this by any positive hereditary right; a previous consent of the states of the kingdom being necessary to the prince's receiving the homage of his people. The succession to the throne rested, therefore, on a mixed hereditary and elective right, as may be shewn in numberless instances among the old Germans, the Franks, the West-Geths, Anglo-Saxons, Danes, and Swedes (*k*). The constitution was the same in Poland under the kings of the Jagellon (*l*) family; but hereditary right has, in process of time, found means to sup-

---

(*k*) Achenwall. Differt. de Regnis mixtæ Successionis, §. iv. 14.

(*l*) Celeber. Lengnich jus Publ. Regni Poloni. Lib. II. c. ii. §. 4.

plant election out of all European states, except Germany and Poland, where election prevails, to the exclusion of hereditary right. The pope, and the doges of Venice and Genoa, are likewise elected.

SECT. XVIII.

The succession in the European hereditary monarchies is either male or mixed. The former takes place in France, in most of the German Imperial fiefs, in Sweden and Prussia. The other hereditary kingdoms admit of the latter. Russia is so far different in this respect from all parts of the European world, that the sovereign has a right to appoint his successor. *[Hereditary succession, either male or mixed.]*

Farther, natural children are debarred from the succession all over Europe; and though instances are not wanting of their being possessed of the throne in Portugal and Naples, yet this has only happened during intestine wars, by violent revolutions, and other singular junctures; and consequently, such cases are to be considered only as deviations from the general rule. *[Illegitimate children excluded from the succession.]*

SECT. XIX.

On the vacancy of a throne in the European elective kingdoms, the election can fall *[Elective kingdoms have only kings.]*

fall on the males only; the fair sex being quite out of the question. This made it the more strange that queen Christina of Sweden should set up for the crown of Poland, on the resignation of John Casimir, as if she would lay aside her sex. (*m.*)

SECT. XX.

Guardians of the realm in elective kingdoms. On the demise of a monarch in the European elective kingdoms, the fundamental laws have appointed guardians, who conduct the administration. Those, in Germany, are the elector of Saxony, with the elector of Bavaria and the elector Palatine alternately. In Poland it is the Archbishop of Gnesna, as primate of the kingdom. In Rome, on the decease of a pope, the college of cardinals superintend affairs both of the church and state.

SECT. XXI.

Regent in the hereditary monarchies. When, by the decease of a monarch, the crown devolves on a minor, tutors or curators are appointed for his person, and regents for the administration; but both these high offices are more often united. In unlimited monarchies the sovereign makes a particular ordinance in his will, appointing

(*m*) Memoires concernant Christine, Reine de Suede. (par Mr. Arkenholz.) Tom. III. p. 338, &c.

the queen dowager both curatrix and regent; of which many inftances occur in France, Spain, Portugal, and Sweden. In the want of a formal appointment, the laws of prefcription turn the fcale.

By thefe are determined the offices of the curator and adminiftrator in limited monarchies. When neither of thefe decide the point, the right of nominating the curator and guardian unqueftionably falls to the ftates of the realm.

SECT. XXII.

Majority of kings. The term of a king's minority is very different in the feveral ftates of Europe. In Germany, the emperor is of age on entering into his eighteenth year; the electors, on their compleating that year; the duke of Saxony, and princes of Anhalt, at the twenty-firft; and the far greater part of the other princes of the empire at their twenty-fifth year, agreeably to the Roman law (*n*). The kings of France enter on their majority at their fourteenth year; thofe of Great Britain at the end of their eighteenth; thofe of Denmark at the beginning of the eighteenth; thofe of Sweden at the conclufion of their twenty-firft year. In Spain and Portugal, the law is filent as to the majority; but the kings

(*n*) Petr. de Ludewig de ætate legitima puberum et majorum, cap. v.

of those nations appear to have assumed the sovereignty at the beginning of their fourteenth year. In other European kingdoms this point is uncertain.

SECT. XXIII.

Right of the states of the realm at the extinction of the royal family.

On the failure of the reigning family, the states of the realm are empowered to elect a new king. The Germans having used this right on the extinction of the Carlovingian male line, Germany has ever since remained an elective monarchy. The Swedes, likewise, on the failure of the royal male line in the year 1719, and 1743, availed themselves of the same right.

Accordingly, on a contest between the branches of the royal family, the states of the realm have decided the competition. This was the procedure of the French, when, on the death of their king Charles IV. both Philip de Valois and Edward III. king of England laid claim to the monarchy. Martin king of Arragon, being dead, nine judges were appointed, and those adjudged the crown to Ferdinand infant of Castile (*p*). The parliament of England in the year 1701, provided, that on the extinction of the Stuart line in the person of queen Anne,

(*p*) Mariana en la historia general de Espanna, Lib. XX. c. 2, 3, 4.

the

the electoral house of Brunswick Lunenburgh should sit on the throne.

SECT. XXIV.

It is not only by death that a monarch's sovereignty ceases, he may likewise divest himself of it by voluntary resignation, of which the European monarchies afford some signal instances. Lotharius the Roman emperor, the kings Alphonso IV. of Leon, Ramir II. of Arragon, Alphonso V. of Portugal, Charles V. Roman emperor and king of Spain, John Casimir king of Poland, Philip V. king of Spain, Victor Amadeus king of Sardinia, voluntarily descended from the throne, and embraced a monastic life, or lived in retirement. Some of these princes indeed, repented of their abdication; but only Alphonso V. and Philip V. had the good fortune to recover their crown.

Resignation of monarchs.

SECT. XXV.

There are still more instances of unhappy sovereigns violently extruded from the throne by a formal deposition. This was the fate of the emperors Henry IV. Adolphus of Nassau and Wenceslaus; of Childeric III. king of France; of Sancho II. and Alphonso VI. kings of Portugal; together with John Lackland, Edward II. Richard II.

Deposition of kings.

II. Henry VI. Charles I. and James II. kings of England. In Sweden Magnus Smeck, Eric XIV. and Sigifmond; in Denmark Chriftian II. and even in Ruffia John III. and Peter III. were depofed. Among all thefe inftances of misfortune, that of Charles I. king of England is without a precedent: his fubjects brought him to a trial as a malefactor, and put him to death by the hand of an executioner, before his own palace.

SECT. XXVI.

<small>Singular good fortune of the French and Danifh royal families.</small> The moft ancient among the fovereign families in Europe is that of France, having by an unparalleled feries of profperity held the throne near 800 years, in an uninterrupted male fucceffion. From the fame houfe are defcended the kings of Portugal. It was for fome time poffeffed of the fovereignty of Naples, and has given more than one king to Hungary and Poland. The royal family of Bourbon at prefent fill three of the European thrones, France, Spain, and Naples. The like good fortune has attended the illuftrious houfe of Oldenburg: it is in poffeffion of the two crowns of Denmark and Sweden, to which in time will be added that of Ruffia, in the perfon of a prince; and thus the fceptres of all the three

three northern monarchies will be in its hands.

Germany has now the honour of giving sovereigns to the greater part of Europe; those of Great Britain, Ruſſia, Denmark, Sweden, Pruſſia, and Hungary, being of German extraction.

SECT. XXVII.

The higheſt title of the European mo- *Emperor* narchs are, emperor and king. Antiently *and king.* the imperial dignity was accounted above that of king, and the Orientals entertain that idea of it to this day; but in Europe other maxims have been adopted, and kings allow emperors no ſuperiority over them. (*q*) The precedency among Chriſtian potentates is indeed allowed to the Roman emperor, on account of his having been conſtantly in poſſeſſion of that ceremonial; but no honorary diſtinction is paid to the emperor of Ruſſia.

The European monarchs and other ſovereign princes, France alone excepted, bear very prolix titles, not only of the countries which they actually poſſeſs, but likewiſe often of ſuch as do not at all belong to them. This is done, 1. When they

(*q*) Moſer's European Law of Nations in Peace, B. I. c. i. §. 5, 3. and c. iii §. 3, 4.

Vol. I.   I   have

have a right to the reversion or succession of certain lands, as the margraves of Brandenburg of the Franconian line to Prussia and Silesia. 2. When they lay claim to certain states, as France to Navarre; and 3. In remembrance of former rights or claims; as the kings of Sicily and the former dukes of Lorrain, now grand dukes of Tuscany, bear the title of kings of Jerusalem; and the dukes of Savoy that of kings of Cyprus *. A particular in the Portuguese title is, that trade and navigation make a part of it.

The arms of the European states are answerable to the titles they assume.

SECT. XXVIII.

Titles of the pope's granting.

But besides these titles derived from countries, some kings bear others, conferred by the pope on themselves or their ancestors, in recompence of some eminent service done to the church or religion. Thus the king of France is termed the Most Christian; the king of Spain, the Catholic; the king of England, Defender of the Faith †; the kings of Portugal, the Most

---

* Both the dukes of Lorrain and Savoy used to place the title of these kingdoms after their ducal stile; but since their becoming crowned heads, Jerusalem and Cyprus come immediately after their first royal title.

† The king of England alone bears this title in the first person, and among his other titles; the other kings commonly use theirs in the third person.

Faithful; and the king of Hungary, the Apoſtolic. In like manner were beſtowed on the Swiſs, the title of Defenders of the Church; and on John Caſimir, king of Poland, that of Orthodox; but the two laſt are grown obſolete.

SECT. XXIX.

Solemnities on a prince's acceſſion to the throne.

The ſolemnities of an European king or emperor's acceſſion to the throne are various. In moſt monarchies, as Germany, France, Great Britain, Denmark, Sweden, Poland, Hungary, and Ruſſia, they are anointed and crowned *. In Spain and Portugal kings are only proclaimed, and the ſtates of the kingdom do homage to them. In Pruſſia and Sardinia, the acceſſion of the new

---

* The cuſtom of kings being anointed and crowned by ſome eminent eccleſiaſtic is of Jewiſh origin; and it is obſerved, that the Eaſtern emperor Juſtin the Younger, ſucceſſor to Juſtin the Great, was the firſt who had himſelf crowned by the patriarch of Conſtantinople. See Selden's Titles of Honours, P. I. c. viii. p. 174. Pepin king of France was crowned by Boniface, archbiſhop of Mentz, and anointed with conſecrated oil; and this ceremony has ever ſince been conſtantly obſerved. Mezeray Abregé Chronol. de l'Hiſt. de France, Tom. I. p. 141. There was anciently a difference between the Imperial and Regal crowns, the former being cloſe and the others open, till Francis I. king of France, made uſe of a cloſe crown, in order to be on a footing with the emperor Charles V. in which he has been imitated by his ſucceſſors and other princes. In Portugal, king Sebaſtian was the firſt who made uſe of a cloſe crown; and the Portugueſe hiſtorians found this very high as an act of great magnanimity.

king is signified to the subjects by public writs, requiring the usual homage.

SECT. XXX.

Houshold. The houshold of emperors and kings, and even of other princes, is very numerous and splendid; all courts having certain high officers, with each his appointed department, in which he is to see that every thing be done in the greatest order and decorum. The principal of these court-officers are the high-steward, the grand-marshal, the great-chamberlain, the great cup-bearer, and the master of the horse, &c. and in Catholic courts there is likewise the great-almoner. Under these are many inferior officers, who receive orders from them. Thus among the several officers at court, there is a gradual dependency; and this constitutes the regular transaction of all public business.

SECT. XXXI.

Orders of knighthood. Orders of knighthood are likewise accounted necessary to the pomp and dignity of a court; and accordingly obtain in most courts of Europe, which are in some measure

Stuck o'er with titles, and hung round with strings (r).

These orders are companies of kings, princes, and nobles, under a grand master, (who is

(r) Pope's Essay on Man, Epist. IV. v. 195.

always the king or sovereign of the country) bound to some particular duties *, and by way of distinction and pre-eminence wear certain marks of honour on their apparel; they are purely honorary, having no salary or income annexed to them, except the order of the Holy Ghost in France.

SECT. XXXII.

Among the excellencies of Europe above the other three parts of the world, we must not omit the Christian religion, as obtaining in far the greater part. Mahometanism is limited to Turkey, Judaism is tolerated only in some countries, and of Paganism there are only a few miserable remains among the North-Laplanders and Samoiedes.

Christianity the prevalent religion in Europe.

SECT. XXXIII.

Many have been the vicissitudes which Christianity has undergone. It no sooner began to spread, than Arianism arose in opposition to the orthodox or true believers.

Three principal religious parties in Europe.

---

* Article VIII. of the laws of the Order of the Elephant, runs thus: "Unusquisque qui in nobilissimum hunc ordinem admittitur, pro ordinis Domini Daniæ et Norvegiæ regis, juribus majestatis, gloria & regnis propugnet, verbi Dei ministros veramque evangelicam religionem defendat, pauperes viduas et orphanos protegat, &c." Vid. Statuta Ordinis Elephant. in Leibnit. Cod. J. G. Diplom. Mantiff. Part II. p. 63 Of the like import is Article II. of the laws of the Danebrog order, ib. p. 72.

These, through the jealousy of the bishops of Constantinople and Rome, and in the seventh century, became divided into two parties, the Greek and Latin churches. In the latter another division was occasioned in the sixteenth century by the Reformation, which gave birth to Lutheranism, Calvinism, and the Church of England. The three last are included under the common name of Protestants: and thus is Christianity in Europe divided into three sects, or religious parties, the Roman, the Greek, and the Protestant.

SECT. XXXIV.

The Greek church.

The Greek is the established religion in Russia, and tolerated in Turkey, Hungary, Poland, and Transilvania. The spiritual head is the patriarch of Constantinople. But in the year 1587, he lost his authority over Russia; Czar Feodor Ivanowits instituting a patriarch of Moscow (*s*); so that, at present, it is only the Greek Christians within the Turkish dominions, who acknowledge the supremacy of the patriarch of Constantinople; and as to his dignity, that absolutely depends on the sultan's, or grand vizir's favour.

(*s*) G. T. Meieri Hist. Relig. cap. v. sect. 16, 17. p. 229, 230.

SECT.

SECT. XXXV.

The Roman Catholic religion prevails in Portugal, Spain, Italy, France, Hungary, Poland, the Auſtrian-Netherlands, part of Germany, Swiſſerland, and Tranſilvania. It is tolerated in the United Provinces, Denmark, Pruſſia, Ruſſia, and Turkey; likewiſe in England and Ireland †, but not with the exerciſe of public worſhip.

Church of Rome.

The head of the Roman Catholick church is the pope, or biſhop of Rome, who, under the humble ſtile of " ſervant of God's ſervants," has uſurped the exalted dignity of a divine vicegerent, and exerciſes a regal prerogative. He is the ſole and ſupreme judge in matters of faith, and his juriſdiction comprehends all eccleſiaſtics, whoſe perſons no civil power, under penalty of excommunication, can lay hands on (*t*). Farther, according to the principles of his politics, the church conſtitutes one large general ſtate, of which the temporal ſtates are but parts, and ſubject to his ſupremacy, which he ſtrengthens in ſome European monarchies, making them in great meaſure tributary to him (*u*.)

---

† In theſe kingdoms it is not tolerated by law; the moſt that can be ſaid is, that the law is not put in execution againſt thoſe who profeſs it. The Tranſl.
(*t*) C. 2. X. de foro comp. c. xxix. X. de Sent. excom.
(*u*) Ludewig. Jur. Feudor. cap. XI. Quæſt. 2. p. 572, ſeq.

And though his loss in Europe by the Reformation be not inconsiderable, yet have the Spaniards and Portuguese by arms, and their missionaries by preaching, made such extensive conquests for him in the East and West-Indies, as have amply compensated for his European losses, his dominion being spread over the face of the whole earth.

SECT. XXXVI.

Supports of the Romish church. This spiritual sovereignty stands on such sure foundations, and is so well strengthened, that nothing seems of sufficient power to overthrow it. Its main pillars are the Inquisition, which, at first, was only a temporary tribunal (*x*), for suppressing the Waldenses and other heretics; but has since been made constant and perpetual in Spain, Portugal, Rome, &c. for the punishment and extirpation of all who depart from the doctrines of the Roman church (*y*). The numberless order of monks scattered over the whole world, are likewise very instrumental in supporting the Pope; but among them all, the Jesuits, being by a particular vow devoted to the see of Rome, have done him the best service. This order,

---

(*x*) Memoires Historiques pour servir à l'Histoire des Inquisitions, Livr. II. c. ii. 54.
(*y*) Ibid c. v. p. 106, 107.

how-

however, after attaining to very extraordinary power and opulence, has lately suffered a violent shock, being suppressed in France, Spain, and Portugal.

SECT. XXXVII.

The religious orders of knighthood were in former times a powerful support of the papal dominions, being by their original institution, bound to defend and propagate the Christian religion by the sword. The principal of these were the Knights of St. John of Jerusalem, the Templars, and the Teutonic knights, who were instituted in Palestine, at the time of the Croisades. The first, who were called Knights of Malta, from the island of Malta, which Charles V. gave them for their residence, are possessed of very large estates in Spain, Portugal, France, and Germany; and their grand master is by the European potentates considered as an independent prince (z.) This order is the only one, which continues acting up to its capital vow, being continually at war with the Turks and African pirates. It is long since the prodigious wealth and licentiousness of the Knights Templars brought their order to a period, attended with many

Spiritual orders of knighthood created for the defence of religion.

(z) Helyot's History of the monastic and military orders.

shocking executions (*a*). The Teutonic Knights, who at firſt were called Mariani and Cruciferi, had conquered Pruſſia, which they loſt in their wars with Poland, as they have by other accidents been deprived of many of their eſtates in Italy, Lorrain, and the United-Netherlands (*b*.) The head of this order is ſtiled the Teutonic Grand Maſter, and has a ſeat and vote at the German diets among the eccleſiaſtical princes. The Brothers of the Sword, or Sword-Bearers, who had made themſelves maſters of Livonia and Courland, and eſtabliſhed Chriſtianity there, have been involved in the loſs of thoſe countries (*c*). But the Spaniſh religious orders of St. Jago, Calatrava, Alcantara, Monteſa, and thoſe in Portugal of Chriſt and Avis, ſubſiſt to this very day.

SECT. XXXVIII.

Proteſtantiſm.

The ſtate of the Proteſtant religion is not in equal proſperity with the Roman Catholic. Inſtead of being properly united, it is ſplit, and not without an acrimony equally

---

(*a*) Nic. Gurtleri Hiſt. Templarior. § 4, 26, 43, 126, &c. Acta quædam ad condemnationem ordinis Templariorum pertinentia in Leibnitii Cod. J. G. Diplom. Mantiſſ. II. N°. V. VI. VII. p. 76, &c.
(*b*) Greg. Rivii (Ge. Burch Lauterback) Monaſt. Hiſt. Occid. cap. lxxvii. p. 117, &c.
(*c*) Conr. Sam. Schurzfleiſch. Diſſ. de Ordine Enſiferorum, §. 5. & ſeq.

unbe-

unbecoming and detrimental, into three principal branches; Lutheranifm, Calvinifm, and the Church of England.

Lutheranifm prevails in Denmark, Norway, Sweden, Pruffia, Livonia, Courland, and part of Germany and Tranfilvania. It is tolerated in England, the United-Netherlands and Ruffia, and in Poland and Hungary; but in the two laft countries, not without many oppreffions.

Calvinifm is eftablifhed in the United-Netherlands, in Scotland, part of Germany, Swifferland, and Tranfilvania. It is tolerated in England, Denmark, Sweden, Ruffia, Poland, and Hungary; but in the two laft countries very much oppreffed; and in France, where it has great numbers of fecret votaries, it is under a downright perfecution.

The Church of England, which is alfo called the High and Epifcopal Church, is eftablifhed in England and Ireland, and tolerated in Scotland. The Englifh have likewife the free exercife of religion in many foreign parts, where they are fettled on account of trade.

Since the Reformation, it has been a ftanding maxim in the papal policy, to weaken, and, if poffible, fupprefs the Proteftants. Such procedures have frequently given

Whether the Roman Catholic or the Proteftant party be the ftrongeft.

given rife to commotions and wars; fo that religion makes a confiderable article in the political ftate of Europe. For two oppofite parties having fprung from it, the queftion is, Which of the two, Catholicifm or Proteftantifm, is the ftronger? or rather, Whether the latter has ftrength enough to defend itfelf againft the former? On comparing the power on both fides, we find the emperor and the greater part of the German empire, the kings of France, Spain, Portugal, Poland, Hungary, Sardinia, Sicily, and the Pope, together with all Italy, and part of Swifferland, to be Catholics; and on the other hand, the Proteftant fide has the kings of Great Britain, Pruffia, Denmark, Sweden, the United-Netherlands, with a part of Germany and Swifferland. Thus with regard to number and extent of countries, the former are by much the ftrongeft. And another no fmall advantage is, their having a general head, which keeps them united, and directs their conduct to the advantage of the religion they profefs; whereas among the latter there is little union, or at leaft not that union which fhould be, even on a political confideration. Notwithftanding thefe circumftances, a writer very intelligent in thefe matters affirms, that the proteftant ftates, being very populous, and many

many of them likewife opulent and powerful, are a match for their adverfaries (*d*.) This indeed feems to be confirmed by the laft war, where the greateft potentates of the two religions were oppofed to each other. Ruffia gave the former a great overpoize; for, on its relinquifhing that party, the fcale immediately turned to the other fide.

SECT. XXXIX.

It is a frequent queftion, Whether the Proteftant or Roman Catholic religion be moft beneficial to a nation? On confidering that the Romifh religion exempts the ecclefiaftics from the jurifdiction of the magiftracy, and makes them dependent on a foreign power, the confequence of which is a ftate within a ftate; that it fubjects the ftate itfelf to fuch foreign power, and by excommunication and the depofition of rulers, which it has affumed, confounds all proper diftinction; and farther, that it does violence to confcience and natural freedom; and by fuch a fyftem, together with the celibacy of the clergy and the monaftic life, hinders the peopling of countries (*e*); and on the other hand, that the Proteftant reli-

Whether the Catholic or Proteftant religion be moft for the national good.

(*d*) See the Prefent State of Europe, by Dr. Campbell, c. ii.
(*e*) Ibid.

gion

gion teaches and practises the contrary of such abuses; all this, I say, considered, the question decides itself.

SECT. XL.

State of the Sciences in Europe. Most countries of Europe, and particularly the northern, owe the introducement of Sciences to the Christian religion. They are at present spread throughout all our part of the world where Christianity prevails; but their prosperity is not in all countries alike. For among the higher Sciences, as they are termed, scholastic philosophy and divinity are still predominant in the Roman Catholic countries, through the restraint laid on freedom of thinking and writing; whereas both these studies are almost exploded every where among the protestants.

Civilians in most European countries used formerly to make the explanation of the Roman and papal laws their chief business; but of late they have applied themselves to the national laws and the nobler parts of jurisprudence, the law of nature and of nations, and the public and municipal system of Laws *.

* Vattel's Law of Nations, B. I. ch. xii. §. 143, 157.

Physic

Phyfic was firft brought into Spain by the Arabs, who blended aftrology with it *; and from Spain it was farther propagated over Europe. It is at prefent greatly improved, which is owing to the many modern difcoveries made in natural philofophy, botany, chemiftry, and anatomy.

SECT. XLI.

On the overthrow of the weftern Roman empire by the irruption of foreign nations, polite literature and the fine arts became totally loft amidft the ignorance and barbarifm, with which Italy and the other Roman provinces were overwhelmed. The fubfequent times afford nothing but very rude productions of hiftory and poetry. This vitiated and ignorant period invented a new kind of compofition, in the fcheme and ground-work not unlike Epic poems, full of love-adventures and feats of arms; and heightened, by way of embellifhment, with the moft incredible and abfurd circumftances. Thefe writings were called Ro-

Of polite literature in particular.

Origin of Romances.

---

* The antient Arabian and Jewifh phyficians ufed, in dangerous cafes, to call in the ftars to the help of their art; of which the Spanifh hiftories give a very remarkable inftance of king John II. of Arragon, in the operation which he underwent for a cataract. Mariana's Hiftory of Spain, Lib. XXIII. c. xii.

mances;

mances*; and for a long time prevailed, to the great injury of taste in Epic poetry; of which Ariosto, in his Orlando Furioso, together with many other Italians, are famous instances. It is, however, the honour of Italy to have first restored Literature according to the models of the Greeks and Romans. So good an example was gradually followed by the other European nations; so that, at present, they all afford men of parts, and ingenious productions in every country.

The Italians likewise formed the general taste in Music; most countries in Europe having adopted their system.

SECT. XLII.

Universities. On the restoration of learning, many universities and inferior schools were erected in all European countries: the number only of the former amounts to an

---

* Romances, which, at first, were short poems, the celebrated Huet in his Traité de l'Origine des Romans, p. 140, 141. has shewn to derive their original from Provence; and not composed in Latin as works of erudition, but in the common Provençal tongue. This was a compound of several languages, in which, however, the Latin predominated, and was called Romance, as the common Spanish is at present: and thus Romance comes to be the general appellation for such poems and books which the Spaniards call Romances, the Italians Romanzi, and the French Romans. See Huet. p. 134, 135.

hundred

hundred and thirty (*f*). Germany, France, Spain, and Italy, have the moſt. They differ greatly in their conſtitution, eſpecially the Proteſtant and Roman Catholic: the former enjoying a much greater liberty of ſpeaking and writing, carried ſcience to a higher degree of improvement than the latter.

SECT. XLIII.

Academies and ſocieties of ſciences.

In every part of Europe, except Poland, there are, beſides univerſities, academies, and ſcientifical ſocieties, which have enriched mathematics, natural philoſophy, phyſic, and other ſciences, with many new diſcoveries, and thus greatly enlarged the boundaries of the learned world; as the Memoirs publiſhed by them glorioufly prove. Some, as the Academy of Sciences at Paris, and others in France; thoſe of Peterſburg and Berlin, together with the Royal Society at Gottingen; annually propoſe certain queſtions to all the learned in Europe; and the beſt anſwer is honoured with a prize, which is uſually a gold medal of no ſmall value.

(*f*) Many curious particulars relating to Univerſities are to be found in Pfeffingeri Corp. Jur. Publ. Tom. IV. Lib. iv. Tit. x. p. 709, 715. with a liſt of the principal academies in Europe, p. 716, 729.

SECT. XLIV.

Painting, sculpture, and architecture, which the Greeks and Romans carried to great perfection, sunk with the Western empire; and the middle ages are monuments of the vicious taste which then prevailed in those arts. The Italians again led the way to a happy imitation of the antients, and the revival of all the exquisiteness of their performances; and long have they maintained their superiority in those arts, which, to this day, are more in vogue among them than in other countries. Italy and France have produced the best masters in sculpture; Italy, France, and England, have had their eminent geniuses in architecture; and many Germans, Dutch, and Flemings, have made a figure among the celebrated painters.

The last mentioned art is divided into three schools, or into a threefold taste and stile in painting; namely, the Italian, Flemish (g), and French. The antients used only water-colours, till John Von Brugge, or, as he is called by others, John Von Eyck, found out the art of painting in oil, (h) to

(g) Memoires de Trevoux, Juin 1762. p. 228.
(h) Ibid. p. 226.

which, however, the English lay claim (*i*). Among the fine arts may likewise be reckoned engraving, which is almost of the same date as printing, tho' cutting figures in wood was practised long before (*k*).

For the improvement of painting, sculpture, and architecture, particular academies have been erected in Italy and France, and lately in Spain.

SECT. XLV.

The general advancement of the sciences, is, among other circumstances, to be attributed to printing, and its consequence bookselling. This is a very great conveniency to the learned, affording them an easy method of publishing their works and to advantage.

Printing and bookselling.

Printing and bookselling have likewise promoted the founding of large public libraries, which, in reality, are the treasures of the Republic of Letters, where the access to them is open. The Vatican library at Rome, that of the French king at Paris, and that of the emperor at Vienna,

Libraries.

(*i*) Anecdotes of Painting in England, collected by George Vertue, and published by Mr. Horace Walpole, Vol. I. c. 2.

(*k*) Dissertation sur l'Origine et les Progrés de l'Art de graver en Bois, par Mr. Fournier le Jeune, à Paris, 1758. VIII. See Journal des Sçavans, May 1748. p. 281, &c.

are accounted the largeſt and moſt valuable in Europe (*l*).

Monthly Writings. The literary monthly journals make known what books are publiſhed, together with their contents; and thus muſt be claſſed among the beneficial inventions, which contribute both to the improvement of knowledge, and the conveniency of the learned *.

SECT. XLVI.

The Roman and canon law. Though all ſtates in Europe have their own laws, yet ſince the thirteenth century, the Roman law has been introduced into many; and in caſes where the laws of the land are not deciſive, it is the ſtandard of juſtice in Italy, France, Spain, Portugal, Germany, and the Low Countries (*m*.) Next to the Roman law, the papal has likewiſe, as celebrated for equity, been adopted almoſt over all Europe, and particularly in judicial proceedings. In ſpiritual and eccleſiaſtical cauſes it obtains even in many Proteſtant countries (*n*.) Theſe foreign laws,

---

(*l*) Keyſler's Travels, Letter LXXXII. Our author ſeems to have forgot the Bodleian at Oxford. T.

* The inventor of theſe periodical pieces was Dennis Sallo, who began with the Journal des Sçavans, 1664. See Raynal. Anecdotes Literaires, Art. Sallo.

(*m*) Arthur Duck de Uſu et Authoritate Juris Civilis Romanor. in Dominiis principum Chriſtianor. Lib. II. c. 9—12.

(*n*) Id. Lib. I. c. 7.

how-

however, are productive of great inconveniencies, both on account of the language in which they are written, and the labour and time in learning them, not to mention their lengthening of suits; so that it is much to be wished they were totally laid aside, and the common laws amended, as Frederic II. king of Prussia has done, to the great happiness of his dominions.

SECT. XLVII.

Several customs gradually arose among the Christian nations in Europe, which, by tacit consent, were admitted as the rule of their behaviour in war and peace; and in consequence of which, more moderation and humanity was observed in the former, and in the latter more civility and decorum, than among the people of the other parts of the world. These usages collectively are called the European law of nations, a happy consequence of the propagation of the Christian religion and the sciences. The reality of this law of nations is unquestionable, but this noble part of jurisprudence has hitherto had but little culture bestowed on it *.

Law of nations in Europe.

---

* The newest and most useful works on this subject are Counsellor Moser's Maxims of the Law of Nations in Time of Peace; Maxims of the European Law of Nations in War; and Mr. Ackenwall's Primæ Lineæ Juris Gentium Practici.

Great military force in Europe. Europe, since the beginning of the sixteenth century, has been harrassed with long and expensive wars; so that this period affords but few years of general peace †. This has occasioned standing armies. Those of Lewis XIV. far exceeded all that had been seen before; and this laid the other states under a necessity of augmenting theirs: hence the military establishment of Europe is now increased to the enormous number of a million and a half, ‡ and this exclusive of the sea-forces.

† From the year 1600 to 1756, Europe has been the scene of forty considerable wars; whereas during the same space of time only three have happened in Asia. Voltaire's History of the War of 1741.

‡ According to M. Busching's Introduction, &c. the European regular forces in time of peace are as follow:

The Ottoman Port	300,000
Russia	250,000
The House of Austria	200,000
France	160,000
King of Prussia	146,000
The other States of Germany	130,000
Spain	70,000
Denmark	59,000
Sweden	48,000
United Netherlands	40,000
Great Britain	30,000
The King of the Two Sicilies	30,000
Venice	28,000
Poland	24,000
King of Sardinia	15,000
The other Italian States	15,000
Portugal	14,000
Total	1,559,000

By this list above a hundredth part of the inhabitants of Europe are soldiers.

The many wars, and formidable armies, have, however, produced great improvements in the art of war and military functions. Thefe muſt principally be aſcribed to French invention, as clearly appears from the many French words in gunnery and military architecture: even the very titles of the military officers, from the higheſt to the loweſt, are French.

The ſtrength of a government chiefly ſhewing itſelf in war, the proportion of European ſtates relatively to their actual force, is to be judged of by its military figure. Baron Bielfeld divides them into four claſſes. The firſt are, thoſe which with a large land and naval force, have alſo a ſufficiency of money; and theſe can maintain a war on their own bottom, without any foreign aſſiſtance or alliance. Theſe, which he terms ſtates of the firſt magnitude, are only France and Great Britain. To the ſecond claſs belong thoſe ſtates which in themſelves are ſtrong, but without all the beforementioned advantages; and in their wars, eſpecially if unfortunate and of any length, ſtand in need of alliances and pecuniary ſuccours: ſuch are the houſe of Auſtria, Ruſſia, Pruſſia, and Spain. The third claſs is compoſed of ſtates which are not able to engage in a war, but as parties in a very powerful alliance, and for a subsidy furnish auxiliaries, whom they cannot maintain in time of peace; in fine, whose territories are too small, and deficient in revenues or inhabitants. Among these he classes Portugal, Sardinia, Sweden, Denmark*, Sicily and the United Provinces. In these three classes are comprehended the great European powers. In the fourth, he places all the other states in Europe which, of themselves, are utterly incapable of undertaking any thing, or have no immediate share in the great transactions; and these he calls the Petty States (*o*.)

SECT. XLVIII.

Maritime powers in Europe.

Most European states confining on the sea, this situation, and the trade and navigation arising from it, have made them maritime powers: these are Portugal, Spain, France, Great Britain, the United Netherlands, Denmark, Sweden, Russia, the Port, Venice, Genoa, and the Knights of Malta; but the precedency so far belongs to Great Britain, that its present navy is respected by all Europe. In the last century, that of the Dutch came pretty near it; and

* Denmark, however, I should be for ranking in the second class, on account of its great trade and marine.
(*o*) Institutions Politiques, par M. le Baron de Bielfeld. Tom. II. ch. iv. §. 14.

never

PRESENT STATE OF EUROPE. 137

never were larger fleets feen than in the wars between thofe two powerful rivals. On this account it is, that they are, by way of preference, termed the Maritime Powers; but the latter is at prefent fo fmall, as fcarce to be compared with the former.

The Dutch fhipping employed in trade is very confiderable; and falls very little, if any thing, fhort of that of Great Britain. Thefe two ftates have more merchant-fhips at fea, than all the reft of Europe put together*.

In the beginning of this century, Europe faw a new maritime power arife in Ruffia. Befides, in moft ftates of our part of the world, both commerce and the marine are

---

* See Campbell's Prefent State of Europe, chap. ii. p. 20, 21, where the author compares the mercantile fhipping of the European nations, as it ftood at the breaking out of the war for the Auftrian fucceffion. On dividing it, fays he, into twenty parts,

Great Britain has — —	6
The United Provinces ———	6
The fubjects of the Northern Crowns —	1
The trading towns in Germany and the Auftrian-Netherlands —	1
France ——— ———	2
Spain and Portugal — —	2
Italy, and the reft of Europe — —	1
	20

But fince that time, many have been the alterations in the European commerce and marine; and Great Britain's fhare muft at prefent be rather greater, fuch large countries in North America having been ceded to it by France and Spain at the peace of Paris, in 1763.

greatly

greatly increased; a circumstance by which ship-building has received considerable improvements, though the palm in this art is generally given to the English (*p*).

SECT. XLIX.

Inconveniency of the different standards of the European coinage. Money being the sinew of war, the great and general wars so frequent in Europe, as likewise the uses of commerce, must occasion a vast circulation of it. Great would be the conveniency to all nations, could one general standard be agreed on for the European coins: but, like the proportion between gold and silver*, this differs considerably in all countries, which causes many inconveniencies in trade, and particularly in exchange of money. The most moneyed country in our part of the world is Holland, which accordingly, in the business of exchange, gives laws to other nations (*q*).

(*p*) Institutions Politiques, par M. le Baron de Bielfeld. Tom. I. ch. xv. §. 20.

* The proportion between gold and silver is,

In Spain, about	1—16
Germany and Swisserland	1—15
The king of Sardinia's dominions	1—14 $\frac{4}{5}$
Holland	1—14 $\frac{2}{3}$
England	1—14 $\frac{3}{5}$
France	1—14 $\frac{9}{13}$

(*q*) Spirit of Laws, Book XXII. ch. x.

SECT.

SECT. L.

Revenues of the European nations very different.

The European countries being not equally rich, and the difference in their extent and inward conftitution being likewife confiderable, there muft of courfe be a great difparity in their revenues. Thofe of France exceed the reft; and there being few ftates in Europe with large crown-lands, or demefnes, their revenues muft arife from taxes and impofts on the fubject. Thefe are higheft in France, Spain, and Holland.

SECT. LI.

Debts of fome European ftates.

The large armies continually kept on foot in Europe, are a very chargeable article, and run away with the greater part of the public revenue; fo that moft European ftates, having no ftock of money in hand, are under a neceffity in time of war, not only to impofe new taxes, or raife the former, but likewife to take up large fums on loans. And hence it is that many of the moft refpectable powers, as France, Great Britain, Spain, Sweden, and the United Netherlands, are encumbered with enormous debts.

SECT. LII.

Alterations and present state of the European commerce.

Next to the confideration of the military ftate, comes that of trade, and efpecially the maritime trade, carried on by the prefent European powers, which has undergone great changes. The overthrow of the weftern Roman empire drew likewife after it the total ruin of the commerce carried on in the Mediterranean and the Archipelago, between the Roman provinces. Venice and Genoa, in the beginning but fmall republicks, in fome meafure reftored it, and conducted a trade, which extended itfelf through the Archipelago into the Black-Sea, and even farther. But this likewife was foon brought to an end, by the irruptions of the Tartars and Turks. After this misfortune, the chief place of refort for the Venetian fhipping was Alexandria in Egypt; from whence they fetched fpices, filks, and other Eaft-India goods, which they diftributed over Europe with very confiderable profit.

In the twelfth century, fome towns in the north of Germany entered into a commercial partnerfhip, and alliance for their mutual defence, which was called the Hanfa; and the allied towns were diftinguifhed by the denomination of Hans-Towns. They not only traded in the Baltic,

tic, but likewife to the Low-Countries, England, France, and Spain; and fuch was the ftrength of their confederacy, that for fome time it was accounted one of the great northern maritime powers.

Thus the Venetians and the Hans-Towns were in poffeffion of the beft part of the trade of Europe, and continued in it till the end of the fifteenth century, when a great change happened to the prejudice of both. For about this time it was that the Spaniards difcovered the New World, and brought from thence many commodities till then quite unknown in Europe, befides prodigious quantities of gold and filver; and the Portuguefe alfo failing to the Eaft-Indies, became mafters of the fpice-trade, and thus totally diverted that branch of the Venetian commerce. The Low-Countries, famous for woollen and linen manufactures, likewife embarked in a trade with Spain and Portugal; which was afterwards carried on with ftill greater fuccefs, when they came under the Spanifh government. The commodities which they purchafed in thofe countries, they carried up the Baltic, and this gave the firft blow to the Afiatic trade; and not long after, the alliance itfelf fell to pieces.

The

The Portuguese, who were become the most opulent nation in Europe by their East-India commerce, were dispossessed of it during their union with Spain. The Dutch, in the long war with that crown, making themselves masters of the best Portuguese settlements in the East-Indies, thereby got the chief part of the spice-trade into their hands, and still continue in possession of it.

The English, who hitherto had but little concerned themselves about foreign commerce, took it in hand in the reign of queen Elizabeth; and under Lewis XIV. the French, from emulation, imitated their example; to which the celebrated Colbert animated them by the most prudent regulations.

In the present century, the northern states have at length engaged in naval commerce with great industry, and the German trading cities have considerably enlarged it. The English and Dutch mercantile shipping continue to exceed those of the rest of Europe.

The trade in home manufactures, being much more beneficial and profitable than any other, great numbers at present begin to be erected in all countries.

SECT.

PRESENT STATE OF EUROPE.

SECT. LIII.

The European nations carry on a confi- *Home-* derable trade with one another; and for its *trade of the Europeans.* confolidation and improvement, feveral have entered into commercial treaties, by which one ftate agrees to allow certain advantages to the fubjects of another, particularly in tolls and duties. It is likewife ftipulated in thefe treaties, in what manner the maritime trade fhall be carried on in time of war, with the enemies of one or the other party; and what goods fhall be permitted or prohibited. It appears, that with regard to permitted goods, the property of the goods was confidered in the former treaties of commerce; but in the latter, the property of the fhip is the point; fo that according to the former, the goods of a friend in an enemy's fhip were free, and the goods of an enemy in a friend's fhip were forfeited: whereas by the latter a friend's fhip faves the goods of an enemy, and the fhip of an enemy fubjects a friend's goods to confifcation.

The Europeans likewife carry on a vaft *To the* trade to the other three parts of the world, *other parts of the* Afia, Africa, and America. From Afia † *world.*

---

† The Afiatic trade includes, 1. a part of the Levant trade; 2. The Eaſt-India trade; and 3. The trade to China. By

they

they fetch spices and drugs, likewise gold and gems, raw silk and cotton, camels hair and mohair; together with several manufactures, as silk and woollen stuffs, china, and all kinds of lacquered ware.

The African commodities are oil, cotton, ivory, gold in ingots and gold dust, gums, skins, copper, leather, almonds, negroes, wine, wheat, wool, sugar.

Coffee. America furnishes timber, cotton, cacao, coffee, cochineal, gems, iron, logwood, fish, gold, hides, indigo, ginger, copper, firs, pearls, pimento, or brazil-pepper, quinquina, rice, sarsaparilla, silver, tobacco, vanillas, Vigogna wool, wax, sugar (*r*).

The American trade is confined to those European nations who have colonies in that

---

the Levant, the Italians mean all the countries lying east of them from Dalmatia to the river Euphrates in Asia, and to the river Nile in Africa, including likewise the islands in those quarters. The French likewise comprehend in it Italy, and all the northern coast of Africa; and the English and Dutch give this appellation, in the most extensive sense, to all the countries lying in the Mediterranean. Busching's Introduction, §. 96. The Levant trade is subject to many inconveniencies from the African corsairs; so that most nations have entered into a treaty with them, and even paid them a kind of tribute under the disgraceful name of presents. The Spaniards and Portuguese, by reason of their situation, might effectually reap great advantages from such an agreement; but their extreme delicacy in point of honour and religion, will not listen to such an accommodation. East-India comprehends all that vast part of Asia reaching from Persia eastward to China, and northward to Great Tartary; likewise all the islands in the Indian-Sea lying within that space.

(*r*) Busching's Introduction, §. 94, 95, 97.

part,

part, importing thither and to Africa their manufactures and fabricks. But little is done this way in the East-Indies and China, that trade requiring ready money; and particularly the Chinese will be paid for their goods in silver, of which they have always shewn themselves fond (*s*).

SECT. LIV.

The East-India and China trade is, on that account, very detrimental to Europe in general, by the annual loss of some millions of gold and silver *. The amazing quantity of silver which America sends over for European goods, is chiefly consumed in this trade; and thus what we receive from the West-Indies, is for the most part swallowed up by the East-Indies and China. The vast gain of this trade † continues enlarging it to a most excessive degree; and

Detriment of the East-India trade to Europe.

(*s*) Maffei Hist. Ind. Lib. VI. p. 249.

* In the year 1753 and 1754, the English East-India Company exported 5,318,580 ounces of silver, and 52,145 ounces of gold. London Evening Post, 1756. N°. 4396. The Danish East-India Company from the year 1731 to 1745, sent over thirty-seven tons of gold in ready money, and only three tons of gold in goods, which annually make a difference of above 260,000 Danish dollars. If to these we add the ready money used by the Dutch, French, Portuguese, Swedes, and the Embden Company, it may be computed that at least seven or eight millions go yearly out of Europe to the East-Indies and China.

† The Danish East India Company has, in return for the abovementioned thirty-seven tons of gold in cash, and three

in all appearance, things will continue going on at the like rate till Europe becomes totally exhausted and impoverished, which a celebrated late writer confidently predicts (*t*). Others again, see nothing so very pernicious in this trade, or the exportation of part of our nobler metals which it occasions; otherwise they would increase too much, and consequently lose of their value. They are, however, and very justly, for limiting the East-India and Chinese trade to tea, coffee, spices, and drugs, with a total exclusion of porcelane, silk, and cotton-stuffs, and other India manufactures (*u*). The East-India and Chinese trade requiring very large sums, is carried on by companies erected for that purpose in several countries; as Portugal, France, England, Holland, Denmark, Sweden, and in East-Friesland, at Emden. Among them all, that of Holland is the most considerable and wealthy, and next to that the English Company.

in manufactures, brought back East-India and China goods to the amount of seventy-four tons of gold; sixty of which were sold to foreigners, and thirteen consumed at home. Patriotisme Tankar. om Manufactur. &c.

(*t*) Mr. de Real dans la Science du Gouvernement, Prem. Partie, Tom. I. p. 155.

(*u*) Mr. de Bielfeld Instit. Polit. Tom. VIII. ch. xiii. §. 20.

SECT.

SECT. LV.

Cardinal Alberoni, if the will attributed to him be really his, and not a work of the editor's, the famous Maubert, has drawn up a project for procuring the whole East and West-India trade, and consequently the dominion of the sea, to the house of Bourbon (*y*). On the other hand, some French writers charge the English with affecting such dominion, and an universal exclusive trade (*z*).

Cardinal Alberoni's plan for procuring the East and West-India trade to the house of Bourbon.

SECT. LVI.

Among the European inventions for the improvement of commerce, must be reckoned the money-trade, which is carried on by bills of exchange and public banks; as at Venice, Amsterdam, Nuremberg, Hamburg, London, Genoa, Stockholm, Copenhagen, and Dantzick. The four former are banks of exchange; the constitution of the others is something different, being likewise loan banks.

Banks of Europe.

For the increase of naval trade, some countries have set up Free-ports, that is,

---

(*x*) L'Espion ou le faux Baron de Maubert, p. 36.
(*y*) Voyez Le Testament Politique du Cardinal Jules Alberoni, ch. vi. p. 96. et suiv.
(*z*) Mr. de Real Science du Gouvernement, Six. Partie, p. 448, 449. Desormeaux dans l'Abregé Chronol. de l' Hist. d'Espagne, Tom. V. p. 348, 531.

such where nothing, or a very small matter is demanded of ships and goods coming thither; and all nations indiscriminately are allowed to trade. Such free-ports are Leghorn, Trieste, Ancona, and Emden.

SECT. LVII.

Advantage of posts. Trade has given rise to a great intercourse between all European nations; and this is carried on by journies and epistolary correspondence, for both which nothing could be better contrived than posts. These seem to have first obtained in France*, and the manifest benefits of such a regulation soon brought them into use all over Europe.

Origin of News-papers. Accounts of what is doing in foreign countries being easily had by means of posts, this gave rise to weekly News-papers, which are likewise a French invention †.

SECT. XLVIII.

Domestic state interest of the European powers. The present politics and administration of the European monarchies and govern-

---

* Horse-posts were first instituted by an edict of Lewis XI. in 1464. Memoires de Comines, Liv. V. c. 10. Henault dans l'Abregé Chronol. de Hist. de France, Tom. I. p. 385. It was an impatience to know what was doing in the kingdom, which put him on this expedient.

† The inventor was Theophrastus Renaudot, a physician of Paris, who, on laying his scheme before cardinal Richlieu in 1631, had a patent given him. Anecdotes Literaires, Vol. II. p. 275. In Portugal the first news-papers were printed in 1715, under the auspices of Mascarenhas, an ecclesiastic. Imperiale Magazine, Feb. 1760.

ments,

ments, is very different from the more ancient. Formerly a true knowledge was wanting of the means for making a state populous, powerful, and respectable. At present all allow that so important an end is chiefly attained by a large trade, manufactures, arts, and sciences; accordingly our princes and statesmen have nothing more at heart than the advancement of those objects. And herein consists the main part of the domestic state-interest of the European powers.

Their relation and conduct towards each other has of late been no less altered. A state formerly little concerned itself about what passed in another, and with the more remote had no manner of connection or correspondence. If ever an ambassador happened to be sent, it was only on some particular business, and on bringing it to an issue, he returned home; but the power of the house of Austria and Spain, in the sixteenth century, awakened the attention of all Europe. Francis I. united himself against Charles V. with very distant powers, as Turkey, Denmark, and Sweden; and this alliance was the more taken notice of, as being the first between France and the northern crowns. It was then likewise, that it became a general maxim in European politics,

Foreign state-interest.

Balance of Europe.

litics, that an over-grown power was dangerous to the liberty and independency of other ſtates; and that its attempts to oppreſs others, and thereby aggrandize itſelf ſtill more, ought to be oppoſed with united forces. This is what conſtitutes the balance of power, ſo much talked of.

Conſequences of it. The preſervation of it againſt the preponderating power of Spain, and ſince of France, having occaſioned ſo many alliances and wars, which produced many and long-winded negotiations betwixt the other powers of Europe, it became a cuſtom, which has been continued ever ſince, to keep envoys in ordinary at foreign courts; by whoſe means one court gets ſpeedy intelligence of what paſſes in another, and frequently comes at its moſt intereſting ſecrets. Such is the riſe of that perpetual intercourſe and connection between the European ſtates; ſo that all are linked together, and any ſlight motion at one end of our part of the world, immediately ſpreads to the other: if the movement be ſuch as may cauſe a conſiderable alteration in the general ſtate of Europe, not only the neighbouring powers, but likewiſe thoſe at a diſtance, take part in it, and by negociations, or openly aſſiſting one or the other ſide, endeavour to bring about an accommodation.

This

This is well known to be an effect, which the balance has never failed producing.

This balance, however, has suffered some important changes. Whilst Spain was the greatest power in our part of the world, France could always depend on allies against that crown; but after France had acquired that envied superiority, all potentates united in support of Spain against the French; and even they who had justly been its most violent enemies, the Dutch, became its most strenuous defenders. At length those two kingdoms, which, for almost two hundred years, had generally been in arms against each other, became united by the accession of a prince of the house of Bourbon to the throne of Spain. Great Britain, which, since the Revolution, interfered more than usual in the preservation of the balance, to this united power opposed the house of Austria, in conjunction with the United Netherlands; and on the demise of Charles VI. saved it from the total ruin which otherwise seemed unavoidable. But the year 1756 produced a strange alteration in the balance and system of Europe; the house of Austria and France entering into a close alliance. This alliance, in which are also

Alterations in the balance.

also included the other branches of the house of Bourbon in Spain and Italy, at present constitutes one of the two principal parties in Europe; the other being Great Britain and its allies. Whether, in this situation of affairs, the balance of Europe can be preserved, time will shew.

Particular balance in the North, Germany, and Italy.

Besides this general, there are likewise three particular balances in Europe; the preservation of which is of great moment; as, should it be weakened or destroyed, the bad effects will be sensibly felt by the whole. The first is in the North, where the Russian power is certainly formidable. The second in is Germany, which consists in the two potent houses of Austria and Brandenburgh remaining in their present condition. The third is in Italy, where the king of Sardinia used to hold the scale between the houses of Austria and Bourbon (*t*); but by the union of those two powers, both his situation and the balance of Italy have but an unfavourable aspect.

SECT. LIX.

Conventions between European powers.

From the continual negociations, and the many alliances and wars of the European

(*t*) See Campbell's Present State of Europe, chap. ii. p. 26, 27.

states,

states, have proceded a multitude of treaties and conventions between them, containing the reciprocal rights and obligations. These conventions, and the history of the present and the two last centuries, are essentially necessary to those, whose station requires a solid knowledge of the present state of Europe.

THE PRESENT STATE OF EUROPE.

CHAP. II.
Of SPAIN.

SPAIN, in the moſt ancient times, was *Name.* called Iberia, and ſince that Hiſpania, which Annius of Viterbo derives from Hiſpanus, a king, and grandſon to Hercules (*a*). But others affirm, that the Phœnicians gave that part of Spain which was known to them, the appellation * of Sphanija, or Spanija (*b*); from whence has been formed

(*a*) Annii Liber de primis temporibus et XXIV. Regibus Hiſpaniæ, cap. xiii. in Beroſi Antiquitatibus ab eo editis, p. 299, &c. Juſtinus, Lib. XXIV. cap. 1. ſays; " Hanc (Hiſpaniam) veteres ab Ibero amne Iberiam, poſtea ad Hiſpano Hiſpaniam cognominaverunt." This Hiſpanus Annius has made a king, and the tenth of the four and twenty, who, according to his account, had reigned over all Spain.

(*b*) Sam. Bochart in Phaleg. Lib. III. cap. vii. p. 190. & in Canaan, Lib. I. cap. xxxv. p. 706. Sphanija, or Spanija, is ſaid to be derived from the Phœnician word Saphan, which ſignifies a rabbit : Spain in former times, according to many writers, producing multitudes of thoſe creatures.

Spania †; and laſtly Hiſpania; which has continued to be the name of the country, though ſeveral times conquered by foreign nations.

SECT. II.

Situation and limits. It lies between the 36th and 44th degree of north latitude; and the 9th and 21ſt of longitude from the meridian of Ferro. Eaſtward, it is bounded by the Pyrenean mountains, which ſeparate it from France; northward, by the Atlantic-ocean, and the Bay of Biſcay; weſtward, it confines on the Atlantic-ocean and Portugal; and ſouthward, on the Atlantic and Mediterranean. Thus Spain and Portugal form a peninſula.

SECT. III.

Temperature and air. The air in Spain is warm, pure, and dry, except in Catalonia and Gallicia, where it is damp; and in the northern provinces, and among the hills, very cold; whilſt up the country, and in the ſouthern provinces, the heat in ſummer is inſupportable, with ſcarce a breeze to cool it; and the winters ſo mild, that the fields are covered with

---

† The manuſcripts of many ancient Greek and Latin writers have Spania, inſtead of Hiſpania. Salmas. ad Jul. Capitolin. in M. Anton. Philoſoph. cap. i.

flowers

flowers and herbage (*c*). The climate of Spain is highly praised by the ancients (*d*); and the Spaniards themselves, travelling but little, are so conceited of the beauty and delightfulness of their country, that they cry it up above all others on the surface of the globe (*e*).

SECT. IV.

But this beauty, and, at the same time, Hills. the fertility of Spain, are much abated, by the many high and craggy mountains with which it is overspread. For, from the Pyrenees, which are eighty-five French leagues in length, and in some places forty broad, three vast arms spread themselves thro' the whole country; one reaching to the Mediterrenean near Tortosa, the second to the streights of Gibraltar, and the third to Cape Finisterre in the ocean (*f*).

SECT. V.

Spain is watered by 150 rivers large and Rivers. small, the principal of which are the Ebro, the Guadalquivir, the Guadiana, the Tagus, the Duero, and Minho. These rivers, how-

(*c*) Vayrac dans l'Etat present de l'Espagne, Tom. I. p. 53, 54.
(*d*) Justinus Lib. XLIV. cap. i. et Latinus Pacat. in Panegyrico Theodof. Aug. dicto. cap. iv. §. 2.
(*e*) Vayrac, Tom. i. p. 41.
(*f*) Ibid. Tom. I. p. 55, 56.

ever, can hardly be called navigable, on account of the many rocks, sand-banks, and water-falls (*g.*)

SECT. VI.

Fruitfulness.

Spain was greatly celebrated among the ancients for its fruitfulness (*h*); but this has of late very much declined, though more by the fault of the inhabitants, than of nature. The Spanish horses were highly valued by the Romans, and by reason of their beauty and swiftness were used for parade, and the course (*i.*) They are in the like esteem at present; but mules being come into great vogue, the Spaniards do not breed such numbers of horses as formerly †.

In the animal kingdom.

(*g*) Vayrac, Tom. I. p. 58, 60, 62.
(*h*) Pompon. Mela de Situ Orbis, L. II. c. vi. says of Spain, " It produces so many men and horses, so abounds in iron, lead, copper, silver, and gold, that though for want of water, it is in some parts, as it were, worn out and unlike itself; yet it yields flax, and esparto, a kind of rush " C. Jul. Solinus in Polyhist. c. xxvi. speaks of Spanish fertility with the like encomiums. Claudian. in Laud. Serenæ. gives this account of Spain,

Dives equis, frugum facilis, pretiosa metallis.

(*i*) Symmach. Lib. IV. Epist 61. et Lib. IX. Epist. 12.
† It is only noblemen of the highest rank who are allowed to drive in Madrid with four mules. Voyage d'Espagne, Tom. II. Lett. viii. p. 120. Count Konigseck, on his coming to Spain in the year 1725, as Imperial minister, went about Macrid and to court in a coach and six mules; which being a privilege particular to the princes of the blood, the count was desired to lay it aside, as the other envoys would affect the like parade. Mem. de Montgon. Tom. I. p. 294.

SPAIN.

Spain abounds in sheep, and their wool is the finest in all Europe †. On the other hand, it is deficient in horned cattle, especially in the inland provinces, but has a sufficiency of game of all kinds, and of wild fowl and poultry (*k*.)

Spain, as environed by the sea on two sides, is provided with variety of fish (*l*), yet not sufficiently to supply home consumption.

In the vegetable kingdom.

The vegetable kingdom, besides great quantities of very good ship-timber growing on the Pyrenees (*m*), affords the finest fruits; as pears, peaches, figs, almonds, oranges, pomegranates, chesnuts, olives, which yield excellent oil; likewise wine* and grapes. The great number of mulberry-trees in Andalusia and Granada, are a nursery for silk-worms; and the sweet-scented herbs and flowers gratify the bees, the honey of which is exquisite. Spain likewise bears the sugar-cane, saffron, rice, hemp,

---

† The number of sheep in Spain is reckoned at above eight millions, and forty thousand shepherds. Ustariz Theorica y Practica de Commercio y Marina. Cap. XI.

(*k*) Bosius in Notit. Hisp. Sect. III. c. i. §. 5.

(*l*) Ibid. l. c.

(*m*) Ustariz en la Theorica y Practica de Marina, c. lxiii.

* The Spanish wines were formerly disagreeable both in taste and smell; but the emperor Charles V. having caused some German vines to be transplanted into Spain, this has given those good qualities for which at present they are in so much repute. Bosius, l. c. p. 53.

and

and flax (*n*), but does not produce sufficient quantity of grain, though formerly it exported wheat to the Low Countries (*o*).

<small>In the fossile kingdom.</small>

Spain antiently surpassed all countries in Europe, and most of the other parts of the world, for valuable minerals, it being almost incredible what a quantity of gold and silver, according to the ancient reports, were fetched away from thence, by foreign nations †. But since the discovery of the New World, the Spaniards have given over searching for those metals in their own mines, which, however, supply them with many other valuable metals and minerals; as iron, lead, tin, quicksilver, cinnabar, alum, lapis-lazuli, calamine, crystal, magnets, and several gems, particularly diamonds and amethysts (*p*); rock, mineral,

---

(*n*) Vayrac. Tom. I. p. 71.
(*o*) Bosius, l. c.

† Though in the most ancient times the Phœnicians, and after them the Carthaginians, carried a prodigious quantity of gold and silver out of Spain, yet was not the country exhausted; the Romans being charged with having brought to Rome 111542 pounds of silver, and 4095 pounds of gold, within the first nine years, after they had, in the second Punic war, driven the Carthaginians out of Spain. Universal Hist. Vol. xviii. p. 517. The province of Asturias was particularly famous for its great quantities of gold. Plin. Hist. Nat. Lib. XXXIII. cap. iv. Silius Italicus, Lib. I. v. 231. makes mention of the Asturians as a very avaricious people.

——————— Astur avarus
Visceribus laceræ telluris mergitur imis,
Et redit infelix effosso concolor auro.

(*p*) Vayrac, Tom. I. p. 70, 71.

and sea-salt; soda, or kali, Spain has in such abundance, as to export great quantities.

SECT. VII.

Division of the kingdom. The Spanish monarchy formerly consisted of two capital kingdoms, Castile and Arragon; but at present the latter is entirely incorporated with the former. Castile included the kingdoms of, 1. New Castile. 2. Old Castile. 3. Leon. 4. Navarre *. 5. Granada. 6. Galicia. 7. Seville. 8. Cordoua †. 9. Murcia. 10. The principality of Asturias. Likewise the provinces of, 11. Estremadura. 12. Guipuscoa. 13. Alava; and 14. the lordship of Biscay.

To Arragon belonged the kingdoms of, 15. Arragon. 16. Valencia. 17. Majorca ‡, and 18. The principality of Catalonia.

These eighteen provinces constitute the present kingdom of Spain, in which are reckoned 1500 cities or walled towns: but in these are different gradations; some,

---

* Ferdinand the Catholic having conquered Navarre in the year 1512, solemnly united it to the crown of Castile, in an assembly of the states held at Burgos, in the year 1515. Mariana, Lib. XXX. c. 24.

† This and the kingdom of Seville make the province of Andalusia.

‡ In this kingdom of Majorca, or Malorca, are comprehended the other three Balearic islands, Minorca, Ivica, and Formentera.

which were the refidence of kings and bifhops, and of the religious orders of knighthood, in virtue of that diftinction, ftill enjoy particular rights and privileges, and are
called ciudades; the others only villas (*q*.)

SECT. VIII.

Dependen-cies. But the Spaniards have likewife many
and great dependencies in the three other
In Africa. parts of the world. 1. In Africa, on the
coaft of Barbary, Ceuta, Oran, and Mafal-
quivir *; and in the ocean the Canary-
Iflands, which abound in wine, fugar, and
valuable fruits.

In Afia. 2. In Afia they have the Ladrones and
Philippine iflands; among which laft the
principal is Lucon, with the famous city of
Manilla.

3. Farther, to the fame nation is fubject
the greateft and beft part of America, to
the extent of above a thoufand geographical miles from north to fouth. In this large
tract, they are poffeffed of California, New-
Mexico, the three kingdoms of Mexico,
or New-Spain, New-Granada, and Peru;

(*q*) Bofius in Notit. Hifp. Sect. III. ch. i. §. 9.
* Thefe three places, which bring in nothing to the crown, and the garrifons of which are very chargeable, are kept purely as a pretence for the king to levy the produce of the Croifade bull. Science du Gouvernement, by M. de Real, Part I. Tom. II. p. 94.

likewise Chili, Tucumannia, Paraguay; together with the island of Cuba, part of the island of Hispaniola, Porto-Rico, the Lucayan islands; as also Trinidad, Margarita, and some of the Caribbee islands.

These countries produce great quantities of valuable commodities of all kinds (*r*); Mexico and Peru, particularly, are very rich in gold and silver *.

The Spaniards ground their right of conquering the New World on the grant of pope Alexander VI. (*s*), and on the war which, in consequence of this bull, they made on that people, with extreme cruelty †.

(*r*) See Chap. II. and Sect. lv.

* Peru at first remitted annually to Spain to the amount of thirteen millions of ducats in gold. Inca Garcilasso de la Vega's History of the Incas of Peru, Book VIII. c. xxiv. p. 354. The silver mines in the mountains of Potosi, the first forty years after the discovery of them, yielded 555,000,000 pieces of eight, exclusive of the unregistered silver, by which the king was defrauded of his fifths, and they likewise were something very considerable. See Antonio De Herrera en los Hechos de los Castellanas en las Islas y Tierra firme del Mar Oceano. Dec. I. Lib. II. cap. xiv. 15. The gold and silver which Spain has received from America, from 1492 to 1724, is reckoned at 5000 millions of pieces of eight. See Don Geronymo de Ustariz in Theorica y Practica de Marina y Comercio. Cap. iii. p. 6, 7.

(*s*) It is to be found in Leibnitii Cod. Jur. Gent. Diplom. N. CCIII. p. 294. and in Du Mont, Corps. Univ. Dipl. Tom. III. P. II. N. CLXI. p. 302.

† The Spaniards are charged with having killed, or put to death in the New World between twelve and fifteen million of people. Istoria della Distruttione dell' Indie occidentali di Bartolomeo de las Casas, p. 11, 12, 14.

They have hitherto been accounted invincible in America (*t*); but in the laſt war the Engliſh have ſhewn the contrary.

SECT. IX.

Its former dependencies in Europe. Spain had formerly very confiderable dependencies in Europe; as the kingdoms of Naples and Sicily, the iſland of Sardinia, the dutchy of Milan, and the Auſtrian Netherlands. But they were all difmembered from it by the peace of Utretcht in the year 1713; which, however, was no real lofs to the crown, the defences of ſuch remote countries being very chargeable *: but the Spaniſh nobility were fufferers by this change, many governments and other lucrative employments ceaſing at that feparation. Not many years after, the fortune of war gave Naples and Sicily to one Spaniſh prince, and Parma and Placentia to another; fo that thefe countries are again become, in fome meafure, dependent on Spain.

SECT. X.

The Gauliſh Celts. The Gauliſh Celts were unqueſtionably the firſt who peopled Spain: the goodnefs

---

(*t*) See De Real, Part I. Tom. II. p. 91.
* The Netherlands alone are faid to have coſt the crown of Spain from the time of Charles V. to 1663, 187,000,000 of livres. Annales Politiques de Saint Pierre, Part I. p. 180.

and

and opulency of the country, in subsequent times, drew thither other foreign nations, particularly the Phœnicians and Carthaginians. The former, for the conveniency of their trade, established colonies on the south and west coasts. The latter forcibly spread themselves up the country; but in the second Punic war were totally driven out by the Romans, who, after several obstinate wars, became masters of Spain, and kept possession above four hundred years; during which time Spain had the honour of giving three emperors to Rome (*u.*)

But in the beginning of the fifth century, this province was over-run by the Vandals, the Suevi, and Alani, who divided it by lot (*x*). The former, however, some time after, passed over into Africa, and the others were subdued by the Visigoths, who erected a vast kingdom; comprehending, besides Spain, part of Gaul, and the province of Mauritania Tingitana in Africa.

409.
429.
584.

This kingdom of the Visigoths was brought to a period by the loss of one deci- 712.

(*u*) Claudian in Laud. Serenæ, v. 60.
    Sola novum Latiis vectigal Iberia rebus,
    Contulit Augustus, fruges. æraria, miles
    Undique conveniunt; totoque ex orbe leguntur:
    Hæc generat, qui cuncta regant.
(*x*) Idatius in Chron. ad ann. 18. Honorii, says expressly: Subversis Hispaniæ provinciis, barbari . . . . forte ad habitandum sibi provinciarum dividunt regiones.

sive battle against the Moors, who, within two years, likewise reduced all Spain, and afterwards Gothick Gaul.

718.

Some remains of the Visigoths sought shelter from the ferocity of the conquerors, in the mountains of Asturias; and under Pelagius, whom they had chosen their king, began to make head against the Moors, and successively dispossessed them of towns and parcels of land, which proved the foundation of the kingdom of Leon; and from its subsequent conquests, arose the county of Castile.

778.

In the like manner Charles the Great, king of France, and afterwards Roman emperor, dispossessed the Moors of the whole country as far as the Pyrenees; and these conquests formed the county of Navarre, which afterwards was raised to a kingdom. Sancho III. one of its kings, very much enlarged his dominions by successful wars; and by his marriage with Nunnia, Countess of Castile, annexed that county to his other territories. The partition of his dominions among his sons, gave rise to two new kingdoms, Castile and Arragon; and with the former Leon became united by a marriage.

1034.

1037.

These kingdoms waged a perpetual war against the Moors, who, weakened by their partitions and dissensions, continually lost ground;

ground; so that in process of time Granada was all that remained to that nation. Particularly Castile on one side, and Arragon on the other, had made considerable conquests upon them; and thus all Spain, except Granada and Navarre, fell under their dominion. To Castile belonged Leon, Galicia, Asturias, Guipuscoa, Alava, Biscay, Estremadura, Andalusia, and Murcia; the kingdom of Arragon comprehended Valencia, Catalonia, and the Balearic islands. The last had also made some foreign conquests, and subdued Sicily and Sardinia.

All these states became united by the marriage of Ferdinand of Arragon and Isabella of Castile. When the new government was thought sufficiently consolidated in both kingdoms, they attacked Granada, and after a ten years war reduced it, which put an end to the dominion of the Moors in Spain. They had conquered it in two years, and by only one pitched battle; whereas the expulsion of them was a work of near 800 years, attended with 3,700 engagements (*y*).

1469.

1481.

Spain was now become a very powerful kingdom. The discovery of the New

1492.

(*y*) Catalogo Real y Genealogico de Espana, por Rodrigo Mendez Silva, p. 158. This author adds, that some encreased the number of these engagements, which he terms Battallas Campales, or pitched battles, to five thousand.

World by Chriſtopher Columbus aggrandized it ſtill more; and the addreſs and courage of Ferdinand the Catholic, brought the kingdoms of Naples and Navarre under his dominions.

1504.
1512.

His grandſon and ſucceſſor Charles I. gave the crown of Spain a greater luſtre and conſideration by the Imperial title, which he obtained, notwithſtanding all the oppoſition of France. The ſingular good fortune which had ever accompanied him againſt all his enemies, and particularly againſt Francis I. he vigorouſly puſhed to the advantage of Spain, adding to it Milan, and the kingdoms of Mexico and Peru. He had the ſame deſign on England in marrying his ſon Philip to queen Mary; and though this was defeated by her dying without iſſue, and though he could not tranſmit the Imperial crown to him, yet he left him the greateſt potentate in Europe, or rather of the whole univerſe.

1519.

1554.

Philip was for realiſing that univerſal monarchy, to which his father had been paving the way for him; and his hopes were the more ſanguine, having united to Spain the kingdom of Portugal, with its large poſſeſſions in the Eaſt and Weſt Indies. But the miſcarriage of his enterprize againſt England and France, and his inability

1580.

1588.

lity to quell the revolted Netherlands, con- 1590.
vinced him of the improbability of such extensive projects.

The Spanish power, which under him had reached its zenith, began to totter, and decline more and more under his successors. Philip III. his son weakened the 1610. state by expelling the Maranes, the most laborious of his subjects, by the misconduct of his privado, the duke of Lerma; and lastly, by engaging in a war against the Protestants in Germany. The latter brought the arms of France on his son Philip IV. the 1635. consequence of which was the defection of the Catalonians; and this drew on the re- 1639. volt of the kingdom of Portugal. By these 1640. disasters Philip IV. was constrained at the peace of Munster to acknowledge the 1648. United Netherlands as a free state; and at the peace of the Pyrenees, to France he 1659. ceded Conflans, Roussillon, the far greater part of Artois, with other considerable parcels of the Netherlands.

At his demise, his son Charles II. was a minor, and left in a labyrinth of misfortunes; so that, at the peace, the ill state of his affairs obliged him to renounce all claim 1668. to the kingdom of Portugal: by three wars with France, in which he lost a great part of Flanders, and other provinces of the Low Countries, together with the country

try of Burgundy, so exhausted was the Spanish monarchy, that this prince, though possessor of the treasures of the West Indies, did not leave ready money enough to defray his funeral (z).

His death and will brought on a long and severe war between Philip V. duke of Anjou, whom he had nominated his heir, and Charles III. archduke of Austria. The former was by the peace of Utrecht established in the monarchy, the latter had the greater part of its European possessions. To Great Britain were ceded Gibraltar and the island of Minorca, which it had conquered during the war. King Philip could not rest till he had recovered the Italian territories, which had formerly belonged to the crown of Spain; but Great Britain and France frustrated this attempt. He, however, made use of another opportunity to place his third son Charles on the throne of Naples and Sicily; and in the war for the Austrian succession, he intended erecting a sovereignty in the upper part of Italy for his fourth son Don Philip. This scheme after the death of Philip V. was in some measure effected by

(z) Francisc. Wagner in Hist. Leopoldi M. P. II. p. 564, says; " Cum ad funerales sumtus (Caroli II.) impar esset ærarium, Portocarrerus factus pro rege fidejussor, mutuatam pecuniam adhibuit, alienoque ære extulit tot regnorum dominum.

Ferdinand V. his succeffor; Parma, Placentia and Guaftalla, being by the peace of Aix-la-Chapelle settled under certain conditions on Don Philip. This king's views were principally directed to the internal improvement of his dominions and the prefervation of peace; so that he declined taking part in the war which had newly broke out between France and Great Britain; but after his demife, his brother and succeffor Charles III. to gratify France, with which he had united himfelf by the Family-compact, as it was called, became a party in it. But the consequences of this ftep proved very unfortunate; the Englifh, besides other conquests, making themselves mafters of the Havannah; and in return for that important place, Florida was ceded to them at the peace.

1748.
1755.
1759.
1761.
1762.
1763.

SECT. XI.

Spaniards, a mixed people.

Spain having been succeffively poffeffed by so many foreign people, the Phœnicians, Carthaginians, Romans, Vandals, Suevi, Alani, afterwards by the Vifigoths, and laftly by the Moors, among whom were great numbers of Jews; it is eafily feen that, generally confidered, the Spaniards muft be a very mixed kind of people: but the defcendants of thefe feveral people did

not

not equally stand their ground, one being overpowered and subdued by another. The Romans expelled the Carthaginians; the Vandals, Suevi, and Alani, after dispossessing the Romans with great slaughter, met with the like treatment from the Visigoths; and these could not withstand the invasion of the Moors, though they were not totally extirpated or driven out of the country, such numbers remaining that they again took up arms against the conquerors; and, in a long succession of years, partly subdued them, and partly compelled them to return to Africa, their mother-country. Thus the Visigoths are the main stock of the Spanish nation, with a considerable mixture of descendants from the Moors, a few from the Romans and Suevi, and fewer still from the Jews, and the fewest of all from the ancient inhabitants (a).

SECT. XII.

Character of the Spaniards.

The Spaniards, as to their persons, are in general of a middle size, or low stature, and withal lean and meagre. They are well limbed, but with weak eyes, which makes spectacles so common among them *.

(a) Bosius in Notit. Hisp. Sect. III. cap. i. §. 11. p. 60, 61, &c.

* Spectacles, besides the use of them for weak eyes, are likewise worn by persons of rank out of parade and affectation. See Gundling's Otia, Vol. I. p. 24.

They

They are of a brown complexion, with something grave or stern and forbidding in their aspect; which, however, relates only to the men; the women, besides their beauty, being more lively and agreeable in their manners (*b*). Among the diseases of both sexes, the venereal is the most common; but they make light of it (*c*).

They are naturally pensive and melancholy; in their deliberations and resolves slow; and in conversation suspicious, discerning, and reserved. They have a large share of ambition, but likewise of firmness and fortitude; are very temperate in eating, and still more in drinking (*d*); they are celebrated for magnanimity, probity, constancy in friendship, and punctual observance of their word (*e*).

This is the bright side of the Spaniards. On the other hand one sees, and sometimes amidst the most sordid poverty, an intolerable haughtiness, and a contempt of other nations (*f*). They are likewise charged with extreme avarice, seizing every oppor-

---

(*b*) Bosius, Sect. III. cap. i. §. 15. p. 67, 68. Gundling's Otia, Part I. p. 21, 24.

(*c*) Relation du Voyage d'Espagne, Tom. III. Lett. XI. p. 85, 86.

(*d*) Barclaii Icon Animor. cap. vii. p. 4. p. m. 439. Bosius, l. c. p. 68, 69.

(*e*) Vayrac, Tom. I. p. 27, 28.

(*f*) Barclaius, ibid. c. vii. p. 439. Vayrac, Tom. I. p. 40.

tunity, however iniquitous, of enriching themselves; an art in which their viceroys, governors, and other officers in America, not excepting even the missionaries in that country, are most infamously expert (*g*). Lewdness is one of their capital vices. Married and unmarried youths and boys, keep mistresses; and from this propensity springs their great veneration and complaisance to the fair-sex, together with that jealousy which is so predominant in them, that they stick at nothing to gratify it. In revenge they are equally vehement, and generally have it executed by bravo's or murderers (*i*); looking on duelling, so much practised by other nations, as giving advantages to an enemy, at one's own peril (*k*). The proceedings of the Spaniards towards the Moors, the Indians, and the Flemings, leave an indelible brand of cruelty on their name (*l*).

Though avaricious, they are slothful, and hate work, by which they might be

(*g*) Relation du Voyage d' Esp. Tom. III. Lett. XI. p. 64.
(*h*) Vayrac, Tom. I. p. 38, 39, 43. See likewise L'Espion dans les Cours des Princes Chretiens, Tom. II. Lett. l. p. 137, 138.
(*i*) Arcana Dominationis Hispanæ, per J. L. W. c. xxv.
(*k*) Relation du Voyage d' Esp. Tom. III. Lett. XI. p. 77, 78.
(*l*) Arcana Dominat. Hisp. cap. xxvi. et xxxiii. See likewise L'Espion dans les Cours des Princes Chretiens, Tom. II. Lett. xxx. p. 85, 86.

SPAIN.

earning fomething, and particularly handicrafts and agriculture. The fource of this indolence lies in their pride, all pretending to be defcended from the Vifigoths; and that to ftoop to fuch low employments would be debafing their illuftrious origin (*m*). This makes the commonalty fo very poor; and perfons of rank are often reduced to exigencies by their negligence and mifmanagement *. The grandees are very profufe in fine furniture, and often expend a great part of their eftates in plate, of which fome have an amazing quantity, though feldom ufed but at nuptials (*n*). The Spaniards are very conceited and tenacious of their old cuftoms and manners, and would equally deteft any alteration in their drefs, as in the ceremonies of the church: the public games and diverfions ufed by their anceftors, fubfift to this very day.

(*m*) Vayrac, Tom. I. p. 47, 48.
(*n*) Relation du Voyage d' Efpagne, Tom. II. Lett. ix. p. 173.

* Their creditors are often very great lofers, it being in the debtor's power to cancel all their claims, by appointing a great number of maffes to be faid for his foul; the fums at which the charge of thefe is computed being previoufly deducted from the inheritance; and thus little or nothing may remain for the creditors. This injurious piece of devotion has given rife to the proverb: Fulano dexado fu alma heredera; "Such a one has made his foul his heir."

(*n*) Relation du Voyage d' Efpagne. Vol. II. Letter IX. p. 173.

Among

Among these, the principal are the bull-fights (*o*); and the pope himself, though so much respected in Spain, never has been able to abolish those sanguinary entertainments *.

SECT. XIII.

Antipathy of the Spaniards and French.

It is not only in their customs and manners, but likewise in their natural disposition, that the Spaniards differ very much from other nations, and particularly from the French (*p*); hence some deduce the violent aversion, or antipathy as it is called, between the Spanish and French nations †.

(*o*) A description of the bull-fights occurs in Voyages en Espagne et en Portugal, p. 94, &c. and in the Relation du Voyage d'Espagne, Tom. III. Lett. X. p. 23, 24, &c.

* The first public and solemn bull-fights were exhibited in the year 1100. Pope Pius V. in 1567, issued an express ordinance against them, but the Spaniards would not give up their favourite diversion; and so far prevailed with pope Clement VIII. that in 1596, he renewed the permission of them, under certain limitations. Rodrigo Mendez Silva Catalogo Real y genealogico de Espanna, fol. 49. a.

(*p*) Gundling's Antipathy of the Spaniards and French; in answer to M. Bayle, in his Otia, Part I. c. 2. §. 5. p. 83.

† Of this opinion is Gundling, in his Otia, §. 7. p. 86. Garsia, a Spaniard, who has wrote a book on this antipathy, ascribes it to the immediate operation of the devil. That evil spirit, says he, was afraid that, should the Spaniards and French, whom he stiles the noblest nations, and the two great luminaries of the earth, close in an union, they would subdue the whole world, and spread the Christian religion every where; and thus his kingdom would come to nothing. In order to prevent this, he kindles such a flame of discord and enmity between them, as should burn with perpetual violence. Antipatia de' Francesi e Spagnuoli del Dottor. D. Carlo Garsia, cap. vii. p. 100, &c.

But

But this antipathy proceeds not so much from natural, as political causes. The jealousy excited by the great power of one crown, the projects on both sides to the prejudice of the other, the opposite views, together with the many and obstinate wars occasioned by such contrariety of interest, are what gave rise to, and have continued, a violent aversion and enmity between them. This, experience undeniably confirms. For the Spaniards coming to have a French king, which united the political views of both, before so directly opposite, the two nations have lived in perfect harmony, and the former enmity is turned into a firm and zealous friendship †.

SECT. XIV.

The Romans, with their sovereignty, introduced their language into Spain. Some Spanish writers, however, ascribe this chiefly to the emperor Marcus Antoninus Pius, and relate, that by an edict he suppressed the several languages which were spoken in Spain, and erected schools for teach-

---

† What Bayle says in his answer to the questions of a country-gentleman, Tom. I. p. 102, perfectly agrees with the French and Spaniards. " Leave neighbouring nations all their difference of manners and customs, but remove from them jealousy and an affectation of equality or superiority, and make their political interests the same, you shall soon see them become friends, and cordially draw together."

teaching the Roman; but that the Cantabrians, who inhabited the kingdom of Navarre, and the provinces of Biscay, Alva, Guipuscoa and Rioja, retained their former idiom (*q*); and are said to speak it to this very day, with only a very slender mixture of the Castilian (*r*). On the successful invasion of the Vandals, Suevi, and Visigoths, the Roman became so adulterated with their languages, as to form a new dialect, into which the Moors likewise introduced many Arabic words. The present Spanish language, accordingly, is a compound of the languages of all these several nations, with the predominancy of the Roman; on which account the Spaniards term their language Romance. It has several dialects, but the Castilian passes for the best and most pure (*s*). The Spanish language, like the people, is grave and majestic. Mariana observes it to be so far analogous to the Latin, that Spanish and Latin may be spoken with the same words, and in the same construction (*t*). During the prosperity of the Spanish monarchy, their language was in the same vogue as the French at present; but since

---

(*q*) Catalogo Real y Genealogico de Espanna, por Rodrigo Mendez Silva, p. 8. a.
(*r*) Bosius in Notit. Hisp. Sect. III. c. i. §. 14. p. 67.
(*s*) Ibid. Sect. III. cap. i. §. 14. p. 67.
(*t*) Mariana's General History of Spain, Book I. c. 5.

Spain

Spain came to lose the far greater part of its European dependencies, it has no longer been so common.

SECT. XV.

Spain is so thinly peopled, that some will allow it only four millions of inhabitants (*u*); but this undoubtedly is too little. A very sagacious Spanish politician in the year 1723 reckoned them at seven millions and a half (*x*); and this is the number at which they are now computed (*y*). The country, with respect to its extent, could maintain many more; but to this augmentation there have been and still are several impediments. 1. The many severe wars. 2. The driving out the Jews and Maranas under Ferdinand the Catholic and Philip III. 3. The West-India colonies * and garrisons. 4. The

Number of inhabitants.

(*u*) M. de Real Science du Gouvernem. Part I. Tom. II. p. 85.

(*x*) Ustariz's Theory and Practice of Trade and the Marine, c 18.

(*y*) The Rev. Mr. Susmilch's Divine Oeconomy, &c. cap. XX. §. 379.

* The emigrations to America Don Geronymo de Ustariz, however, will not admit as a principal cause of the thinning of Spain; Gallicia, Biscay, Navarre, &c. from whence emigrations are most frequent, being very populous; whilst the countries of Toledo, la Mancha, Guadalaxara, &c. whence very few go to visit the New World, are the barest of inhabitants. And thus in his account the decay of trade and manufactures, and the poverty consequential to those evils, together with the heavy taxes on the inhabitants, are the chief causes of the depopulation. Theory and Practice of Commerce and the Marine, cap. XII. p. 21, 22.

great number of ecclesiastics and religious of both sexes. 5. The inquisition, which deters foreigners from settling in Spain. 6. The sterility of married women; the blame of which, however, is not so much to be charged on the sex, as on the premature licentiousness of the men. 7. The barrenness of some parts, which is such, as not to bear many inhabitants; and 8. The taxes, too heavy for the comfortable support of a family (*z*). King Philip IV. indeed, endeavoured to promote population by granting privileges and conveniencies to those who married early and had children; but all his good intentions have failed of their desired effect (*a*).

SECT. XVI.

Upper and lower Spanish nobility.

The principal among the Spanish nobility were formerly called Ricos homes or Ricos hombres, perhaps, from their estates and wealth *. But this title has ceased since

---

(*z*) Bosius in Notit. Hisp. Sect. III. c. i. Sect. III. p. 63, 65. See likewise Science du Gouvernement, par M. de Real.

(*a*) Bosius l. c. p. 65. Thomas Campanella in Discursu de Monarchia Hispan. c. xxxi. p. 318, 319. advised to remove Indians and Africans into Spain. "Nothing is more absurd, says he, than to make that country a storehouse of gold and silver, and not rather of men and women, these being much more valuable and useful than both those metals put together."

* The Ricos hombres were made by the delivery of a banner and a kettle to them, as tokens of a right to bring troops

those

those of dukes, marquesses, counts, viscounts, and barons, have been adopted † (*b*). These constitute the upper nobility in Spain, and are stiled Titulados or Titulos, with the word Don before their names, which, however, is likewise taken by the knights of the three religious orders, and other persons in respectable employments.

The lower nobility or gentry are called Hidalgos; and among these are likewise reckoned the Cavalleros and Escuderos. Spain is particularly favourable to foundlings, who by custom are accounted Hidalgos (*c*.)

It was anciently a singular custom among the Spanish nobility, that on any one's having cause of discontent, or imagining he had, from any real or supposed affront or injury, he solemnly revoked his allegiance to the king, and renounced his country. This

into the field, and of their being able to maintain them. Selden's Titles of Honour, Part II. c. iv. Manoel Severim De Faria nas Noticias de Portugal, p. 127.

† Rodrigo Mendez Silva en el Catalogo Real y Genealogico, fol. xxxi. b. & 133. says, that Ferdinand the Catholic suppressed the title of Ricos hombres, substituting in lieu of it, that of Grandee; but this is a mistake, the latter title having been used long before.

(*b*) See Selden's Titles of Honours, Part II. c. iv.

(*c*) Memoires Instructifs pour un Voyageur, Tom. II. p. 72. Concerning this custom the Spaniards say, that, in doubtful cases, it is better to give nobility to one who had it not, than to deprive one whose right it was.

was called Defnaturalizarfe; and a nobleman, after this formality, might go over to the enemy, and even to the Moors, and carry arms againſt his king and his country, without being chargeable with any crime or violation of his duty (*d*).

SECT. XVII.

Grandees of Spain. Among the upper nobility of Spain, the dukes, fome marqueſſes, and fome counts, have particular honours and privileges; on which account they are ſtiled Grandees; a title uſed, at leaſt, under king John I. (*e*). One of their greateſt privileges is their being covered before the king; a ceremony, however, that formerly admitted of fome difference. Some put on their hats before ſpeaking to the king; others, not till they had done ſpeaking; and others, not before taking leave of the king, and going away from his preſence; and on this account the grandees were divided into three claſſes: but this diſtinction is at preſent laid aſide, the king making only grandees of the firſt claſs (*f*). They take place of all officers

(*d*) Mariana, Book XI. chap. xi. Book XII. chap. xii. Book XIV. chap. 12. and Oſor. de Reb. Eman. Lib. XI. p. 23.
(*e*) Vavrac, Tom. III. p. 182, 183.
(*f*) Clarke's Letters concerning the Spaniſh Nation. Letter VII. Part II. p. 119.

of state, or those belonging to the court, the constable and admiral of Castile excepted. They are allowed to keep heralds, and to have a sword carried before them. In chapel they sit on a bench on one side of the king. They cannot be put under arrest, but by his majesty's express order. They put themselves on a footing with the electors of the empire and the princes of Italy (*g*). They likewise had formerly a dispute with the peers of France, which in the year 1701 was adjusted on these terms; that the grandees of Spain, when in France, shall enjoy the privileges of peers, and these in Spain shall be treated as grandees (*h*).

King Lewis I. to the extreme mortification of the grandees made the captain and lieutenant-general, their equals in respect of precedence at court (*i*).

SECT. XVIII.

The form of government in the Spanish monarchy, and of its particular kingdoms, has undergone several vicissitudes. The Visigoth kings were elected with a limited prerogative, the consent of the great and

(*g*) Vayrac, Tom. III. p. 201, 206.
(*h*) Ibid. p. 177.
(*i*) Delormeaux dans l'Abregé Chronologique de l'Hist. d'Espagne, Tom. V. p. 382.

the lesser nobility being requisite in every important step of government. King Reccared I. having embraced the Catholic religion, the prelates and other dignitaries soon rose to great consideration, not only in the concerns of the church and religion, but even in the discussing of state-affairs, so that laws were made in their assemblies (*k*); which thus were become both synods and diets.

Several kingdoms springing up in Spain on the extinction of the monarchy of the Visigoths, the royal prerogative was in all very much curtailed by the states of the country. In Castile, the upper nobility, the clergy, the three orders of knighthood, who with the principal cities made the states of the kingdom, could levy troops, and sometimes used this privilege against the kings themselves *.

The states of Arragon, who consisted of the clergy, the nobility, and the cities, were possessed of very great privileges and immunities; and king Alphonso III. under penalty of forfeiting his crown, bound himself and his successors to the observance of

---

(*k*) See the decrees of the fourth, fifth, and sixth council of Toledo, in Ferrera's General History of Spain, Vol. II. p. 366, 371, 375.

* Of this are instances in the histories of John II. and Henry IV.

them.

them (*l*). Nay, the kings of Arragon in any difputes with their fubjects were obliged to fubmit to a judge, who was ftiled El Jufticia, and who kept the king's prerogative within due limits (*m*).

Thefe two kingdoms becoming united by the marriage of Ferdinand of Arragon and Ifabella of Caftile, each retained its particular form of government. Under this joint fovereignty, however, the power and exorbitant privileges of the Caftilian grandees were very much abridged; but the Arragonians preferved all their ancient liberties; king Ferdinand apprehending that it might be of ill confequence to infringe them (*n*). They were, however, fo offenfive to him, that having in the year 1515 conquered the kingdom of Navarre, he united it with Caftile, becaufe, as Mariana obferves, the Navarrians might lay claim to the liberties of the Arragonians; for otherwife he might better have united Navarre with Arragon: thefe two kingdoms had been formerly united, and he himfelf was immediately king of Arragon (*o*). Under the emperor Charles V. the ftates of Caf-

(*l*) See the decrees of the fourth, fifth, and fixth councils of Toledo, as before cited, Vol. IV. p. 427.
(*m*) A. Perez obras y Relaciones, p. 141. Mariana, Book VIII. cap. i.
(*n*) Anton. Perez, p. 143.
(*o*) Mariana, Book XXX. chap. xxiv.

tile loft the greater part of their ancient confideration; for that prince having at the diet of Toledo, held in 1538, demanded an extraordinary fupply, and the nobility and cities refufing their confent, he abruptly diffolved the affembly; and this was the laft diet of Caftile in which the ftates affifted (*p*). The kings ever after omitted the archbifhops, bifhops, and nobility, and fummoned only eighteen cities, each of which fent two reprefentatives (*q*).

The Arragonians, fome time after, met with the like treatment. In the year 1591, a ftate prifoner, the celebrated Anthony Perez, who had been fecretary of ftate, was releafed by an infurrection of the people of Saragoffa; and king Philip II. fending a body of troops into Arragon to chaftife the infurgents, the Jufticia John de la Nuza oppofed it with an armed force: but the king caufed his head to be taken off, without the leaft examination or trial (*r*); in flagrant violation of the Arragonian liberties. They, however, ftill retained their conftitution, and their peculiar council of ftate, as inftituted by Ferdinand the Catholic, till the war for the Spanifh fucceffion, in which

(*p*) Ferreras, Vol. IX. p. 236, 237.
(*q*) Science du Gouvernem. par M. de Real, Part I. Tom. II. p. 102, 103.
(*r*) Anton. Perez, p. 158, 159, &c.

Arragon, Valencia, and Catalonia, had declared for the Auftrian party. On this account Philip V. deprived them of all their privileges; and totally abolifhing the form of government, which had fubfifted fo long, united them to the crown of Caftile, and fubjected them to its laws (s). Thus the kings of Spain, at prefent, exercife an unlimited power in all parts of the kingdom: and as for the Cortes, or affembly of the ftates, it is only on certain folemnities, or for fettling the fucceffion, that they are convened.

SECT. XIX.

Each of the feveral kingdoms and provinces of which the Spanifh monarchy has been gradually compounded, had its own fundamental laws; but fince their being united, and ftill more fince the prerogative grew to be unlimited, few of thofe laws remain, and thefe chiefly relate to the fucceffion. The Spanifh kings at firft divided their dominions among their children, as appears from the example of Sancho the Great, king of Navarre; Ferdinand I. Alphonfo VI. Alphonfo VIII. kings of Caftile and Leon; and James I. king of Arragon. But time

Fundamental laws.

(s) Deformeaux, Tom. V. p. 272, 273. Miniana de Bello ruftico Valentino, Lib. III. c. xix. Mr. de Real, Part I. Tom. II. p. 108.

fhewed

shewed the inconveniency of these divisions; and Ferdinand III. king of Castile, established the right of primogeniture by law (*t*). Pursuant to this regulation the crown devolves to the eldest son, and after him to his descendants in a right line; and in the want of a male issue, to the king's eldest daughter. If the eldest son dies before his entering on the succession, and leaves a son or daughter by a legitimate marriage, he or she is to have the crown; and in failure of all these, it is to go to the nearest of kin *.

Another law was made by the same prince against any division or partition of the kingdom, in virtue of which it is always to remain consolidated, without any alienation or division; and this law was to be sworn to by the sovereign at his accession, and by

---

(*t*) This occurs in the code published by king Alphonso XI. called Las Siete Partidas, Partida II. Tit. 15. Ley. 2. from which Mr. Rousset has inserted it, though not so correctly as could be wished, in the Supplement au Corps Universel Diplomatique, Tom. I. Part I. 101.

* This kind of succession is termed Successio linealis cognatica, or likewise Castellana. In it regard is first had to the line, and then to the degree; so that the nearest relation to the deceased king in the same line is to succeed him. After the line and degree, regard is had to the age and sex, the elder being preferred to the younger, and the princes to the princesses, that is to say, in the like line, and the like degree. H. Grot. de Jure Belli & Pacis, Lib. II. cap. vii. §. 23. and Mr. de Real Science du Gouvernem. Part I. Tom. II. p. 95.

the

the people at their taking the oath of fealty (*u*).

In Arragon, under the reign of James II. it was likewise enacted by a diet held at Tarragona in 1319, that Arragon, Valencia, and Catalonia, together with their privileges and incomes, should be for ever incorporated, without any future separation (*x*).

These fundamental laws have both before and since the conjunction of the two kingdoms, been constantly observed down to our times.

But king Philip V. in the year 1713 altered the former mixed succession by a new law, that the princes should always take the lead of the princesses, who were never to inherit, except in case of a total failure of the male line (*y*). By this ordinance, the succession in the royal family was better secured, and not so frequently transferred by marriage into foreign families; which in Castile was the case three times, in Arragon twice, in Navarre seven times, and twice since the conjunction of the monarchy.

By that part of the treaty of Utrecht between Philip V. king of Spain, and Victor

---

(*u*) Las Siete Partidas, Partida II. Tit. xv. Ley. 5. And in Suplem. au Corps Universel Diplomat. par Mr. Rousset, Tom. I. Part I. p. 102.
(*x*) Ferrera's General History of Spain, Vol. IV. p. 592.
(*y*) Deformeaux, Tom. V. p. 312, 313.

Amadeus duke of Savoy, the fucceſſion to the throne, on the extinction of the line of the former, is to devolve to the latter and his family (z). This arrangement having been previouſly agreed to by the ſtates of the kingdom, is juſtly accounted among the fundamental laws of Spain.

The king's majority. The king's majority being not determined in Spain by any law, ſome minor kings have taken the reins of government ſooner, and others later, into their hands; as Alphonſo XI. king of Caſtile, on his entering into his fifteenth year; Henry III. at the age of only thirteen years and ten months; and John II. at the very beginning of his fourteenth year; from which it is probable, that the term of the king's minority does not at moſt reach beyond his being full fourteen years of age. For as to Charles II. having reached his ſixteenth year before he aſſumed the government, this was owing to particular circumſtances; among others to his being of a ſickly habit, and weak both in body and mind. Beſides, the queen-regent his mother, Mary-Anne of Auſtria, was for keeping her place at the helm as long as poſſible.

(z) Art. III. du Traité de Paix entre Philippe V. Roy d'Eſpagne, & Victor Amadée, Duc de Savoye, fait à Utrecht le 13me Aout 1713. See Corps Univerſel Diplom. de M. du Mont, Tom. VIII.

The king appoints the regency, and the guardianship of the minor; and where no such provision has been made, the right belongs to the states of the kingdom.

SECT. XX.

The Spanish kings have, in ancient times, Title. and long before the conjunction of the monarchy, affected very lofty and high-sounding titles, and not a few stiled themselves emperors of Spain; as Sancho the Great, king of Navarre; Ferdinand the Great; Alphonso VI. Alphonso VII. Alphonso VIII. kings of Castile, and others (*a*). The latter imagined, that as sovereign of several kingdoms, namely, Castile, Leon, and Gallicia, and the kings of Navarre and Arragon being his vassals, he had a right to the title of emperor (*b*); so that he caused himself to be crowned as such at Leon, with great pomp (*c*). But his successors have not thought fit to imitate him. The king of Spain's present title is very diffuse, contain-

(*a*) Chifletius in Vindic. Hisp. cap. xi. p. 101, &c. et in Luminib. Prærogativ. X. p. 369, 370.
(*b*) Chiflet. in Lum. Prær. X. p. 371.
(*c*) Mariana, Book X. c xvi. Ferreras, Vol. III. According to the latter, only king Alphonso VIII. solemnly assumed the Imperial dignity; and his French translator thereupon observes, that the other abovenamed prince did not bear that title; but Chiflet has sufficiently proved it, at least of Ferdinand the Great, and Alphonso VI.

ing

ing the several kingdoms and countries, from the union of which the Spanish monarchy is formed; likewise the foreign conquests, together with the Austrian and other dominions, of which they have long since been deprived. This title in Spanish runs thus.

Don —— — por la gracia de Dios, Rey de Castilla, de Leon, de Aragon, de las dos Sicilias, de Jerusalem, de Navarre, de Granada, de Toledo, de Valencia, de Galicia, de Mallorca, de Sevilla, de Cerdenna, de Cordova, de Coreega, de Murcia, de Jaen, de los Algarves, de Algecira, de Gibraltar, de las Islas de Canaria, de las Indias Orientales y Occidentales, Islas y Tierra Firme del Mar Oceano, Archiduque de Austria, Duque de Borgonna, de Brabante y de Milan, Conde de Abspurg, de Flandres, de Tirol y de Barcelona, Senor de Vizcaya y de Molina, &c. *

* This was the title of king Ferdinand VI. in the ratification of the Assiento treaty with Great Britain, on the 5th of October 1750, at Madrid. See Recueil d' Actes, par M. Rousset, Tom. XX. p. 356. It is something singular that the king of Spain, being so stiled by all Europe, instead of taking that title, always calls himself king of Castile, Leon, &c.

And

SPAIN.

And in LATIN.

— — — Dei gratiâ Castellæ, Legionis, Aragoniæ, utriusque Siciliæ, Hierosolymarum, Navarræ, Granadæ, Toleti, Valentiæ, Galliciæ, Majoricæ, Hispalis, Sardiniæ, Cordubæ, Corsicæ, Murciæ, Giennæ, Algarbiæ, Algeziræ, Gibraltaris, Insularum Canariæ, Indiarum Orientalium et Occidentalium, Insularum et Continentis Maris Oceani Rex, Archidux Austriæ, Dux Burgundiæ et Mediolani, Comes Habspurgi, Flandriæ, Tirolis et Barcinonis, Dominus Biscajæ et Molinæ, etc.

When the king of Spain signs an instrument, instead of subscribing his name, he writes, ' Yo el Rey, i. e. I the king;' but in letters to foreign princes he subscribes his own name (*d.*)

Besides the many titles which the king of Spain derives from his countries, he is also peculiarly stiled his Catholic Majesty. This surname pope Alexander VI. conferred in the year 1496 on king Ferdinand, in recompence of the extraordinary zeal for religion shewn by him and queen Isabella in

---

(*d*) Ceremonial de la Cour d'Espagne, Liv. II. c. vi. §. 2. n. 5. dans le Ceremonial Diplomatique de M. Rousset, Tom. II. p. 366.

making war on the Moors, expelling the Jews, and introducing the inquisition (*e*). The ancient Spanish councils had indeed, in their decrees, given that title to some Visigoth kings; and the popes in their letters to several kings of Leon and Castile (*f*). But this was rather a compliment than an authentic title, as the pope now accounts it *.

SECT. XXI.

Arms. The king of Spain's arms are as complicate as his titles. These consist of a shield quartered, together with a shield sur tout. The first quarter is counter-quartered: in the first and fourth quarters, is a castle, Sol, with three battlements in a field, Mars, for Castile; in the second and third, a crowned lion, Mars, in a field, Luna, for Leon. Between the two lower fields, are the arms of Granada, being a pomegranate, Venus, opened and seeded, Mars; and a sprig, Ve-

---

(*e*) Mariana, Book XXVI. c. xii. He says likewise, that the pope was disposed to confer the title of Christantissimus on king Ferdinand; but that did not take place, lest France might be displeased. There are, however, some gold coins, on which king Ferdinand is stiled Catholicus Christianissimus. Kopler's Muntz, V. Lust. Hart. III. p. 49, 50.

(*f*) Diego de Saavedre Faxardo, in Corona Gothica, Part. I. and p. 274.

* The superscription of the pope's letters were formerly, Regi Castellæ Illustri, but at present Regi Hispaniarum Catholico, but which the kings of Portugal would not for a long time allow. Mariana, Book I.

nus,

nus, in a field, Luna. The second quarter is paly: on the right are the arms of Arragon, four pallets, Mars, in a field, Sol; and on the left, those of Sicily, a shield quartered oblique; above and below, four pallets, Mars; on both sides an eagle, Saturn, in a field, Luna. The third quarter is parted: above is a chevron, Luna, in a field, Mars, representing Austria; below is bendy of six pieces, Sol and Jupiter, bordered, Mars, the ancient arms of Burgundy. The fourth quarter is likewise parted. In the upper part are the modern arms of Burgundy, being a shield, Jupiter, semee with flower-de-luces, Sol, with a bordure compone Luna and Mars: and beneath the arms of Brabant, a lion, Sol, in a field, Saturn. The sur tout contains the arms of Anjou, or three flower de-luces, Sol, in a field, Jupiter, with a bordure, Mars. The shield is surrounded with the collar of the order of the Holy-Ghost, and surmounted with a royal crown. The supporters are two lions.

A smaller shield is sometimes used, with only the arms of Castile and Leon, and those of Anjou (g).

(g) Mr. J. P. Reinhard's Introduction to the Knowledge of the principal States in Europe and Africa, p. 30, 31.

SECT. XXII.

Precedency. As the kings of Spain claim a superior rank before all Christian kings, they have, particularly since the reign of Charles V. endeavoured to obtain the precedence before the kings of France *; which, however, they have not been able throroughly to compass, the French generally maintaining the pre-eminence †: and, at length, Philip IV. in the year 1662 plainly gave it up, in a declaration made to the French court; at

---

* The celebrated Chiflet has with great zeal maintained the Spanish cause in this dispute about rank, and given them the precedence for the following reasons. 1. That the family of the kings of Spain (of the Austrian line) is of greater antiquity than the French royal family. 2. That several kings of Spain have borne the title of emperor. 3. As being in number of countries and strength, far superior to the kings of France. And 4. That the title of Catholic king, and the greater antiquity of the Christian religion in Spain, and their zeal to maintain it pure and undefiled, necessarily intitle it to precedence and respect. Chifletius in Vindic. Hisp. cap. x. p. 90. cap. xi. p. 101. c. xiv. p. 130. c. xv. p. 149. et in Lumin. Prærogat. xi. p 406, 407. Add. Fern. Vasquius in Illustr. Controv. Part. I. Præf. p. 48. n. 131.

† The French side alledged their long and continued possession; and that in disputable cases, the decision has been always in favour of France. Vid. Jac. Gothofredi, Diatr. de Præcedentia, P. I. cap 2. §, 6, 7, 11. At the council of Trent, the Spanish ambassador left no stone unturned to obtain the precedence before the French, but without effect. See Father Paul's History of the Council of Trent, Book VII. and VIII. And some relate, that the Spaniards sollicited the pope to declare their king emperor of the New World, conceiving, that thus they should make sure of the precedence in question. Vid. Hubert. Languet. Lib. II. Epist. 89.

least

least such was the construction put on it by Lewis XIV.

SECT. XXIII.

Coronation of the Visigoth kings. The ceremonies of unction and coronation were not in ancient times constantly observed in Spain. Vamba, a Visigoth king, and his successors, down to king Roderigo, caused themselves to be anointed and crowned (*i*): but nothing of this is mentioned concerning the subsequent kings of Asturia and Leon. After the junction of the kingdoms of Leon and Castile, we meet with three kings, Alphonso VIII *. Sancho IV. and John I. whose accession to the government was attended with these solemnities (*k*). *Of the kings of Castile and Leon,* The crowned kings among those of Arragon are, Peter II †. Peter III. Alphonso III. James II. Alphonso IV. and Peter IV. (*l*). *and of Arragon. Coronations discontinued.* But since the great union of Castile and Arragon, coronations have been laid aside as unnecessary. The king, at present, on

---

(*i*) Ferreras in the year 672, 680, 686, 700.

* This prince, according to Mariana, Book X. chap. xvi. had himself crowned three times; first, at Leon, as emperor of Spain; and afterwards at Toledo and Compostella; so that he might, even in this particular, be on a footing with the Roman emperors, who used to be crowned three times.

(*k*) Ferreras, in the years 1135, 1284, 1319.

† This Peter was crowned at Rome by pope Innocent II. and in return for this favour, engaged to pay the see of Rome an annual tribute of 250 doubloons. Ferreras, in the year 1204.

(*l*) Ferreras, in the years 1204, 1276, 1286, 1291, 1336.

on his accession to the crown, is proclaimed *; and after taking his oath, the states of the kingdom do him homage (*m*).

SECT. XXIV.

Title of the hereditary prince of Spain.

The hereditary prince of Spain is stiled prince of Asturias; a title which has been used ever since 1388, when the eldest son of king John the first, of Castile, married the princess Catherine, daughter to John duke of Lancaster (*n*). The succeeding kings have ever since declared their eldest son prince, or, in want of sons, their daughter princess of Asturias (*o*). This is accompanied with great solemnities, as proclamation by heralds, and taking the oath of fealty, by which the states of the kingdom, who are convened on that occasion, acknowledge him heir to the crown on the demise of the king (*p*).

The other royal children are called Infants and Infantas; and the estates which

---

* The ceremonies with which the proclamation is performed at Madrid, are to be found in the Ceremonial d'Espagne, Liv. II. ch. iii. §. 1. dans le Ceremonial Diplomat. des Cours de l'Europe, par M. Rousset, Tom. II. p. 343.

(*m*) Vayrac, Tom. II. p. 98.

(*n*) Mariana, Book XVIII. ch. xii. makes this the origin of it, that the king of England's eldest son being stiled prince of Wales, king John, in imitation of this custom, conferred the title of prince of Asturias on his heir.

(*o*) Vayrac, Tom. II. Liv. iii. p. 228, &c.

(*p*) Ibid. p. 237, &c. Ceremonial d'Espagne, Liv. II. ch. 3. Ceremonial Dipl. par M. Rousset, Tom. II. p. 344.

formerly were assigned for their maintenance, were termed an Infantado or Infantazgo.

SECT. XXV.

Descent of the royal family.

The present royal family of Spain is a younger branch of that of Bourbon. Philip V. duke of Anjou, grandson to Lewis XIV. and Maria Teresa, Philip IV's eldest daughter, was, by the will of Charles II. his grandmother's brother, nominated successor, and after a long and ruinous war, remained in possession of the crown. In 1724, he resigned it to his eldest son Lewis; but that prince dying early he reascended the throne *, an event almost unparalleled in history. He was succeeded in 1746, by his second son, Ferdinand VI. who had for successor his brother Charles III. the fourth king of the house of Anjou.

SECT. XXVI.

Madrid, the residence of the kings of Spain.

Toledo was formerly the residence of the Visigoth kings, and afterwards of most of

---

* This occasioned the following epitaph on king Lewis:

Posterior patre sum, sed sum tamen & prior illo:
Hoc cedente rego, meque cadente regit.

The Escurial monks were at a great loss where to place Philip V's corpse in the Pantheon, as he had reigned both before and after his son. See Memoires Instructifs, Tom. II. p. 112. They might have saved themselves this anxiety, that prince being interred at St. Ildephonso.

thoſe of Caſtile: but Philip II. finding that city too ſmall, made choice of Madrid, on account of its advantageous ſituation, its healthy air, and conveniency for hunting; and it has continued ſuch ever ſince (*q*). The Spaniards prefer Madrid, and its court, to all the cities and courts in the world*: it has indeed fine ſtreets and fountains, but the former are withal very filthy (*r*), the dirt of the houſes being continually thrown into them; though diſpoſitions are now in hand for removing this inconveniency †.

The principal royal ſeats are Buen-Retiro, Aranjuez, Caſa del Campo, La Flo-

---

(*q*) Ferreras, in the year 1560.

* Alphonſo Niunnez de Caſtro has wrote a book on this pre-eminence, with the title of Solo Madrid es Corte, y el Corteſano de Madrid. Vid. Gerh. Ern. De Franckenau. Biblioth. Hiſpan. Hiſt. Geneal. Herald. p. 12. n. 36.

(*r*) Memoires Inſtructifs, Tom. II. p. 60, 62.

† An Italian has made a ſonnet on Madrid, which gives no very advantageous idea of that city, or the manner of living there.

> Stemprato cielo, ambitioſe genti,
> Di fangoſo lavor tugurii anguſti,
> Carni ritroſe a denti, ingrate a guſti,
> Peſci guaſti, agri frutti, ogli fetenti,
> Di ſtercorato humor Strade correnti,
> Stronzi d'ogni color, molli & aduſti,
> Donne ſpolpate e di — — fruſti,
> Carche non men il vis ch'il—d'unguenti.
> Di sforzato valor moneta infame,
> Uſar acqua per vin, per fuocco il Sole,
> Tripudiar ne' tempi e mercar Dame,
> Ridiculo veſtir, mangiar beſtiale,
> Mori infiniti, Sbirri,
> Furman il bel Madrid, villa Reale,
> L'Ambaſciata di Romolo à Romani, p. 77.

rida, El Pardo, Villa Viciofa, St. Ildefonfo, and St. Lorenzo el Real, or the Efcurial, as it is commonly called *.

SECT. XXVII.

The great officers of the kingdom of Caf- tile were the chancellor (Chanciller), the conftable (Condeftabile), the admiral (Admirante). But as thefe were officers of great power, the kings have long fince fuppreffed the fubftance of them, leaving only the bare title †. _{Antient great-officers.}

SECT. XXVIII.

The king of Spain's houfhold is very confiderable and fplendid, exceeding moft Eu- _{Court-officers.}

---

* This vaft and ftately building was erected by Philip II. in honour of St. Lawrence; it is an oblong quadrangle, 280 paces in length, and the breadth a little lefs. In it is a palace, a convent for 200 monks, and a church. The laft has an amazing quantity of gold and filver utenfils and ornaments, befides jewels, and gorgeous veftures. Under the great altar of this church is the Pantheon, or Royal Vault, begun by Philip II. continued by Philip III. and finifhed by Philip IV. It is only the kings, and thofe queens who have borne fons, that are buried in the Pantheon. The other queens, and the infants and infanta's, lie in two vaults under the church. The Efcurial is particularly celebrated for its library, in which are a great number of rare Arabic manufcripts; but, through the ignorance of the monks, this treafure is of little benefit to the public. Mem. Inftruct. Tom. II. p. 96—115.

† Thus the archbifhop of Toledo ftiles himfelf Chancellor of Caftile, and the title of Admiral of Caftile is hereditary in the houfe of Henriquez, as that of Conftable in the family of Velafco. Vayrac, Tom. I. p. 123, 124.

ropean

ropean courts in the number of officers. The principal are, the lord-almoner (Limofnero Mayor *), the lord-fteward of the houfhold, (Mayor domo Mayor), the lord-chamberlain (Sumiller de Corps) the mafter of the horfe (Cavallerizo Mayor), the great-falconer (Halcohero Mayor), and the great-huntfman (Montero Mayor). But the laft two offices are generally filled by one perfon (*s*).

SECT. XXIX.

Order of the Golden-Fleece.

An additional fplendor to the Spanifh court, is the ancient and celebrated order of the Golden-Fleece, inftituted in the year 1431, by Philip the Good, duke of Burgundy (*t*). The emperor Charles V. as heir to the Burgundian dominions, transferred the grand-mafterfhip of this order into Spain, and from him the fucceeding kings inherited it. On the deceafe of Charles II. the two kings Philip V. and Charles III. afterwards emperor of Germany by the name of Charles VI. claimed

---

* This dignity was once annexed to the archbifhoprick of Compoftella; but fince the year 1572, the Patriarch of the Indies is always lord-almoner. Vayrac, Tom. II. p. 101.

(*s*) Concerning all thefe offices, fee Vayrac, Tom. II. p. 100—122. And for the lower court employments, p. 142, to 247.

(*t*) See the rules of this order in Leibnitz. Cod. J. G. Diplom. Mantiffa II. p. 17, &c.

the

the sovereignty of this order, and remained in possession, without taking any notice of it in the peace concluded between them at Vienna, in the year 1725. But Charles VI. dying, his daughter Maria Teresa queen of Hungary and Bohemia, conferred the grand-mastership on her husband the great duke of Tuscany, afterwards emperor by the name of Francis I. Philip V. king of Spain, conceiving that the grand-mastership now belonged solely to him, opposed that resignation (*u*); and afterwards, at the treaty of Aix la Chapelle, asserted his exclusive right by a solemn manifesto; but the like was also done by the empress-queen (*x*).

SECT. XXX.

Christianity was preached very early in Spain, and, according to the common notion of the Spaniards, by the Apostle James the Elder himself *. The Goths, who re-

State of religion in Spain.

(*u*) Vid. Illustr. Ayreri Dissert. de magno Magisterio Equestris Ordinis Aurei Velleris Burgundo-Austriaco feminino-masculino, Sect. III. §. 11, 15.

(*x*) Recueil Historiques d'Actes, Negociations, &c. par M. Rousset, Tom. XX. p. 220, 223.

* This is likewise zealously maintained by Ferreras, in his first volume; though Baronius himself denies it, or at least looks upon it as very doubtful. Mariana speaks somewhat ambiguously concerning both the Apostle James's preaching, and, his being buried in Spain, Book IV. c. ii. Lib. VII. c. xv. for which some, however, are much displeased with him.

ceived

ceived their first knowledge of the Faith from Arian teachers, brought their errors into Spain, and extremely molested the orthodox Christians; till at length, king Reccared became a convert to the catholic faith, on which the Arians were, in their turn, persecuted, and totally suppressed. The Spaniards have ever since shewn a singular zeal for the tenets of the Romish church; and no people pay a more blind obedience and submissive reverence to the papal see. They expend great sums on devout institutions and donations, as appears from the amazing riches of their churches (*y*). But this is their greatest merit with regard to religion; for, besides their superficial knowledge of it, their worship has a strange mixture of levity and ridicule. The absurd paintings and decorations in the churches, the indecent salutations in their religious processions, the gorgeous attire of the images of the saints, and particularly of the Blessed Virgin, whom they stile the Mother of God (*z*), and worship rather more than her Son (*a*); displease the very Catholics themselves of other countries.

(*y*) Mem. Instruct. Tom. II. p. 71, 72.
(*z*) Mem. de Montgon. Tom. II. p. 275, 276. Tom. VII. p. 196, 197.
(*a*) Vayrac, Tom. I. p. 36, &c.

If

If these be gross offences against decency, the like may very well be said of the verses and songs made by many Spanish rhymers on religious subjects, being often stuffed with such ridiculous conceits as would raise a smile even in the most phlegmatic reader *.

> * Little copies of verses called Villancicos, are made for the festivals, and sung in churches. The contents are sometimes, like the expression, extremely ridiculous, as two instances will shew, though taken from a versifier, who, for this kind of poesy, is in high repute among his countrymen. In one, the mayor of Bethlehem, on the nativity of Christ, summons the taylors to clothe the naked Saviour. Among other lines are these:
>
> > Xabon pidio un Sastre al Ninno
> > Para cortale una gala;
> > Pues non vendra sin Xabon
> > El, que viene aquitar manchas.
>
> "A taylor required soap of the child to make him a holiday-coat, as certainly he who came to take out stains, would not come without soap."
>
> In another madrigal, or ballad on the festival of the Epiphany, the trees celebrate a masquerade in honour of the infant Jesus. They all act their parts with a high glee.
>
> > El Almendro, que su fruta
> > En las colaciones gasta
> > Al Rey le Dió Almendras dulces,
> > Y al demonio muy amargas.
> > La Vid alegró la Fiesta,
> > Y negandole la entrada,
> > Dixo a la puerta un Tudesco:
> > Entre, que mas vale que agua.
>
> "The almond-tree, which plentifully distributes its fruit at collations, to the king gave sweet almonds, but to the devil the bitterest it had. The vine was for enlivening the feast; and on its being denied admittance, a German called out, "Let him in, by all means, it is much better than water."

SECT. XXXI.

Archbishops and bishops. The upper clergy in Spain consist of eight archbishops and forty-five bishops. The archbishops are,

I. The archbishop of Toledo, who, besides being stiled primate of Spain, bears the title of chancellor of Castile, and counsellor of state. His diocese is the largest, and his income not less than 300,000 ducats a year. His suffragans are, 1. Carthagena. 2. Cordova. 3. Cuenza. 4. Siguenza. 5. Jaen. 6. Segovia. 7. Osma. 8. Valladolid.

II. The archbishop of Seville. His suffragans, are, 1. Malaga. 2. Cadiz. 3. Canaria. 4. Ceuta.

III. The archbishop of Santjago, to whom are subordinate the bishops of, 1. Sa-

---

In a panegyrick on St. Francis, the author enumerates the many miracles performed by him; and among others, is the following,

  Sanó mil endemoniadas
  Sin saber, si avia librado
  Al diablo de las mugeres,
  O à las mugeres del diablo.
  Y al conjurarlas
  Vió como eran las feas
  Endemoniadas.

" A thousand female demoniacs he cured, but without knowing whether he had driven the devil out of the women, or women out of the devil; and at the conjuration he saw that the ugly were possessed."
Obras Poëticas Posthumas de Maestro Don Manuel De Leon Marchante, p. 1, 2, 11, 77.

lamanca. 2. Tuy. 3. Avila. 4. Coria. 5. Plasencia. 6. Astorga. 7. Zamora. 8. Orense. 9. Badajoz. 10. Mondonedo. 11. Lugo. 12. Ciudad-Rodrigo.

IV. The archbishop of Granada, who has under him, 1. Guadix. 2. Almeria.

V. The archbishop of Burgos, within whose jurisdiction are, 1. Pampeluna. 2. Calahorra. 3. Palencia. 4. St. Andero.

VI. The archbishop of Taragona, whose suffragans are the bishops of, 1. Barcelona. 2. Girona. 3. Lerida. 4. Tortosa. 5. Vique. 6. Urgel. 7. Salsona.

VII. The archbishop of Saragossa, within whose diocese are the bishops of, 1. Huesca. 2. Barbastro. 3. Xaca. 4. Taragona. 5. Albaracin. 6. Teruel.

VIII. The archbishp of Valencia, whose suffragans are, 1. Segorbe. 2. Orihuela; and 3. Mallorca (*b*).

The bishoprics of Oviedo and Leon are immediately subject to the see of Rome (*c*).

The annual income of all these archbishoprics is computed at 1,363,000 ducats; and that of the chapters of the cathedrals and collegiate churches, is as much (*d*).

(*b*) Clarke's Letters concerning the Spanish nation, Letter II. p. 20, 21.
(*c*) Vayrac, Tom. II. p. 379.
(*d*) Busching's Geography, Part II. p. 123.

In

In New-Spain are six archbishoprics *, with twenty-eight bishops; and in the Philippine-islands one archbishop, whose see is Manilla, and three subordinate bishops (*e*).

SECT. XXXII.

The king nominates the archbishops and bishops.

The disposal of ecclesiastical benefices in Spain, was formerly, for the most part, lodged in the pope, who, on a requisition from the king, appointed archbishops and bishops; and likewise nominated to many inferior dignities and benefices; till by an agreement between the emperor Charles V. and pope Adrian VI. the nomination to the archbishoprics and bishoprics was yielded up to the king (*f*). Pope Clement VII. farther granted to the kings of Spain, the right of conferring other ecclesiastical offices and benefices (*g*). Notwithstanding such cessions, frequent differences arose between

---

* Of these the principal is that of St. Domingo, in the island of Hispaniola, and the archbishop bears the stile of Patriarch of India.

(*e*) Clarke, Letter II. p. 22, 23.

(*f*) Mariana, Book XXVI. c. v. and in the Summary of the History of Spain, anno 1523. Thus the kings recovered their antient right, which rests on the sixth decree of the XIIth council of Toledo. Ferreras, Vol. II. Year 681. Cont. Fern. Vasquii Controvers. Illustr. c. xxii. n. 16. p. 213, et Didaci Covarruvias Oper. Tom. I. p. 440, 441. n. 4, 5, 6.

(*g*) This bull, which is dated on the 10th of May 1528, is to be found in the Supplement au Corps Universel Diplomat. par M. Rousset, Tom. II. Part. I. p. 169, et suiv.

them

them and the fee of Rome, till the year 1753, when by a new convention between Ferdinand VI. and Benedict XIV. the pope referving to himfelf fome fpecified leſſer dignities and benefices, abfolutely gave up all the others to the king, in confideration of a fum of money (*b*).

SECT. XXXIII.

The power of the pope has always been very great in Spain; and Gregory VII. was for fcrewing it up to the very higheſt pitch, requiring of the kings in his time to acknowledge themfelves his vaffals, and pay him an annual tribute. But this demand, notwithſtanding their great obfequioufnefs and refpect towards the fee of Rome, they could not digeſt (*i*). Spain, however, has been the golden mine to the apoſtolic-chamber, on account of the large fums which are annually remitted to Rome *. Even the pope's nuncio has his particular jurifdiction in ecclefiaftical and fpiritual matters, which he exercifes with great ri-

Great power in Spain of the pope and his legates.

(*b*) See Europe's New Fame, Part CLXXXIX. p. 691, 692.
(*i*) Ferreras, in the years 1074, 1075.
* Thefe amount to 132,000 fcudi d'oro, which make fifty thoufand pounds fterling. Table au de la Cour de Rome, p. 111.

gour*; and would stretch it beyond all bounds, did not the council of Castile sometimes take the liberty to reduce him to order (*k*). This assembly maintains the rights of the sovereign and the state, against the invasions of that foreign power; and in many cases, the pope's bulls and briefs are of no force, till they have undergone the examination of the royal tribunals (*l*).

SECT. XXXIV.

Inquisition, its basis.

The chief foundation of the papacy and the papal power in Spain is the inquisition, which queen Isabella introduced into Castile, and her husband Ferdinand the Catholic into Arragon. The first court of inquisition was held at Seville, towards the end of the year 1480, at the instigation of the archbishop of that city, cardinal Mendoza; for great numbers of the new converted Jews

---

* The persons who, by order of king Charles II. carried off the famous Valenzuela, his mother's favourite, out of the convent in the Escurial, were excommunicated for violating that sanctuary, and the exemption of ecclesiastical persons. And though there were among them persons of the first rank, they were obliged to make their appearance with halters about their necks, and in their shirts, before the nuncio Molini, who, at their absolution, gave them some strokes with a wand. Mem. de la Cour d'Esp. Part. I. p. 66.

(*k*) Domenico Zanetornato nella relatione della Corte di Spagna, p. 68, 69.

(*l*) Didac. Covarruvias in Oper. Tom. II. Pract. Quæst. c. 35. p. 513.

and

SPAIN.

and Moors relapsing into their former errors, he proposed such a course, as the best means to prevent this evil (*m*). A like court was appointed in the year 1483, in Castile and Leon, on the same account. Thomas de Torquemada, a Dominican, was the first inquisitor-general (*n*); and during the term of his office, caused 2000 people to be burnt (*o*). There are at present in the Spanish monarchy eighteen courts of inquisition, namely, at Seville, Toledo, Granada, Cordova, Cuenza, Valladolid, Murcia Ellerena, Logrono, Santjago, Saragossa, Valencia, Barcelona, Majorca, the Canary-islands, Mexico, Carthagena, and Lima (*p*). The supreme court of inquisition is at Madrid; and its president, besides the title of Inquisitor-general, is likewise stiled the pope's vicar. He is nominated by the king, confirmed by the pope, and, in other respects totally independent (*q*). This supreme court of inquisition, besides the president, consists of six counsellors, called apostolic inquisitors, a fiscal, a pri-

(*m*) Ferreras, Vol. VII. p. 578, 579, 590.
(*n*) Ibid. p. 632.
(*o*) Mariana, Book XXIV. c. xvii. Others say, that in fourteen years he brought above 100,000 persons to a trial, of whom 6000 were burnt. See Mr. Estor's Observations on the Civil and Ecclesiastical Power, cap. xvii. p. 391.
(*p*) Vayrac, Tom. II. p. 365.
(*q*) Ibid. p. 364.

vate secretary, two other secretaries, a receiver, two referendaries, four serjeants or messengers, a solicitor, and several qualificators, or law-counsellors; among whom, by an order of Philip III. in 1618, one must be a Dominican friar (*r*). The other courts of inquisition have only three inquisitors, two clerks, a messenger, a receiver, and a certain number of qualificators and law-counsellors (*s*). All these officers, high and low, must be men of irreproachable morals, and of pure blood; making proof that none of their ancestors were either heretics, Jews or Moors (*t*). The inquisition, besides these officers, has not less than 20,000 familiars, as they are called, dispersed over the whole kingdom, and whose chief business is to apprehend those against whom an information lies (*u*). The proceedings of this tremendous court are singular, and contradictory to the common forms of law; the person informed against being imprisoned on a bare information, without seeing or knowing his accuser, or the witnesses

---

(*r*) Vayrac, Tom. II. p. 384.
(*s*) Ibid. p. 385.
(*t*) Vayrac, là même, Memoires pour servir à l'Histoire des Inquisitions, Tom. I. p. 141.
(*u*) Vayrac, Tom. II. p. 387. The origin of these familiars is to be found in the Memoirs of the Royal Academy of Portuguese History, in the year 1723, p. 384—390.

who depose against him (*x*). When the enquiry is gone through, sentence is pronounced on the prisoners; and formerly it used to be accompanied with striking solemnities *. The crimes within the cognizance of the inquisition, are heresy, Judaism, Mahometanism, sorcery, sodomy, and polygamy. The punishments are various. Jews obstinately refusing to embrace Christianity, are burned alive; they who are convicted of heresy or infidelity, and will not acknowledge it, or profess themselves Catholic Christians, are strangled (*y*). The possessions of the persons condemned, are confiscated; and for a person to have been in the inquisition, is an indelible ignominy to all his descendants (*z*).

(*x*) Mariana, Book XXIV. c. xvii.

* Namely, in those Autos da Fé, at which the king and court assisted; these were attended with pompous processions and exhibitions, of which a description is to be found in the Ceremonial d'Espagne, Liv. I. c. iv. §. 19. in the Ceremonial Diplomatique de Mr. Rousset, Tom. II. p. 219, et suiv. These dismal solemnities, at first very common in Spain, are not at present so often repeated. From the year 1632, when king Philip IV. permitted an Auto da Fé to be held, no other was seen till 1680, when the nuptials of Charles II. were celebrated by a like sanguinary scene. Memoires pour servir à l'Hist. des Inquisitions, Tom. I. p. 199. Two were held under Philip V. in 1720, and 1721; and under Lewis I. in the year 1724, on the occasion of his accession to the throne. Deformeaux, Tom. V p. 367, 370, 384.

(*y*) See Noticias reconditas del Procedimiento de las Inquisiciones de Espana y Portugal. Part I. p. 73.

(*z*) Mariana concludes his account of the erection of the inquisition with these words: " Præsens remedium adversus

SECT. XXXV.

Great number of the clergy.

By such violent procedures is the Catholic religion in Spain sufficiently secured against all innovations; and the numerous clergy are a farther support to it. These, amidst the depopulation of the kingdom, have been continually increasing, new foundations being frequently made for them; and their present number is computed at 250,000 seculars and regulars (*a*). The greater part of these live in convents, which in Spain are very numerous; there being 2146 monasteries, and 1023 nunneries (*b*).

SECT. XXXVI.

Religious orders of knighthood.

The continual wars against the Moors gave rise in Castile and Leon, to the three religious orders of St. James, Calatrava, and Alcantara. Their chief vow was to fight against the infidels. The first adopted the rule of St. Austin, and the two others that of the Cistercians (*c*). But all this has been pretty much altered by length of time.

impendentia mala, quibus aliæ provinciæ exagitantur, cœlo datum; nam humano consilio adversus tanta pericula satis caveri non potuit."

(*a*) Voyez Don Geronymo De Uſtariz dans la Theorie et Pratique du Commerce & de la Marine, ch. xviii. p. 85.

(*b*) Busching's Geography, Part II. p. 123.

(*c*) Helyot's History of Religious and Secular Orders, Vol. II. c. xl. Vol. VI. c. xlv.

James

James II. king of Arragon, after suppressing the order of the knights Templars, founded, out of their effects, a new order, which received its name from the city of Montesa, in the kingdom of Valencia, as its residence (*d*).

But this never attained to that consideration and opulence, as the three beforementioned orders of St. Jago, Calatrava, and Alcantara, which acquired such possessions and revenues, that their grand-masters, being absolutely independent of all jurisdiction, became formidable even to the kings themselves. On this account, Ferdinand the Catholic prevailed on pope Innocent VIII. to invest him with the grand-mastership of those three orders during his life; pope Alexander VI. afterwards extended this right to queen Isabella, in case she should survive the king; and lastly, pope Adrian VI. to gratify the emperor Charles V. annexed the three grand-masterships to the throne (*e*).

Besides the above four orders, the knights of St. John or Malta are possessed of such revenues and estates in Spain, as yield them

---

(*d*) Mariana, Lib. XV. cap. xvi.
(*e*) Ibid. Lib. XXVI. c. v. and in the Sumario de la Historia d' Espana, al anno 1523.

near sixty thousand pounds sterling per annum (*f*).

SECT. XXXVII.

State of the sciences in Spain.

By the number of universities, literature and the sciences should be very common, and flourish greatly in Spain. It has no less than twenty-two: Salamanca, Valladolid, Siguenza, Toledo, Avila, Alcala de Henares, Sevilla, Granada, Baeza, Ossana, Huesca, Saragossa, Valencia, Gandia, Orizuela, Lerida, Tortosa, Terragona, St. Jago de Compostella, Onnate, Oviedo, Pampelona (*g*). Others raise them to thirty, adding Osina, Oropesa, Murcia, Barcelona, Girona, Luchenite, Hirache, Estolla (*h*).

The principal are Salamanca, Alcala de Henares, and Valladolid. The first is said to have seventy-two professors (*i*).

SECT. XXXVIII.

Academies of sciences.

Several academies of polite literature and sciences, were likewise founded in Spain

(*f*) Busching's Geography, Part II. p. 140.
(*g*) Vayrac, Tom. II. p. 395, 397.
(*h*) Noticias de Portugal, por Manoel Severim de Faria, p. 207—223, though he himself allows that some of them are only colleges. Vayrac, p. 396, places Palencia likewise among the universities; but Faria, p. 207, remarks, that this never was a real university, nor, as some would have it, removed to Salamanca.
(*i*) Vayrac, Tom. II. p. 396.

under

under the reign of Philip V (*k*). In Madrid is, 1. La Real Academia Eſpannola, the object of which is the improvement of the Spaniſh language *. 2. La Real Academia de la Hiſtoria; and 3. La Real Academia Medica. Seville, Valencia, and Barcelona, have academies of polite literature, and Valladolid an academy of geography.

SECT. XXXIX.

The Spaniards are by their penetrating and comprehenſive genius qualified for ſciences of all kinds, and particularly for poetry, of which they have given eminent inſtances, even in the time of the Romans. Seneca, Lucan, Silius Italicus, Martial, Prudentius, and other poets, were natives of Spain. Modern times have likewiſe produced many among them, who have written in Spaniſh, and diſtinguiſhed themſelves in every ſpecies of poetry. The characteriſtic of their works is wit and ſublimity; but affecting the ſublime rather in the expreſſion than in the ſubject, they not ſel-

Spaniſh poets.

(*k*) Deſormeaux, Tom. V. p. 200—328, is very laviſh of his encomiums on king Philip V. though it does not appear that he had immediately any great ſhare in thoſe foundations.

* This academy, which is conſtituted from the model of the French, and conſiſts of twenty-four members, was founded in 1713, by the duke of Eſcalona. It has publiſhed an excellent Spaniſh Dictionary of ſix folio volumes.

dom

dom run into the turgid and unnatural. The moſt celebrated modern poets are Garcilaſſo de la Vega, don Diego Hurtado de Mendoza, don Luis de Gongora, don Alonzo de Ercilla, Lopez de Vega, don Franciſco de Quevedo, don Franciſco de Borja, prince Squillace, don Manuel de Leon Marchante, &c.

SECT. XL.

Philoſophy. The dread of the inquiſition lays the literati in Spain under a painful reſtraint; ſo that they dare not always venture to make known their real thoughts, but muſt take up with writing and teaching even as their forefathers wrote and taught (*l*). To this check it is owing, that the ſchool-philoſophy has ſo long ſtood its ground in Spain; as to diſturb its authority *, would be extremely dangerous.

SECT. XLI.

Divinity. Divinity in Spain ſhares the ſame fate with philoſophy; nay, to advance any thing

---

(*l*) Memoires Inſtructifs, Tom. II. p. 53, 54, 114, 116.

* John Wendlinger, a Jeſuit of Bohemia, has, however, ventured to aſſert literary freedom; he is the king's geographer and hiſtorian for the two Indies, and has inſtructed Charles III's ſons in mathematicks, hiſtory, geography, and the German language. He is ſaid to have publiſhed a ſyſtem of the Wolffian philoſophy in Spaniſh.

contrary to the doctrines of the fathers, would rather be attended with worfe confequences, as the inquifition would not overlook the leaft innovation even in the moft dignified ecclefiaftic; which, among others, Bartholemew de Carranza, archbifhop of Toledo, experienced. They ftick to the fchooldoctrines of their fathers, and little concern themfelves about the learned languages, or the explanation of the facred writings, applying themfelves to cafuiftical divinity, in which they are very expert, and which likewife is in fome meafure neceffary to confeffors (*m*).

CHAP. XLII.

The number of Spanifh lawyers is very extraordinary: moft of them have written on the Roman and canon law, and their works were formerly in fuch efteem, that foreign countries printed many editions of them. The principal are Anthony Gomez, and his grandfon Diego Gomez; Diego and Anthony de Covarruvias, Ferdinand Vafquez, Menchaca, Anton Auguftinus, Emanuel Gonzales Telez, Anthony Perez, John de Solorzano Pereira, Gregory de Mayans, and Sifcar.

Lawyers.

(*m*) Clarke's Letters concerning the Spanifh Nation, Letter IV. p. 52.

SECT.

SECT. XLIII.

Phyſick.

In phyſick and ſurgery the Spaniards are far inferior to their neighbours the French, and other European nations. One proof of the unſkilfulneſs of their ſurgeons is the venereal diſtemper, with which the country is ſaid to be over-run; an effectual method of cure being beyond their ſkill. The part of medicine moſt ſtudied here is botany (*n*); and king Ferdinand VI. being a great lover of natural hiſtory, founded a phyſic-garden at Madrid *.

SECT. XLIV.

Painting, ſculpture, and architecture.

The ſame king was pleaſed likewiſe to take painting, ſculpture, and architecture, under his protection, and founded an academy in Madrid for the advancement of thoſe arts.

SECT. XLV.

Printing and engraving.

That the Spaniards have made no great improvement in printing and engraving, is

---

(*n*) Clarke's Letters concerning the Spaniſh Nation, Letter IV. Part II. p. 55.

* Accounts of the Life and Writings of learned Spaniards are found in the following works.

D. Nicolai Antonii Bibliotheca Hiſpana Vetus, ſeu Hiſpanorum qui ab Octavii Auguſti imperio uſque ad annum MD. floruerunt, notitia. 2 Tom. Romæ 1696. fol.

Ejuſdem Bibliotheca Hiſpana, ſeu Hiſpanorum qui poſt annum MD. floruerunt, notitia. 2 Tomi. Romæ, 1672. fol.

SPAIN.

evident from their books, especially those published in the preceding and the sixteenth century. In the present, they have something mended their hands, and but something. This induced Charles III. to found a printing academy at Madrid, in which youth sdesigned for that art, are instructed in the languages and other requisites at the king's expence.

SECT. XLVI.

Amidst the different revolutions in the Spanish monarchy, the laws must likewise be supposed to have undergone several alterations. The Romans with their dominion introduced their laws. The Visigoths at first followed their old customs, till their king Eric gave them written laws (*o*). Of these and the edicts of the succeeding princes, and the decrees of councils, was composed under king Sisenand, or more probably, under Egiza, the Fuero Juzgo, or Forum Judicum (*p*). Ferdinand III. and

---

(*o*) See Mascou's History of the Germans, Vol. I. B. X. p. 490.

(*p*) Mariana, Lib. VI. cap. v. These laws were first published by Peter Pithoeus, under the title of Codex Legum Wisi-Gothorum, Libri XII. (Parisiis, 1759. fol.) And afterwards by Alphonso de Villadieco, with a Spanish Comment. (Madrid, 1600, fol.) Vid. Buderi Biblioth. Jur. Selecta, c. vi. §. 2. They are likewise to be found in Fred. Lindenbrogii, Codex LL Antiquarum, and in Petr. Georgisch Corpore Jur. Germ. Antiqui.

Al-

Alphonso X. kings of Castile, ordered a new code to be made, which, in the year 1348, king Alphonso XI. published under the title of Las Siete Partidas (*q*). Ferdinand the Catholic employed Alphonso Diaz de Montalvo to digest into one body all the royal ordinances; and these he published under the title of El Ordenamiento Real (*r*). Under the same king, in the year 1505, were made public the Leyes de Toro, so called from their being passed into laws at the diet of Toro (*s*). Lastly, Philip II. had a new code made by a sett of lawyers; and it was published by the title of Nueva Recompilacion de las Leyes de Estos Reynos (*t*): this collection has been augmented by several of his successors (*u*).

(*q*) Vid. Leyes de Toro, pr. These Siete Partidas are, for the most part, translated from the Roman and Canon law into that of Castile. Didac. Covarruvias, Var. Resol. Lib. I. ch. xiv. n. 5. in Operib. Tom. II. p. 61. Several Spanish lawyers, and among others, Gregory Lopez, have written comments on them. Buder. in Biblioth. Jur. Sel. cap. vi. §. 2.

(*r*) Buder. L. C. §. 3. The said Montalvo has to this Ordenamiento Real, added illustrations and comments.

(*s*) Mariana, Lib. XXVIII. cap. xiii. Anthony Gomez, and his grandson Diego Gomez, have illustrated the Leyes de Toro with remarks.

(*t*) Buder, L. C. §. 3.

(*u*) Vid. Leyes de Toro. pr. & Anton. Gomezii Commentar. ad illas, 5. A compleat account of all the Spanish law is to be met with in Gerh. Ern. de Franckenau. Sacr. Themidis Hispanæ Arcanis. Hannoveræ 1703 4.

SECT.

SECT. XLVIII.

The judges or chief magistrates in the *Lower Courts.* Ciudades, or large cities, are called Corregidores, in some Alcaldes mayores, and their assessors have the title of Regidores. In the villas or towns, the judges are called Alcaldes or Bayles. These magistrates superintend not only the administration of justice, but likewise that of the police. The Corregidore cannot be a native of the place which is the seat of his office; but the Regidore must absolutely be such (*x*).

SECT. XLIX.

The king's court has likewise a particular tribunal, with a president, eight alcaldes, a fiscal, two referendaries, four clerks, and four serjeants, or messengers. These alcaldes are termed Alcaldes de Corte; and have both the civil and criminal jurisdiction within the verge of the court, which extends to the distance of twenty miles, and over those who attend his majesty in any of his journies (*y*). *Court of justice and police in the king's palace.*

Cases appertaining to the police come under the cognizance of twelve alcaldes, each having his department, which he

(*x*) Vayrac, Tom. III. p. 272, 274.
(*y*) Ibid. p. 266, 267.

some-

sometimes visits, attended by his clerk and serjeant, for the preservation of good order (z).

SECT. L.

Upper Courts.

There are, besides, in the provinces of Spain certain courts of justice, to which lie appeals from the above mentioned city and town judges, and which likewise try several cases in the first instance. These courts are, 1. The royal chancery (Chancilleria Real) at Valladolid; and 2. at Granada; each having a president, and sixteen counsellors, called oydores, or auditors, two or three judges in criminal causes, a fiscal, and other officers (a). In the kingdom of Navarre is, 3. The royal council, (Consejo Real de Navarra) in which the viceroy presides, when so disposed. This tribunal consists of a regent, six oydores, four alcaldes, and other inferior officers (b). Next to these are various courts, called Audiencias; namely, 4. Audiencias Real de la Corunna. 5. De Sevilla. 6. D'Oviedo. 7. De Saragossa. 8. De Valencia. 9. De Barcelona. 10. De Mallorca. The president of these courts is stiled regent, and

(z) Vayrac, Tom. III. p. 269.
(a) Ibid. p. 256, 257, &c.
(b) Ibid. p. 250.

SPAIN.

the affeffors Alcaldes Majores. In civil cafes, where the fum exceeds ten thoufand maravedis; and in criminal matters, touching life, or corporal punifhment, or banifhment for ten years, an appeal has been made from their fentence.

Laftly, 11. There is alfo an Audiencia in the Canary-iflands; and at Cadiz is the Audiencia de la Contractacion de las Indias. Spanifh America has twelve Audiencias (c).

SECT. LI.

Spain was formerly under a neceffity of keeping on foot a very large military force, on account of its many dependencies in Europe; but the far greater part being difmembered from it at the treaty of Utrecht, that neceffity ceafed: yet by reafon of the feveral wars, both in Italy and Africa, the Spanifh military eftablifhment has continued ftill very confiderable. The Spaniards, both cavalry and infantry, are excellent foldiers (d), and ftill maintain all the ancient glory of their martial forefathers.

Land-forces.

In the year 1760, the Spanifh forces confifted of the following troops.

(c) Vayrac, Tom. III. p. 270, 271.
(d) Ibid. Tom. I. p. 35.

1. INFANTRY.

Thirty-two Spanish regiments, which made seventy-eight battalions, among which were six battalions of Spanish, and six battalions of Walloon guards, with two battalions of matrosses, and eight battalions of marines:

		Men.
Total — —		46876

		Battal.	
2	Italian regiments — —	4	2120
3	Walloon — —	6	3180
3	Irish — —	6	3180
3	Swifs — —	6	4440
33	Militia — —	33	23100
4	Invalids — —	8	4800
			87696

2. CAVALRY.

Twenty-two regiments, containing forty-six squadrons, and in which are included the horse-guards -   } 6114

3. DRAGOONS.

10 Regiments, 20 Squadrons — 2560

4 INDEPENDANT COMPANIES.

15 — — — 2005

(e) In all 98375

(e) Clarke's Letters, Number XII. p. 211, 214.

SECT. LII.

Nature itself has secured Spain against France by the Pyrenean mountains; and those parts which are easiest of access, have several strong fortifications, as St. Sebastian, Fuentarabia, Pampelona, Rofes, Girona, &c. On the frontiers of Portugal are Tuy, Xamora, Ciudad Roderigo, Valenza de Alcantara, Badajoz, and others. [Fortified places.]

SECT. LIII.

The situation of Spain, the discovery of the New World, the distance of its European dependencies, gradually produced a navy, which at length became very considerable, and under Philip II. was, after the conquest of Portugal, the most powerful in Europe. But since the miscarriage of its expedition against England in 1588, it has continually declined, and under Charles II. was at a very low ebb. Philip V. and his successors attending to the restoration of it, in the year 1760 it consisted of [Marine.]

Ships of the line	47
Frigates	21
Chebecs	14
Packet-boats	4
Bomb-ketches	7

which required 4016 guns, 712 gunners, 6870 marines, and 45960 seamen (*f*).

The stations for the men of war are, Cadiz, Corunna, Ferrol, and Carthagena; the harbours of which, together with those of Barcelona and Malaga, are strongly fortified.

SECT. LIV.

Coins.

The Spaniards reckon by hundreds, thousands, and millions (cuentos) of maravedis; in larger sums, by reals, dollars, ducats, and doubloons.

2 Maravedis make 1 ochavo.

4 Maravedis make 1 quarto.

1 Real = $8\frac{1}{2}$ quartos = 17 ochavos = 34 maravedis.

1 Peso, or piece of eight, = 8 reales = 272 maravedis.

1 Ducado = 11 reales = 374 maravedis*.

1 Doubloon or pistole = 4 pesos = 32 reales = 1088 maravedis.

By these appellations are understood either silver (moneda de plata), or (moneda de velon) copper-money. The former is about $88\frac{8}{17}$ per Cent. better than the latter; so that the proportion between these two coins is as follows:

(*f*) Clarke's Letters, XII. p. 219, 222.
* That is in trade, but in exchange the ducat is equal to 275 maravedis.

17 Reales

SPAIN.

17 Reales de plata = 32 reales de velon.

1 Real de plata = 64 maravedis de velon.

1 Peso de plata = 15 reales, 2 maravedis de velon.

1 Ducado de plata = 20 reales, 24 maravedis de velon *.

1 Doubloon de plata = 60 reales, 8 maravedis de velon.

But these are only ideal coins, the real being minted on quite another standard, and are as follow.

1. In GOLD.

Doubloons (pistoles) = 40 reales de plata = 75 reales, 10 maravedis de velon.

Double doubloons = 80 reales de plata = 150 reales, 20 maravedis de velon.

Quadruple doubloons = 160 reales de plata = 301 reales, 6 maravedis de velon.

Half doubloons, or escudos de oro = 20 reales de plata = 37 reales, 22 maravedis de velon.

Pesos fuertes de oro = 11 reales, 6 maravedis de plata = 20 reales de velon.

* In trade: in exchange the ducado de plata fetches 20 reales, 25$\frac{15}{17}$ maravedis de velon.

2. In SILVER.

Pesos fuertes = 11 reales, 6 maravedis de plata = 20 reales de velon. These are likewise called piastres.

Half pesos fuertes = 5 reales, 20 maravedis de plata = 10 reales de velon. These are commonly called escudos de velon.

Quarter pesos fuertes = 2 reales, 27 maravedis de plata = 5 reales de velon.

Reales fuertes = 1 real, $13\frac{1}{2}$ maravedis de plata, 2 reales, 17 maravedis de velon.

Half reales fuertes = $23\frac{1}{4}$ maravedis de plata = 1 real, $8\frac{1}{2}$ maravedis de velon.

There are besides:

Reales de Sevilla = 1 real, 4 maravedis de plata = 2 reales de velon.

Double = 2 reales, 8 maravedis de plata = 4 reales de velon.

Half = 19 maravedis de plata = 1 real de velon.

3. In COPPER.

Quartos = 4 maravedis.
Double = 8 maravedis.
Ochavos = 2 maravedis.
Single maravedis and blancas = half a maravedi.

The Spanish coinage or specie suffered great alterations by raising the money. The most detrimental was that of Philip III. doubling the current worth of copper-money: foreigners coined vast quantities, and filled the whole kingdom with them, at the same time draining it of its gold and silver (*g*); since which, this inconveniency has remained, with this farther grievance, that most payments are made in copper-money (*h*).

SECT. LV.

A late writer says, that the revenue of Philip II. amounted to thirty millions of ducats (*i*). If so, it must have been extremely diminished under his successors, yielding only seven or eight millions of French livres in the last years of Charles II (*k*). The president Orry, in the year 1714, raised the royal revenue to forty millions of French livres, and higher; but by such means as rendered him detestable to the whole Spanish nation (*l*). In the year 1722,

Revenue.

(*g*) Don Diego de Saavedra Faxardo Idea de un Principe Politico Christiano, Empresa LXIX. p 639.
(*h*) Ustariz's Theory and Practice of Commerce, and the Marine, ch. civ. p. 504
(*i*) Voltaire's Univ. Hist. Tom. V. c. iv.
(*k*) Vayrac, Tom. III. p. 304.
(*l*) Ibid. 307.

it amounted to 23,510,154 escudos de velon (*m*); and since 1747, the total has been about 27,246,302 escudos de velon (*n*). The taxes and duties from whence this revenue arises, are extremely numerous, and divided into general and provincial contributions: Rentas Generales y Provinciales.

To the former belong,

1. Some regalia, as the stamp-paper, the post and coinage.
2. The monopoly of salt, tobacco, quickfilver, and lead.
3. The duties of 15 per Cent. on all imports and exports; and these are levied under different denominations and in different manners.
4. The grand-masterships of the three religious orders of knighthood; the horse-tax paid by them; and the priorate of St. John.
5. The taxes on the clergy, and the tenths of the income of their possessions, levied by the king with the pope's consent; likewise the contribution paid by the church for supporting the military hospitals in time of war.

(*m*) Uftariz, ch. xix. p. 93, 94.
(*n*) Confiderations fur les Finances d' Espagne, p. 8. in Vol. II. of the Memoires fur le Commerce d'Espagne.

6. The

6. The Croisade-bull, by virtue of which some kinds of indulgences, and certain ecclesiastical exemptions, are sold for the king's benefit.

7. The spear-tax, (Servicio de las Lancas) paid by the upper nobility, in lieu of the twenty-four spearmen, whom they were formerly to provide.

8. The pension tax (Media Annata).

9 The Madrid excise (Effetos y Sisas de Madrid).

10. The cattle-tax, (Montazgo de los Ganados) raised on the cattle put to pasture.

11. The meadow tax.

12. The excise of the kingdom of Navarre.

13. Revenues from Arragon, Valencia, Catalonia, and Majorca [*].

14. The quartering-money, paid by these countries and some others.

15. Tax on negroes imported into the Spanish colonies in America (Assiento de los Negros).

16. West-India revenues, as the Croisade-bull, and the taxes on the clergy, the

---

[*] Into these countries, since their union with Castile, have likewise been introduced the monopoly of salt and snuff, the stamp duty, and customs; before, the kings had only some tithes, and what was called the patrimonial incomes. Ustariz, ch. xix. p. 92.

fifths of the profits of mines, the profit from the quickfilver exported thither.

17. Profits on the Weft-India trade, to which belong the indulto, or licence for the galleons and regifter-fhips, the freight of them, the duties, &c. (*o*).

The provincial contributions are levied only in Caftile, which in this refpect is divided into twenty-two provinces. 1. Burgos. 2. Leon. 3. Galicia. 4. Zamora. 5. Toro. 6. Palencia. 7. Valladolid. 8. Avila. 9. Soria. 10. Salamanca. 11. Segovia. 12. Murcia. 13. Madrid. 14. Toledo. 15. Guadalaxara. 16. Cuenza. 17. Eftremadura. 18. Seville. 19. Cordova. 20. Granada. 21. Jaen. 22. La Mancha *.

In thefe provincial contributions are included,

1. The tenth penny of all things bought or exchanged (Alcavala) †, and this has been gradually increafed to four additional pennies per Cent.

(*o*) Uftariz, ch. xix. where likewife is to be found the neat produce and total of all thefe feveral payments.

* Uftariz, ch. cv. p. 508-511, reckons only the firft twenty-one provinces; but in the Table, p. 512, 573, where he fets down the produce of the provincial contributions, according to the new farm, there are twenty-two, and among them La Mancha.

† This tax is of a very ancient ftanding: the twentieth penny was granted to king Alphonfo XI. in the year 1341, for the war againft the Moors. Under Henry II. the ftates of Caftile raifed it to the tenth penny, which has been paid ever fince. Mariana, Lib. XVI. chap. ix. XVII. chap. viii.

2. The

SPAIN. 235

2. The twenty-four million-tax, of which four and a half has been laid on salt, and the remaining nineteen and a half, on wine and vinegar, oil and flesh.

3. An impost of four maravedis on each arrob (about three gallons English) of wine (el fiel medidor).

4. A duty of 4 reals 3 quarters, per hearth, payable by those who are not noble (Servicio ordinario y extraordinario).

5. Duty on brandy, which is made personal since the king gave up the monopoly of brandy.

6. Duty on soap, snow, cards, and other little matters (*p*).

The provincial taxes are all farmed, whereas the general are under administration, and accounted for (*q*).

The provincial contributions being all levied from the necessaries of life, prove such a heavy load to the commonalty, that some wise financiers have lately advised an alteration in those impositions (*r*).

A considerable part of the provincial contributions is assigned to the creditors of the crown as interest, and not a little has been given away to private persons (*s*).

(*p*) Concerning these imposts, see Considerations sur les Finances d' Espagne, p. 32, & suiv.
(*q*) Uſtariz, ch. xix. p. 89.
(*r*) Considerations sur les Finances d' Espagne, p. 43, 44.
(*s*) Voyez Uſtariz, ch. xix. p. 92.

SECT.

SECT. LVI.

Expences and debts of the crown.

The revenue of the crown of Spain, considering its yearly amount, is nothing very confiderable: this proceeds from the former abufes and diforders which have long prevailed in the finances, the want of due population, and likewife the low ebb of manufactures and trade; whereas the court, the navy, and army, and the multitude of ftate and law officers, are articles of prodigious expence *. Befides, the almoft continual wars fince Charles V. have funk the kingdom into an abyfs of debts, from which it cannot emerge under fome centuries of tranquillity and good management, there being debts in arrear of all the kings as far back as Charles V. (*t*)

SECT. LVII.

Agriculture neglected in Spain.

Agriculture has been utterly neglected by the Spaniards fince the difcovery of the New World. Philip III. and Philip IV. endeavoured to promote it by feveral ordinances in favour of fuch as would employ

---

* Vayrac, Tom. III. p 309, 310, has given an account of the expences of the Spanifh court; according to which, the annual amount of them is about 16,592,356 ducats; but he adds, that king Philip very much diminifhed his expences both in his court and other particulars, and that the annual expence may now but little exceed half that fum.

(*t*) See the New General Hiftory in German, p. 63, 64.

them-

themselves either in tillage or graziery; but they proved without effect (*u*), not so much from the barrenness of the country, as the pride and laziness of the people (*x*), who prefer hunger and penury to an occupation which they conceit to be greatly beneath them.

> Furfureo cum pane domi vescatur egenus,
> Sordeat et vacua semper inops que casa,
> Non artem exercet, non terram sulcat aratro,
> Accinctus gladio nobilis esse studet.
> Hinc inculta jacent camporum millia passim,
> Atque deest vastis gnavus arator agris (*y*).

SECT LVIII.

Under Charles V. some manufactures in Spain were in a thriving condition. Segovia, Herencia, and some other towns in Castile, grew noted for making cloth; Granada and Andalusia for damasks, sattins, and other silks; Biscay for fire-arms, and Cuenza and other places for paper (*z*): but since the beginning of the seventeenth century, and especially since the expulsion of

State of Spanish manufactures.

(*u*) Vayrac, Tom. I. p. 48.
(*x*) Saavedra en la Idea de un Principe Politico Christiano, Empresa LXXI. p. 711.
(*y*) Corn. Kiliani Lusus de Nationib. in Arcanis Dominationis Hispanæ, cap. xxxiv. p. 205.
(*z*) Memoires sur le Commerce d'Espagne, Tom. I. Ch. X. p. 286. It farther says, that in the year 1552, the woollen manufactures in Segovia employed above 13,000 hands.

the

the Moors, things are so much altered for the worse, that in Spain there is a want even of the most necessary crafts and trades. The duke de Riperda, indeed, set up some linen and other manufactories in Guadalaxara, and invited workmen from Holland and other countries; but, at his fall, all these promising beginnings dropped, and the foreign manufacturers returned home (*a*). Ferdinand VI. and Charles III. were likewise very intent on the same object; and the present Spanish administration seem to apply themselves in good earnest to redress such a capital defect: at least, according to the public accounts, several cloth and silk looms, with other manufactures and fabrics, are already at work *.

SECT. LIX.

Of home-trade.

By these means the Spanish home-trade is in a fair way to prosper, whereas hitherto it was cramped by several other discouragements, besides the want of manufactures;

(*a*) Memoires Instructifs, Tom. II. p. 43, 44, 45. The author relates, that some unknown people distributed money among these manufacturers secretly, and as it were out of pity, yet upon condition that they should return back into their own country again; and afterwards, on any delay, threatened them with the inquisition.

* Philip V. besides erecting manufactures and fabrics, bestowed many encouraging privileges on the undertakers and workmen. See Ustariz, chap. lxii. lxiii. lxiv.

for the many tolls and imposts made the goods too dear, and the badness of the roads rendered it extremely chargeable and troublesome to transport them from one province into another. King Philip V. to remove these difficulties, suppressed the inland tolls, and replaced some on the harbours (*b*). He likewise intended to provide for the conveniency of home-trade by good roads, canals, and making rivers navigable †; but these views have remained long unexecuted.

SECT. LX.

The Spanish foreign commerce is very considerable, almost all European nations trade to Spain, but especially the English, Dutch, and French (*c*). In the latter half of the former century, the two first nations had the greatest traffic, which was likewise established by several treaties, very much to their advantage (*d*): but since the house of Bourbon

Foreign commerce.

(*b*) Uftariz, chap. lv. p. 189, &c.

† Few of the large rivers in Spain can be said to be navigable. Some Dutchmen, in the reign of Charles II. laid a proposal before the council for making the Manzanares and the Tagus navigable, and thereby open a communication between Madrid and Lisbon; but this proposal was rejected on reasons deduced from religion. Vayrac, Tom. III. p. 315, 316.

(*c*) Uftariz, chap. xlix.

(*d*) Memoires sur le Commerce d'Espagne, Tom. II. ch. vii. viii.

has possessed the Spanish throne; the French are most favoured (*e*). However, instead of the Spaniards exporting much themselves, foreigners bring their goods and carry away Spanish commodities in return. It is only the Biscayners who go to France, England, and Holland, and sometimes as far as Hamburgh and Dantzick; and some Spanish seaports on the Mediterranean carry on a trade to the south coasts of France, to Genoa and Leghorn (*f*). The Spaniards are in general losers by the foreign trade, since their importations from abroad far exceed their exports; and consequently the balance must be made up in specie *. Spain otherwise is excellently well situated for maritime trade, and has many good harbours both on the ocean and the Mediterranean, among which Cadiz is the principal: it is, indeed, the center of the Spanish, European, and American trade.

(*e*) Ustariz, ch. v. p. 163, 166.
(*f*) Vayrac, Tom. III. p. 316. Memoires sur le Commerce d'Espagne, Tom. II. ch. iii. p. 121.
* Ustariz, ch. ii. complains greatly of this, and of the millions which go every year into the pope's Datary for ecclesiastical merchandize; and to these two causes it is owing, as he says, that Spain is so bare of gold and silver. He moreover thinks, that notwithstanding the prodigious quantities of those noble metals which are brought from America, scarce a hundred millions of coined and wrought silver are to be found in all Spain. See Ustariz, ch. iii.

The

SECT. LXI.

The Spaniards do not trade to Africa, Turkey, or the East-Indies: their traffic to the Canary-Islands, indeed, is an article of pretty good account, but in which other European nations come in for a share. The most considerable trade of the Spaniards is to their American possessions, from which all foreign nations are absolutely excluded. This trade is carried on from Cadiz, under the inspection of the India-council (Casa de la Contractation a las Indias). 1. In the Flota, as it is called, which consists partly of king's ships, and partly of merchant-ships, and sails to Vera Cruz. A little before their departure, two or three frigates, called the Flotilla, are dispatched to carry intelligence of them. 2. In the galleons, which are eight or ten men of war, serving as convoy to twelve or fifteen merchant-ships, which first go to Carthagena, then to Porto-Bello; thence again to Carthagena, afterwards to the Havannah, and from thence proceed back to Spain. 3. In the register-ships, which merchants, with licence from the council of trade, send to several parts of the West-Indies. Besides these, the king likewise, at certain times, sends the azogue or quick-silver ships to Vera Cruz, which carry quick-

quickfilver for the Mexico mines (g). All the above-mentioned ships carry Spanish and other European goods to the West-Indies, and bring back an amazing quantity of gold and silver, with other very valuable commodities. The Spaniards not having goods by far sufficient for this trade, the greater part are consigned to them by the French, Italians, English, Dutch, and others; and the merchants at Cadiz, for an acknowledgment, or part of the profit, send the goods under their respective names to America. Thus most of the gold and silver comes ultimately into the hands of foreigners; so that, in this important trade, the Spaniards are little more than factors (h); in which, however, it is agreed that they act with very uncommon probity and honour (i).

SECT. LXII.

Trade between Manilla and Acapulco.

By favour of the Spanish court, a considerable trade is likewise carried on from the city of Manilla in the island of Lucon, to Acapulco in Mexico; but with as little advantage to the crown of Spain, as to the

(g) M. de Real Science du Gouvernement, Tom. II. p. 92.
(h) Id. ibid. Memoires sur le Commerce d' Espagne, Tom. II. p. 131. where is likewise an inventory of goods sent to the West-Indies.
(i) Memoires de Montgon, Tom. IV. p. 63, 71, 72.

Spa-

Spanish subjects, it being entirely given up to the convents in Manilla, and particularly the Jesuits*, for the support of their missions, as they are called. Every year, two ships, furnished by the king, usually go from the said city to Acapulco, with a cargo of all kinds of East-India goods, for which they seldom bring back less than three millions of piastres (*k*).

SECT. LXIII.

That the Spanish administration is more intent at present on the advancement of trade than formerly, appears from a company being set up in 1728, for trading from St. Sebastian's to the Caraccas in South-America; and another in 1756, for a traffick to the Island of Hispaniola, the Bay of Honduras, and those parts.

[marginal note: Trading companies in Spain.]

SECT. LXIV.

The administration of the affairs of the Spanish monarchy, is conducted by several assemblies.

[marginal note: Administration of government and state affairs.]

1. La Junta del Despacho Universal, or the cabinet council, in which the most important affairs, and matters of favour, both domestic and foreign, come under delibe-

---
* This must have admitted of some alteration, since the expulsion of the Jesuits. Transl.
(*k*) Anson's Voyages, Book II. ch. x.

ration. The secretary to this cabinet council (Secretario del Despacho Universal) is accounted the most considerable among the ministers, the king frequently discoursing of affairs, and forming resolutions with him only; and whatever concerns the crown goes through his hands (*l*).

II. El Consejo de Estado, the council of state, which manages the general affairs of the kingdom, and consists of the greatest state officers. Its president is always the senior counsellor; and the archbishop of Toledo is, by virtue of his dignity, a counsellor of state (*m*).

III. El Consejo Supremo de Guerra, the great council of war, which is divided into two chambers; one taking cognizance of every thing relating to the military, and the other decides law cases. The counsellors of state are by their office counsellors of war, and in the meetings of this council take precedence (*n*).

IV. El Consejo Real de Castilla, the royal council of Castile, consisting of a president and sixteen counsellors. It has four divisions, viz.

(*a*) Sala de Govierno, which takes care of the king's prerogative in ecclesiastical affairs.

(*l*) Vayrac, Tom. III. p. 211, 212.
(*d*) Ibid. p. 218, 219.
(*n*) Id. Ibid.

(*b*) Sala

SPAIN.

(*b*) Sala de Mil y Quinientos (*o*), where proceſſes, on a petition from a decree of the council, are reviſed.

(*c*) Sala de Juſticia, where the papal bulls and penal cauſes are examined.

(*d*) Sala de Provincia, which takes cognizance of cauſes brought before the council of Caſtile, by appeal from the lower courts.

The council of Caſtile, by an order of Philip IV. in the year 1623, confers the profeſſorſhips in the univerſities of Salamanca, Valladolid, and Alcala de Henares (*p*).

V. La Real Camara de Caſtilla, the royal chamber of Caſtile, which is annexed to the council of Caſtile; and the preſident of which, with three or four counſellors, a referendary, and three clerks, conſtitutes this council: and here, by virtue of the king's right of patronage, are iſſued nominations to church and law employments, as likewiſe matters of favour and pardons of delinquents and malefactors (*q*).

VI. El Conſejo Real y Supremo de las Indias, the ſupreme royal council of India.

(*o*) For the origin of this name, ſee Vayrac, Tom. III. p. 22. and Montgon, Tom. VI. p. 96.
(*p*) Vayrac, Tom. III. p. 222, 229.
(*q*) Ibid. p. 229. and foll.

To its inspection belong the whole Spanish American dominion, and likewise the Audiencia de la Contractation, or the Cadiz council of trade. They who have been viceroys in the West-Indies, or held other great employments in that part of the world, are generally appointed members of this council (*r*).

VII. El Consejo Real de Hazienda y Contaduria Mayor, the royal council of finances and accounts. This council manages the king's revenue; and here all farmers, contractors, or other officers concerned in it, must give in their accounts (*s*).

VIII. El Consejo de la Suprema y general Inquisition, the president of which is inquisitor-general. All the other courts of inquisition within the kingdom are subordinate to this, which likewise has the disposal of all their vacant employments (*t*).

IX. El Consejo Real de las Ordines, the royal council of the orders of knighthood, to which belong two departments; one for the order of St. James, and the other for those of Calatrava and Alcantara (*u*).

(*r*) Vayrac, Tom. III. p. 233, and foll.
(*s*) Ibid. p. 244. 250.
(*t*) Ibid. Tom. II. p. 384, 385.
(*u*) Ibid. Tom. II. p. 394.

SPAIN.

X. La Commiffaria y Direccion general de la Cruzada, the Croifade-bull commiffion *. Its prefident is ftiled Commiffario-General, and has two affeffors, who are members of the council of Caftile, and one of the council of India, with feveral other officers. His jurifdiction comprehends the whole monarchy, with all its dependencies; and takes cognizance of all matters relating to the tax levied on the Spanifh clergy by the pope's confent, and the trade (*x*) with the croifade-bulls.

SECT. LXV.

The Spanifh provinces and dependencies are under the adminiftration of governors, who in thofe provinces which are kingdoms bear the title of viceroy (Virey); in the others they are ufually ftiled captain-general; but otherwife their power is equal, and

Government in the Spanifh dependencies.

---

* In the year 1457, pope Calixtus II. fent to king Henry IV. of Caftile, for defraying the expences of the war againft the Moors, the firft Croifade-bull, containing an indulgence for the dead and living; and of which all might be partakers, who either ferved againft the infidels, or paid 200 maravedis to the king towards carrying on the war againft them. This bull, however, was granted only for twenty-four years. Mariana, Lib. XXII. cap. xviii. But the fucceeding kings have from time to time procured it to be renewed, and extended to feveral religious privileges; fo that a licence for eating butter, eggs, cheefe, milk, in a time of faft, is to be purchafed by a printed copy of this bull, on paying eight reals to the king. Vayrac, Tom. II. p. 389.

(*x*) Vayrac, Tom. II. p. 388, 389.

very

very great it is, all officers, civil and military, being under their command. They have the difposal of moft vacant employments, or recommend perfons to the king (*y*). The governors have many opportunities of raifing a fortune, and are very expert at making the moft of them *. This is particularly the cafe in America, where the adminiftration is the more arbitrary, by being fo remote from court, and by the great difficulty of laying any complaint before the throne †.

SECT. LXVI.

The domeftic ftate of Spain is fufceptible of many improvements; and matters would be exceedingly mended by promoting agriculture and manufactures, which would tend to the increafe of population, the chief ftrength of a ftate. Her domeftic and foreign trade would revive and flourifh; and inftead of being obliged to deal the greateft part of her Weft-India treafures among

---

(*y*) Vayrac, Tom. III. p. 273, 274.

* The Spaniards themfelves fee nothing amifs in this; and not only the viceroys, but likewife their officers and fervants ftick at no means to raife a fortune. See Relatione della Corte di Spagna, da Domenico Zanctornato, p. 85, 86.

† See Don Emanuel de Lira's reprefentation delivered to king Charles II. in the Memoires fur le Commerce d'Efpagne, Tom. II. ch. i. p. 12. & foll.

foreigners, she might supply not only her own people, but likewise her American colonies, with all necessary commodities.

The foreign concerns of the Spanish monarchy are greatly altered since Spain has been under a king of the house of Bourbon. The former enmity against France is changed into amity and union. If policy on one side requires the careful maintenance of such harmony, on the other France is not to be so indifferent about the real advantage of Spain, as it has sometimes shewn itself (z).

Foreign interests of Spain.

Portugal is of itself too weak to hurt Spain; yet is it adviseable for Spain to cultivate the friendship of Portugal, as by means of its proximity, it may, in conjunction with other powers, give Spain a good deal of trouble; and Spain must also give over all thoughts of reducing Portugal, as in such a case Great-Britain will always step in to its assistance.

With the see of Rome Spain has almost continually preserved a good understanding, which by reason of the Spanish territories in Italy, was once of absolute necessity; and at present, one Spanish prince being possessed of Naples and Sicily, and another of Parma and Placentia, which connects these

(z) Campbell's Present State of Europe, ch. xi.

countries clofely with Spain, it appears to be no lefs neceffary.

Great Britain is the chief object of Spain's jealoufy, which ſtill looks with an evil eye on its holding Gibraltar and Minorca; but the ſtrength of the Britiſh navy checks all hopes of recovering thofe places, and ſhould likewife be a motive for Spain to avoid a rupture with that crown; recent inſtances having ſhewn of what detriment it may prove to her Weſt-India treafures and poffeffions. But the Spaniards may be fure that Great Britain will never quarrel with them, whilſt they obferve the commercial treaties between the two nations.

Their quarrels with the houfe of Auſtria have ceafed fince Spain has been difpoffeffed of the greater part of the Italian territories formerly belonging to the Spaniſh monarchy, or to which it laid claim. But ſhould the royal family of Spain, befides Parma and Placentia, which purfuant to the treaty of Aix-la-Chapelle were, on the demife of king Ferdinand VI. to have devolved to the emprefs queen, likewife extend its views to Milan and Tufcany, this would be oppofed both by the king of Sardinia and the pope. The beft way for Spain is to leave things in Italy as they are at prefent.

Spain

SPAIN.

Spain and the United-Netherlands (since the other parts of the Low-Countries no longer belong to that crown) have little or no concern with each other, but in what relates to commerce; and it is in the same situation with regard to Denmark and Sweden.

The distance from Spain to Russia, Poland, and Prussia, is too great for them either to succour, or annoy, each other. A connection, however, with the last of those three powers may be convenient for Spain, in case of an Italian war with the house of Austria.

SECT. LXVII.

The most interesting conventions of the crown of Spain with other powers, are the following. *Conventions with other powers.*

I. With FRANCE.

1. The peace of Vervins, 2d of May 1598 (*a*). The peace of the Pyrenees, 7th of November 1659 (*b*). 3. The peace of Aix-la-Chapelle, 2d of May 1668 (*c*). 4.

(*a*) Corps Universel Diplomat. par M. Du Mont, Tom. V. Part. I p. 561.
(*b*) Du Mont, Tom. VI Part. II. p. 264. Le Droit Publique de l'Europe, par M. l'Abbé de Mably, Tom. I. ch. i. p. 21 et suiv.
(*c*) Du Mont, Tom. VII. P. I. p. 89. Mably, Tom. I. ch. iv. p. 141.

That

That of Nimeguen, 17th of September 1678 (*d*). 5. The peace of Ryſwick, 20th of September 1697 (*e*). And laſtly, the Family-Compact, 15th of Auguſt 1761 (*f*).

II. With PORTUGAL.

1. The peace of Liſbon, the 13th of February 1668 (*g*); 2. That of Utrecht, the 8th of February 1713 (*h*); and 3. That of Paris, 10th of February 1763 (*i*).

III. With GREAT BRITAIN.

1. The treaty of peace and commerce at Madrid, 27th of May 1667 (*k*). 2. Convention relating to American affairs, of the 8th of July 1670 (*l*). 3. Of Utrecht, 13th of July 1713 (*m*). 4. That of Aix-la-Chapelle, the 18th of October 1748 (*n*); and

---

(*d*) Du Mont, Tom. VII. P. II. p. 208. Mably, Tom. I. ch. iv. p. 202.

(*e*) Ibid. P. II. p. 408. Mably, Tom. I. ch. v. p. 231.

(*f*) An abſtract is to be found in Faber's New Secretary of State for Europe, written in German.

(*g*) Du Mont, Tom VII. P. I. p. 70. Mably, Tom. I. ch. iii. p. 141.

(*h*) Du Mont, Tom. VIII. P. I. p. 444. Mably, Tom. II. ch. vii. p. 185.

(*i*) Antony Faber's New Secretary of Europe, Part VIII. p. 117, 118.

(*k*) Ibid. Tom. VII. P. I. p. 27. Mably, Tom. II. ch. xii. p. 351.

(*l*) Ibid. P. I. p. 137.

(*m*) Ibid. Tom. VIII. P. I. p. 393. Mably, Tom. II. ch. vii. p. 127.

(*n*) Recueil d'Actes & Traités, par Mr. Rouſſet, Tom. XX. p. 179.

SPAIN.

5. The peace of Paris, 10th of February 1763 (*o*).

IV. With the House of AUSTRIA.

1. The peace of Vienna, 30th of April 1725 (*p*); 2. Of Vienna, 18th of November 1738 (*q*); and 3. Of Aix-la-Chapelle, the 18th of October 1748 (*r*).

V. With the House of SAVOY.

1. Cession of the kingdom of Sicily, 10th July 1713 (*s*); and 2. The peace of Utrecht, 13th of August 1713 (*t*).

VI. With the UNITED-NETHERLANDS.

1. Peace of Munster, 30th of January 1648 (*u*); and 2. That of Utrecht, 26th of June 1714 (*x*).

(*o*) Faber's New Secretary of State for Europe, P. VIII. p. 117.
(*p*) Du Mont, Tom. VIII. P. II. p. 106. Mably, Tom. II. ch. vii. p. 157.
(*q*) Rousset, Tom. XIII. p. 421, 527. Mably, Tom. II. ch. ix. p. 222.
(*r*) Art. VII. Rousset, Tom. XX. p. 188.
(*s*) Du Mont, Tom. VIII. P. I. p. 389. Mably, Tom. II. ch. viii. p. 138.
(*t*) Ibid. P. I. p. 401. Mably, Tom. II. ch. viii. p. 137.
(*u*) Ibid. Tom. VI. P. I. p. 429. Mably, Tom. I. ch. i. p. 67.
(*x*) Ibid. Tom. VIII. P. I. p. 427.

SECT.

SECT. LXVIII.

The most celebrated Spanish warriors and statesmen have been, under Sancho VI. and Alphonso VI. kings of Castile, Don Rodrigo Dias de Vivar, commonly known by the name of el Cid, the Spanish Hercules. Under Ferdinand the Catholick, Christopher Columbus, who discovered the New World; in consideration of which he was made admiral of the Indies for him and his heirs; Gonsalez Ferdinand de Cordova, surnamed El Gran Capitan; Francis Ximenes de Cisneros, cardinal of Spain, and archbishop of Toledo. Under Charles V. Ferdinand Cortes, the conqueror of Mexico; Francisco Pizarro, who reduced Peru under the Spanish dominions; Mercurius Alborius de Gattinara, and Nicholaus Perenot de Granvelle, who rose from the most abject condition to the most exalted dignities. Under Philip II. Ferdinand Alvarez de Toledo, duke of Alva, whose rigour occasioned the revolt of the Netherlands, but afterwards made some amends to Spain by reducing the kingdom of Portugal; Cardinal Anthony Perenot de Granvelle, Nicholas Perenot's son; Don John of Austria I. who gave that famous blow to the Turkish navy at Lepanto. Under Philip III. Don Francis

cis de Sandoval, duke, and afterwards cardinal, of Lerma, who engrossed the management of all affairs, as prime minister of state. Under Philip IV. Don Gaspar de Guzman, count of Olivares, and duke of St. Lucas, commonly called el Conde-Duque, who had the like vicissitudes of fortune as the duke of Lerma; and his sister's son Don Lewis Mendez de Haro, duke of Montoro, and marquis Del Carpio. Under Charles II. Eberhard Neithard, a German Jesuit, afterwards Inquisitor-General of Spain; and Don John of Austria II. natural son to king Philip IV. Under Philip V. Cardinal Julius Alberoni; John William, baron, and afterwards duke of Ripperda; and Don Joseph de Carillo, count of Montemar, and duke of Bitonto.

SECT. LXIX.

The sources of the Spanish history are contained in some collections published by Andreas Schottus, John Pistorius, and Francis Schottus (*y*). The principal authors of the general histories of Spain are, Stephen de Garibay (*z*), Ma-

---

(*y*) Under this title: Hispania Illustrata, opera et studio doctorum hominum. IV. Tomi; Francofurti, 1603, 1606, 1608, fol.

(*z*) Los quarenta Libros del Compendio historial de las Chronicas y Universal Historia de todos los Reynos de Esparianz,

riana,

riana (*a*), Saavedro Faxardo (*b*), and Ferreras (*c*).

Accounts of the ſtate of Spain have been given by Goes (*d*), De Laet (*e*), Boſius (*f*), Abbe Vayrac (*g*), and others (*h*).

---

na, compueſtos por Eſtevan. De Garibay in Barcelona, 1628. IV. Tomos, fol.

(*a*) 10. Marianæ Hiſtoriæ de rebus Hiſpanicis, Libri XXX. Accedunt Joſephi Emmanuelis Minianæ Continuationis Novæ Lib. X. cum Iconibus Regum; Hagæ comit. 1733. IV. Tomi fol. Mariana himſelf has farther tranſlated his hiſtory into Spaniſh. It was publiſhed at Madrid in 1608, in two volumes folio, and has ſince gone through ſeveral editions. Mariana's own countrymen, however, are not much pleaſed with him, and condemn him for the freedom with which he cenſures their baſe actions. See Saavedra's Corona Gothica, P. 1. c. ix. p. m. 130. and the ſame writer's Republica Literaria, p. 59. Mariana's Hiſtory, however, has been continued by Medrano in a large work: Continuation de la Hiſtoria General de Eſpanna, de Anno 1516. a 1700. 3 Tom. fol. Madrid, 1748. See Clarke's Letters, p. 68.

(*b*) Corona Gothica Caſtellana y Auſtriaca, en Munſter, or in reality, Amſt. rdam, 1646, 4to. This is the firſt part of the work, which afterwards was augmented with three others by Don Alphonſo Nunnez de Caſtro. It has been ſeveral times printed in Spain, but the beſt edition is that of Antwerp, in four volumes folio, publiſhed in 1687.

(*c*) Synopſis Chronologica de la Hiſtoria de Eſpanna, XV. Partes IV. Mr. d'Hermilly has tranſlated this work into French, under the title of Hiſtoire Generale d'Eſpagne, (à Paris, 1751. X. Tomes IV.) and from this was taken the German tranſlation. As Ferrares breaks off with king Philip II. Mr. Profeſſor Bertram of Halle has entered on a continuation of it, which is very well written; and two volumes have already appeared.

(*d*) Damaini a Goes Hiſpania, in Hiſpania illuſtrata, Tom. I. p. 1106.

(*e*) Hiſpania, ſive, de Regis Hiſpaniæ Regnis & Opibus Commentarius, Lugd. Bat. 1629. in form. min.

(*f*) Hiſpaniæ, Ducatus Mediolanenſis & Regni Neopolitani Notitia e Muſeo 10. Andr. Schmidii. Helmſtadii, 1704. 4.

(*g*) Etat

SPAIN.

(*g*) Etat present de l'Espagne, à Amsterdam; 1719. 3 Tomes. 8.

(*h*) Among others: Hispaniæ et Lusitaniæ Itinerarium nova & accurata descriptione iconibusque loca eorundem præcipua illustrans. Amstelod. 1656. 12.

Annales d'Espagne et de Portugal, avec la Description de tout ce qu'il y a de plus remarquable en Espagne et en Portugal, par Don Jean Alvarez de Colmenar, à Amsterd. 1741. IV. Tomes. 4.

Letters concerning the Spanish Nation; written at Madrid during the years 1760 and 1761, by Edward Clarke; London, 1763 4.

This work has been translated into the German language, by Mr. Professor Kohler of Gottingen, with notes and illustrations.

Of the Spanish laws, a good account is given by Peter Joseph Perez Valiente, Apparatus Juris publici Hispanici, printed at Madrid in 1751, in 2 vols. 4to.

Concerning the former interest and policy of Spain, see Campanellæ de Monarchiâ Hispanicâ Discursus. Hardervici, 1653. 12. Hispanicæ Dominationis Arcana, per I. L. W. Lugd. Bat. 1653. 12.

The Spanish finances, manufactures, and trade, are discussed with great accuracy and judgment in Theoria y Practica de Commercio y de Marina, que se procuran adaptar à la Monarchia Espannola, por Don Geronimo de Ustariz, en Madrid, 1742. fol. This excellent work is likewise translated into some foreign languages. Another good treatise on the same subject is, Memoires et Considerations sur le Commerce et les Finances d'Espagne, à Amsterd. 1761. 8. 2 Vol.

For the character of the Spanish nation, see Mr. Gundling's Discourse on the Morals, Capacities, and Dispositions of the Spaniards, in his Otia, P. I. ch. i.

THE PRESENT STATE OF EUROPE.

CHAP. III.
Of PORTUGAL.

SECT. I.

THE kingdom of Portugal was anciently a part of Spain, and generally comprehended under that province to which the Romans gave the name of Lusitania. The present appellation was derived from a place at the mouth of the Douro, which, on account of its excellent harbour, was called Porto, and the adjacent town of Cale or Calle (*a*); from which at first was compounded Portucalia or Portucallia, and afterwards, by a slender alteration, Portugallia. At first, no more was understood by it than the present province of Entre Minho e Dou-

Name.

(*a*) Mariana, Lib. I. cap. iv. Universal History, Vol. XVIII. p. 478.

ro, which the kings of Leon had wrested from the Moors: but when count Henry and his son Alphonso began to enlarge their conquests in these parts, the name was given to the whole country (*b*).

SECT. II.

Situation and bounds.   Portugal is the most western land in Europe, and lies between the 37th and 42d degree of northern latitude, and the 7th and 11th western longitude, from the meridian of Ferro. Towards the south and west, it confines on the Atlantic Ocean; and towards the north and east it is hemmed in by the Spanish provinces of Galicia, Leon, Estremadura, and Andalusia. Its extent is about 1545 square geographical miles (*c*).

SECT. III.

Air and temperature.   The air and temperature is more agreeable and moderate than in Spain; for though the summer heats in the southern provinces be extreme, yet are they seldom of any long continuance, being very much abated by the frequent westerly winds. The winter is mild; but by reason of the violent rains, very disagreeable.

(*b*) M. Schmaufen's State of the Kingdom of Portugal, written in German, P. I. p. 83.
(*c*) Busching's Geography, Vol. II.

PORTUGAL.

SECT. IV.

The great branches of the Pyrenean mountains which spread all over Spain, shoot likewise into Portugal, and form several new chains. The most known are Estrella, Marvan, Sintra, Arabida, Tagro, or Sagro, and the Algarves mountains, which separate that kingdom from Portugal (*d*). Hills.

SECT. V.

From these mountains issue a great number of rivers and streams, delightfully watering the vallies and plains; but its chief rivers, as the Minho, the Lima, the Douro, the Tagus, and the Guadiana, come from Spain. Rivers.

SECT. VI.

Portugal is by nature one of the most happy and fruitful countries in Europe. Its beef is excellent, yet the inhabitants are deficient in breeding horned cattle; the wool of its sheep, besides the delicacy of the flesh, is scarce inferior to the Spanish. It abounds in swine, and its pork excels that of most other nations (*e*). The Portuguese horses Products in the animal kingdom.

(*d*) Manuel De Faria y Sousa en la Epitome de las Historias Portuguesas, Parte IV. cap. vi. p. 357, 358.
(*e*) Faria y Sousa, P. IV. cap. viii. p. 361.

have in all ages been celebrated for fwiftnefs (*f*); but the breeding of them is at prefent much decreafed, affes and mules having been found fitter for ufe (*g*). Of poultry and wild-fowl it has plenty, and the rivers and fea fupply it with fifh of the beft kinds (*h*).

In the vegetable kingdom. The vegetable kingdom yields the moft delicious fruits, lemons, Seville and China oranges *, almonds, figs, chefnuts; likewife grapes, olives and oil, in fuch quantities as to fupply many countries in and out of Europe. Every part of Portugal affords wine: the preference, however, is given to that of Lifbon growth, and that of the province of Alentejo. The fields and woods are covered with fcented flowers, herbs, trees, and plants, of which the bees make the beft of honey; yet the latter has loft not a little of its efteem, fince fugar is come fo much in vogue. Portugal, till the reign of king Ferdinand, produced corn for exportation; but fince its great maritime difcoveries, and the eager application of the people to navigation and commerce, confe-

---

(*f*) Juftin, Lib. XLIV. cap. iii. Faria y Soufa. L. C.
(*g*) Schmauff. P. I. p. 74, 75.
(*h*) Faria y Soufa, P. IV. cap. viii. p. 361.

* Thefe, as appears from their names, were brought from China to Portugal, and there tranfplanted.

quential

quential to those discoveries, and turning to better account, agriculture is fallen into such neglect (*i*), that, instead of exporting, they purchase grain from foreigners, and more especially from the English.

Portugal, like Spain, antiently yielded great quantities of the more noble metals; and the Portuguese boast of their country, that there is not a mountain or river in it without gold (*k*). The Tagus is often mentioned by the Romans for its gold *; but at present, the Portuguese receiving such treasures of that metal from the East-Indies and Brazil, have given over searching for it in their hills and rivers. Several parts have silver, tin, lead, and iron; yet the mines of these ores are not worked †. Portugal, farther, is not without some kinds of gems, as turquoises and hyacinths, chrystals, agates, and many others; its marble is exquisite both in grain and colours; and the Portu-

In the mineral kingdom.

(*i*) Faria y Sousa, P. IV. cap. viii. p. 360, 361.
(*k*) Ibid. p. 361.

* See Plin. Hist. Nat. Lib. IV. cap. xxii. Martial, Lib. I. Epigr. 50, calls it " Aureus Tagus;" and Lib. XII. Epigr. 12, " Aurifer Tagus." King Dionȳfius is said to have had a sceptre and crown made of Tagus gold, and king John III. another sceptre.

† There is a famous silver-mine by the side of the Guadiana, called Via de Plata, and some others in the northern parts of the kingdom; but for particular reasons of state, these, like the abovementioned, are made no use of. Memoires Instructifs pour un Voyageur, Tom. 1. p. 211.

guese mill-stones are of such a goodness as to be carried to Spain and the Indies (*l*). A rich salt-petre mine has been discovered by a foreigner in Estrella-hills (*m*). Salt, and particularly sea-salt, is made in such quantities, as to be a considerable article in exportation (*n*). In some places are mineral waters, and warm baths, or, as the Portuguese call them, As Caldas (*o*); those in the country of Leria are said to do wonders in venereal diseases (*p*).

SECT. VII.

Division of the kingdom. Portugal is divided into six provinces: two north of the Douro, namely, 1. Entre Minho e Douro; 2. Trafs os Montes (in Spanish Tra los Montes) two in the middle between the Douro and Tagus; 3. Beira; 4. Estremadura: and two are inclosed within the Tagus, the Guadiana, and the Ocean; namely, 5. Alem-Tejo, or Entre-Tejo e Guadiana; and, 6. Algarves, which has the title of a kingdom. In all these provinces are nineteen large cities, and 527 towns.

(*l*) Faria y Sousa, P. IV. cap. viii. p. 362, 363. Schmauss. P. I. p. 75—80.
(*m*) Memoires Instructifs pour un Voyageur, Tom. I. p. 176, 178.
(*n*) Faria y Sousa, cap. viii. p. 361. Schmauss. P. I. p. 45, 48, and Part II. p. 429.
(*o*) Ibid. P. IV. cap. vii. p. 360.
(*p*) Memoires Instruct. Tom. I. p. 52.

SECT. VIII.

Portugal's dependencies in the other three parts of the world are much larger than the mother-kingdom itself; for though the Portuguese have lost a great part of them, what still remains in their hands is very considerable. Among these are,

1. In the Atlantic Ocean, the Azores islands, otherwise the Flemish islands; the principal of which is Tercera; likewise the island Madera or Madeira, so famous for its wine, sugar, and other products; and Porto Santo: next are the Cape de Verd islands, or Ilhas do Cabo Verde, but of which sea-salt is the only merchantable product; and lastly, on the African coast under the Equator, are the islands of San Thome, do Principe, Fernando Pao and Anno Bono.

2. In Africa their western possessions are, Mazagan, a fort in the kingdom of Morocco, and several places and forts in the kingdoms of Loango, Congo, and Angola; particularly Loanda da San Paulo in the East: they here carry on a very considerable and lucrative trade, but the principal article of it is slaving. On the eastern coasts of Africa, they have several forts in Soffala, which yields great quantities of gold, and in the island of Mosambique, besides many

small

small islands known by the general name of Quirimba.

In Asia.

3. They have large territories in Asia; particularly in the kingdom of Cambaia, to them belong Diu, a strong place, likewise Duncan, Bazaim, and others; in the kingdom of Decan, Chaoul; in the kingdom of Cuncan, Goa, the capital of the Portuguese East-India possessions; and lastly, the city of Macao, in a small island on the coast of China *.

4. In America they have possessed themselves of Brazil, under which general name is also comprehended a part of Guiana and Paraguay. The whole Portuguese dominion is divided into fifteen Capitanias or governments; and the principal places therein are, Para, Olinda, San Salvadore, the residence of the Portuguese viceroy, and San Sebastian, commonly called Rio Janeiro. The country abounds in sugar, tobacco, Brazil wood, spices and drugs; likewise gold and diamonds †. Hence Brazil is justly

---

* This city intirely depends on the courtesy of the Chinese, who, at their pleasure, may make themselves masters of it, or starve it; and the Portuguese governor there is treated pretty much on a footing with a Chinese subject. Anson's Voyage round the World, ch. vii.

† Gold was discovered in Brazil towards the end of the last century, merely by accident; and the annual amount of it is now computed at twelve millions of dollars. Anson's Voyage round the World, Book I. c. v. The dif-

accounted the most considerable of all the Portuguese dependencies, and in the present century has been peopled and cultivated accordingly. In order to promote its population, king Joseph in 1755, declared that marriages between Portuguese and Indians should be legal and valid, and the issue of such marriages be capable of employments and honours (*q*).

The founding of the colony of San Sagramento, on the river de la Plata, by the Portuguese in 1680, occasioned great differences between them and the Spaniards, which at length were determined by the peace of Utrecht *, in 1713.

---

covery of diamonds is of a later date; but to prevent too busy a search after them, and keep them up to a proper value, king John V. erected a Diamond-Company, which, in consideration of a sum of money, have an exclusive right of gathering diamonds. Anson's Voyage, Book I. ch. v.

(*q*) New Genealogical Historical Accounts, written in German, p. 74.

* Philip V. however, reserved to himself, in the VIIth article of the treaty of Utrecht, the giving the crown of Portugal an equivalent for San Sagramento, on which that colony was to be ceded to Spain, the clandestine trade between that place and Buenos Ayres being exceeding detrimental to the Spaniards. Likewise, in the year 1750, it was agreed between the two courts, that San Sagramento should be exchanged with the Spaniards for a piece of land in Paraguay; but in 1753, when this came to be put in execution, and the limits were to be settled by commissaries on both sides, the Indians, at the instigation of the Jesuits, opposed it, and the agreement came to nothing. See a Short Account of the Republic erected by the Jesuits of the Provinces of Portugal and Spain in the transmarine Countries and Dominions of those two Monarchies, p. 7—24.

The

The possession of these important countries the Portuguese acquired by arms; and their right rests partly on several papal grants *, and partly on the convention made with Spain at Tordesillas, in the year 1494; by which king Ferdinand the Catholic king of Spain, and John II. of Portugal, made a formal division of their new discoveries of the globe between them †.

SECT. IX.

Origin and revolutions of the kingdom.

As Lusitania was formerly a part of Spain, so has it partaken of its destiny. In the second Punic war, the Carthaginians being driven out of Spain, it fell under the domi-

---

* Pope Nicholas V. in the year 1452 and 1454, gave to Alphonso V. king of Portugal two grants relating to the Portuguese conquests in Africa, both which were confirmed by pope Calixus III. in the year 1455: the first of these grants is to be found in Raynaldi Contin. Annal. Baronii, Tom. XVIII. ad Ann. 1452. N°. XI. the 2d. ib. ad Ann. 1454. N°. VIII. and the Confirmation, ibid. ad. Ann. 1455. N°. VII.

† The occasion of it was this: On Christopher Columbus's return from his discovery of the New World, Ferdinand procured a bull from pope Alexander VI. by which all the countries of the infidels, to the extent of one thousand leagues, from the Azores and the Cape de Verd islands, were given to the crown of Spain. In this John II. king of Portugal would not acquiesce, but appealed to other papal grants. Hereupon the two kings determined to settle the dispute amicably; and this was done by the convention of Tordesillas, which extended the pope's partition line to 390 leagues west of the Cape de Verd islands. Faria y Sousa in Europa Portuguesa, Tom. II. Part III. c. iv. N° 80, 82. This partition gave the Portuguese a right to Brazil.

nion

nion of the Romans, and so remained till the beginning of the fifth century, when the Alani, Suevi, and Vandals, over-ran Spain. The Alani were the first who seated themselves in Lusitania; and afterwards the Suevi set up a kingdom in this country, but which 534. Leovigild king of the Visigoths overthrew. The Moors, in process of time, conquering 712. Spain, Lusitania likewise became subject to them; but Alphonso III. king of Leon, and Ferdinand I. king of Castile, gradually dispossessed them of the country between the Minho and Douro, which was then called Portucale or Portugal; and Alphonso VI. 1095. king of Castile, conferred it in full right by a testamentary bequest on his son-in-law Henry of Burgundy, with the title of 1109. count. His son Alphonso I. by his successes against the Moors, enlarged his dominions; and after the signal victory obtained over them at Ourique, assumed the 1139. title of King. This Alphonso VIII. king of Castile and Leon would not allow of, looking on Portugal as a fief of Leon; but Alphonso I. being supported by Rome, whose countenance he purchased by making his kingdom tributary to that see, kept possession of his new dignity. His successors, Sancho I. Alphonso II. and Sancho II. had violent contests with the clergy concerning

eccle-

ecclesiastical immunities, for which the latter was deposed by the sentence of pope Innocent IV. His brother and successor Alphonso III. reduced Algarves, since which the kingdom of Portugal has continued within its present limits. His son Dionysius made up his differences with the clergy by agreement, greatly to the advantage of that body and the pope; consequently inglorious and detrimental to the regal dignity: otherwise he behaved as a wise prince, particularly encouraging tillage; and he was both a judicious and liberal patron of the sciences. Alphonso IV. his son, chiefly distinguished himself in war; and his successor Peter I. was a just prince, but, at the same time, too rigid. His son Ferdinand, who succeeded him on the throne, was himself the cause of the misfortunes which embittered his reign.

The kingdom after his death became involved in great troubles. John I. king of Castile, who had married Beatrix, Ferdinand's only daughter, laid claim to the crown. But the Portuguese, detesting a foreign sovereign, made choice of John, a natural son of Peter I. who obtaining a decisive victory over the Castilians, shewed himself worthy of the throne, and reigned with great applause. He took from the Moors the

the town of Ceuta on the coast of Africa; and under his auspices it was that the Portuguese discovered the Azores islands, and that of Madera. His son Edward, endeavouring to enlarge his African conquests, proved unfortunate; but Alphonso V. in the prosecution of the like views, was as successful, and reduced Alcassar, Tangier, and Arcilla; and soon after were discovered Guinea and Congo. His successor John II. humbled the Portuguese nobility, and principally directed his views to extend the Portuguese navigation as far as the East-Indies; to which country, under his successor Emanuel, Vasco de Gama made the first voyage with great success. By these and the suc- 1497. ceeding conquests on the south coasts of Asia and Africa, the Portuguese became masters of the East-India trade, which poured in such riches, that Emanuel's reign was termed the Golden Age. This prosperity likewise continued under his son John III. but Sebastian, grandson and successor to the latter, rashly undertaking an expedition to Africa, in which he himself lost his life, 1578. occasioned a fatal revolution to Portugal.

For his grandfather's brother, cardinal 1580. Henry, who succeeded him in the throne, died after a short reign, and with him the male line of the royal family became extinct.

Here-

Hereupon Philip II. king of Spain, claimed the kingdom in right of his mother Isabella, daughter to king Emanuel; and maintaining his claim by force, he united Portugal with Spain; an union by which the former kingdom was a great sufferer. Under the two following kings, Philip III. and Philip IV. the Portuguese lost the most considerable part of their East-India trade, and of their East and West-India conquests, which were all wrested from them by the inhabitants of the United Netherlands, then at war with Spain.

These misfortunes, and more especially the domestic oppressions, exasperated the Portuguese to such a degree, that they universally revolted, and proclaimed the duke of Braganza king, by the name of John IV. who kept possession of his new crown. Under his son Alphonso VI. the Spaniards, indeed, strained every nerve to recover Portugal; but were so far from succeding, that, at the peace which terminated this war, they were obliged to renounce all claim and pretenfion to this kingdom, retaining only the single town of Ceuta. Alphonso VI. however, had no share personally in these glorious events; and even before the peace had been deposed, as unfit for government. His brother Peter II. being greatly instrumental

1640.

1668.

in

in this revolution, was recompenfed not only with the throne, but, what was ftill more extraordinary, with the fpoufe of the late king: he governed with great prudence, juftice, and magnanimity, reftoring the laws to their due vigour, which they had loft amidft the confufions of the former reign, and punifhed all offenders without refpect of perfons. John V. trod in the foot-fteps of 1706. his father, and made the prerogative more independent than it had been before his time. He promoted arts and fciences with royal munificence; but his expences in ecclefiaftical buildings and foundations were carried to fuch an enormous profufenefs, that the ftate groaned under the load, by fuch miftaken devotion. His fucceffor Jofeph, finding many abufes had crept in under the former adminiftration, very carefully applied himfelf to correct them, and place things on a better footing. This paternal care of his fubjects, however, did not fecure him from many calamitous events: he faw a great part 1755. of his capital city Lifbon, laid in ruins by a moft terrible earthquake and a conflagration; and his perfon very narrowly efcaped the 1758. murderous attempt of a powerful confpiracy. Farther, the war waged againft him by France and Spain, from a very fingular pretence, threatened him with the lofs of his

Vol. I.   T   king-

kingdom; but the open assistance of Great Britain and the speedy restoration of peace prevented the consequences, which had so dangerous an appearance in respect to the very existence of Portugal.

SECT. X.

The Portuguese, a mixed people.

The Portuguese, like the Spaniards, are a mixed people, descended from the several foreign nations which successively settled in that kingdom. Among them are no small number of Moorish, and still more of Jewish extraction; for king John II. having kindly received the Jews who had been driven out of Spain in the year 1492, and his successor Emanuel, on the contrary, taking violent measures for converting them, thousands offered themselves for baptism, and in process of time became, by marriages, more and more intermixed with the Portuguese. But not a few of these new christians retained their former religion, secretly practising its observances, and propagating it among their descendants. Hence the great number of latent Jews, and these even of all ranks (*r*).

SECT. XI.

Their character.

The Portuguese are very like the Spaniards both in body and mind; and have most

(*u*) Schmauss. Part II. p. 280, 281.

of their virtues and vices. They are naturally ingenious and subtle; cautious, flow, and taciturn; sparing in their diet, and particularly in drinking (s). They have the character of being courteous to strangers, faithful in friendship, and cordially benevolent to their relations (t). They value themselves on their courage, learning, zeal for religion, and loyalty to their kings (u).

Their own countrymen allow, that in pride, pomp, and vanity, they exceed all nations (x). Their orators and poets, and even historians, are notoriously exaggerating in their relations of the atchievements performed by their ancestors against the Castillians (y), and in the East-Indies (z). Covetousness and usury prevail among them to an enormous degree, which is attributed to the great mixture of Jewish blood (a). Their jealousy is without a parallel, their

(s) Description of Portugal, by J. M. Van Gobel, in German.
(t) De Real Science du Gouvernem. Part I. Tom. II. p. 114.
(u) Faria y Sousa en la Epitome de las Historias Portuguesas, P. IV. c. ii. p. 342.
(x) Id. ibid.
(y) Ibid. in Europa Portuguesa, Tom. II. Part III. c. i. No. 135, 136.
(z) Colleccam dos documentos e memorias du Academia Real da Historia Portuguesa de Anno 1724. Noticias do 22. Outubre, p. 14, 15.
(a) De Real, Part I. Tom. II. p. 114.

women scarce ever going out of doors, unless in Passion-week, when they may visit churches day and night; a liberty of which they are said passionately to avail themselves in carrying on intrigues (*b*): otherwise, their confinement is so rigid, that it is only at the Auto da Fé processions, and those of Corpus-Christi-day, that they dare so much as be seen at the window (*c*); and here the husbands closely watch them, and sometimes on a bare suspicion make them the victims of their revenge (*d*). They are slow to anger; but when once roused, they are furious and cruel (*e*); which is experienced by their slaves, who often meet with very inhuman treatment from them (*f*).

The wealthy Portuguese are mighty lovers of finery, extremely ceremonious, and keep a great number of servants (*g*).

The principal and most favourite public diversions among the Portuguese are, as in Spain, the bull-fights. The festival of St. Anthony of Padua is annually solemnized at Lisbon by such an exhibition, he being both a native and the tutelar saint of this

---

(*b*) Memoires Instructifs, Tom. I. p. 135, 136.
(*c*) Ibid. Tom. I. p. 135. Tom II. p. 164.
(*d*) Ibid. Tom. II. p. 165.
(*e*) Faria y Sousa in Epitome, Part IV. c. ii. p. 342.
(*f*) Relation d' un Voyage de Mr. Froger, p. 154, &c.
(*g*) Schmauss. Part. II. p. 593.

city;

city; and these dangerous spectacles, in which king Peter II. extremely delighted, are given on other occurrences of public rejoicings (*h*).

SECT. XII.

Though the Portuguese and the Spaniards are of one origin, have the same religion, and are alike in manners, yet does a violent enmity prevail between them, and by the former is carried to the utmost extremity (*i*). The many contests and wars between these two nations ever since Portugal became a distinct kingdom, have produced and fomented this rancorous disposition; and the oppressions which the Portuguese suffered under the dominion of the Spaniards, have so increased the hatred of the former, that it seems inextinguishable.

Antipathy of the Portuguese and Spaniards.

SECT XIII.

The Portuguese language is derived from the Latin, which in the time of the Romans was general in the country, and afterwards became intermixed with not a little French and Spanish. If the Portugese themselves

Portuguese language.

(*h*) Relation de la Cour de Portugal sous D. Pedre II. Tom. I. p. 11. The Description of a Lisbon bull-fight occurs in Memoires Instructifs, Tom. II. p. 131.

(*i*) Espion dans les Cours des Princes Chretiens, Tom. I. Lettre LXIX. p. 195. Memoires d'Ablancourt, p. 32.

do not boast much of its sublimity and energy, they account it a very pretty, engaging, and tender language. The best Portuguese is said to be spoken in Entre Minho e Douro, where it had its origin; and the worst in Tras os Montes (*k*). There is, however, no small difference between the Portuguese and the Spanish; the Portuguese translating Spanish, and the Spaniards Portuguese books.

SECT. XIV.

Number of inhabitants. The kingdom of Portugal contains about eighteen hundred thousand, or two millions of souls*. It was formerly much more populous; but since the year 1500, the number of its inhabitants is very much diminished. This a Portuguese writer imputes to three causes: 1. The conquests in Asia, Africa, and America; the voyages to which countries, together with the wars and colonies, carried away great numbers. 2. The

---

(*k*) Faria y Sousa in Epit. Part. c. 342.

* Busching's New Geography, where he produces a computation from a Portuguese geographer, according to which the number of the inhabitants in Portugal about the year 1732, did not exceed one million seven hundred forty-two thousand two hundred and thirty; but as he thinks the clergy, monks, and nuns, are not included in that account, he makes a round number, and settles the whole at two millions. M. de Real Science du Governement, Part. I. Tom. II. p. 115, estimates the number of inhabitants only at between thirteen and fourteen hundred thousand souls.

want

want of manufactures and handicrafts; and 3. The neglect of agriculture (*l*). To these may be further added, 4. The expulsion of the Jews under king Emanuel. 5. The great number of ecclesiastics and religious; and 6. The inquisition. That the nobility likewise are so very much declined, the said author accounts for, from many estates falling to one proprietor, which, of course, lessens the number of marriages; and from young ladies of quality having too large portions; so that it is only few noblemen who are able to marry only one daughter, and scarce any who can portion out two (*m*).

SECT. XV.

The Portuguese nobility were formerly very numerous and considerable; and before the accession of the house of Braganza to the throne, possessed two-thirds of the kingdom (*n*). In former times the principal of the nobility, as in Spain, were stiled Ricos homens; but this appellation is grown quite obsolete, being superseded by the titles of duke, marquiss, count, viscount, and ba-

High and low nobility in Portugal.

(*l*) Manoel Severim de Faria Noticias de Portugal Discurso I. §. 2. p. 6—9.
(*m*) Ibid. p. 9, 10.
(*n*) Faria y Sousa in Epit. Part IV. c. x. p. 367.

rons (*o*). These at present constitute the high, or titular nobility, who are all grandees of Portugal, and place the respectable word Don before their names (*p*). In the want of lawful issue, or heirs, the illegitimate children of the high nobility succeed to the estates and title (*q*). The lower nobility in general are called Fidalgos; though some are distinguished by the title of Cavalleiro and Escudeiro (*r*).

King Emanuel endeared himself very much to the Portuguese nobility in causing the arms of all the families to be searched for in records, chapels, and on monuments; and draughts of them, in the exact rules of blazonry, methodically to be arranged in a book; and to this end he instituted a herald's office (*s*). This appeared the more necessary, as the converted Jews and new Christians at their baptisms assumed the name of their godfathers, which occasioned inextricable confusion in the genealogical registers of the ancient nobility (*t*).

(*o*) Manoel Severim de Faria y Noticias de Portugal, Disc. III. §. 20. p. 126, 127, 128. The same author gives an account of all these several titles and dignities, Disc. III, §. 23, 24, 25, 26.
(*p*) Ibid. Disc. III. §. 1. p. 88, and Schmauffen's State of Portugal, Part. II. p. 68.
(*q*) Memoires Instruct. Tom. I. p. 225, 226.
(*r*) Schmauff. Part II. p. 68.
(*s*) Faria y Sousa in Epit. Part IV. cap. xi. p. 370.
(*t*) Ibid. p. 375.

PORTUGAL.

Thofe noblemen who hold employments at court, ufed to receive from the king a certain falary, which defcended to their fons. This was called Moradia, and was anfwerable to the employment; and, though generally no great matter, was very much fought for by the nobleffe, for the largenefs of the Moradia added a luftre to their nobility (*u*): but of late thefe Moradias have been difcontinued (*x*). It was cuftomary among the Portuguefe nobility, as among thofe of Spain, on any difcontent againft the government to renounce their country, and go over to the enemy.

SECT. XVI.

Form of government.

The prerogative of the kings of Portugal was formerly limited by the ftates of the kingdom. Thefe confift of the clergy, the nobility, and the cities. The clergy are reprefented by the archbifhops and bifhops; the nobility by the dukes, marquiffes, counts, vifcounts and barons; and the cities fend their deputies (Procuradores) to the diets (Cortes), which the king convenes at his pleafure (*z*). The limits of the royal

---

(*u*) Oforius de reb. Eman. Lib. XI. p. 322.
(*x*) Schmauff. P. II. p. 64.
(*y*) Oforius de reb. Eman Lib. XI. p. 323.
(*z*) Faria y Soufa, in Epit. P. IV. cap. xi. p. 346.

prerogative, and the power of the states of the kingdom, having never yet been rightly settled, some kings have assumed more power than others; and on the other hand, the states of the kingdom have, at different times, claimed a different share in the government. In the beginning of the reign of John IV. they had great weight both in foreign and domestic affairs; and every thing of any moment, relative to war, peace, or taxes, went through their hands (*a*). But under John V. who very much humbled the nobility (*b*), their consideration totally declined, and no diet has been held ever since; so that now the king of Portugal's power is unquestionably unlimited, except in determining the succession, and an arbitrary imposition of new taxes (*c*).

SECT. XVII.

Fundamental laws.

The first and capital laws of the kingdom of Portugal occur in the resolutions of the diet held at Lamego (*d*) in 1143. By

(*a*) Vid. Caietani Paffarelli Bellum Lusitanum, Lib. II. p. 58. a. Don Luis de Menezes, Conde De Ericeira na Historia de Portugal Restaurodo, Part. I. Liv. III. p. 129, 130. Memoires d'Ablancourt, p, 349, 352. Relation de la Cour de Portugal sous Don Pedre II Tom. II. p. 510, 511.
(*b*) Memoires Instructifs, Tom. I. p. 83, 84.
(*c*) Voyez La Relation de la Cour de Portugal, sous Don Pedre II. Tom. I. p. 26.
(*d*) The laws of Lamego are to be found in Latin in Anton. Brædao's Monarchia Lusitania, Tom. III. Lib. X. cap.

these

these the states have established the hereditary succession to the throne, in such a manner, that the king is to be succeeded by his sons, according to the right of primogeniture; next by his brother, but not by a brother's son, unless elected; and lastly, by the daughters, yet with this provision that they marry a Portuguese *. This ordinance was confirmed in a diet held at Lisbon, 1641, after the inauguration of John

The succession to the throne.

---

xiv. fol. 142. and a French translation of them in Rousset's Supplem. au Corps Univ. Diplom. de Mr. Du Mont, Tom. I. Part. I. p. 37, 38.

* The act concerning the succession to the throne runs thus:

Si habuerit (Dn. Rex Alfonsus) filios varones, vivant et habeant regnum.—Ibunt de isto modo. Pater si habuerit regnum, cum fuerit mortuus, filius habeat, postea nepos, postea filius nepotis, et postea filii filiorum in secula seculorum per semper.

Si fuerit mortuus primus filius, vivente Rege patre, secundus erit Rex; si secundus, tertius; si tertius, quartus; et deinde omnes per istum modum.

Si mortuus sit Rex sine filiis, si habeat fratrem, sit Rex in vitâ ejus; et cum fuerit mortuus, non erit Rex filius ejus, si non fecerint eum Episcopi & Procuratores et nobiles curiæ Regis. — —

Si Rex Portugalliæ non habuerit masculum, et habuerit filiam, ista erit Regina, postquam Rex fuerit mortuus, de isto modo: non accipiat virum, nisi de Portugal; nobilis, et talis non vocabitur Rex, nisi postquam habuerit de Reginâ filium varonem; et quando fuerit in congregatione, maritus Reginæ ibit in manu manca, et maritus non ponet in capite corona regni.

Sit ista lex in sempiternum, quod prima filia Regis accipiat maritum de Portugalle, ut non veniat regnum ad estraneos; et si casaverit cum Principe estraneo, non sit Regina, quia nunquam volumus nostrum regnum ire for de Portugalenfibus. — —

IV.

IV. and explained by the will of king John I. and on this occasion the Roman Jus Repreſentationis was ſettled in the royal ſucceſſion (*e*). In the decrees of this ſame diet, the ſtates expreſsly aſſumed the right of deciding all diſputes or conteſts concerning the ſucceſſion, and, when neceſſary, to deprive a bad king of his ſovereignty.

SECT. XVIII.

Majority of the kings. The majority of the kings of Portugal is not ſettled by the laws or preſcription. Alphonſo I. forcibly took poſſeſſion of the government when he was eighteen years of age, his mother Tereſa having ſat at the helm during his minority. Alphonſo V. aſſumed the ſceptre at the age of ſixteen, though his tutor, and uncle by his father's ſide, Don Pedro, duke of Coimbra, had laid down the regency two years before (*f*). King Sebaſtian began to reign by himſelf at his entering only on his fourteenth year; whereas Alphonſo VI. remained under the guardianſhip of his mother Louiſa de Guſman, till his nineteenth year; but this was

---

(*e*) See this Act in Gio. Bat. Birago Avogaro, Hiſtoria della Diſunione del Regno di Portogallo dalla Corona di Caſtiglia, Lib. III. p. 284, to 301. And in Du Mont, Corps Univerſ. Dipl. Tom. VI. Part I. p. 202, 203.

(*f*) Hiſt. of Portugal, in the Modern Univerſal Hiſtory, Vol. XXII. Lib. XIX.

partly

partly owing to that princefs's ambition, and the bodily and mental weaknefs of her fon. It is, however, commonly thought, that a king of Portugal's minority ceafes on his entering into the fourteenth year (*g*). The regency and guardianfhip were generally appointed by their kings in their laſt wills, and fettled on their conforts; but it appears from the hiftories of the kings Alphonfo V. and Sebaftian, that thefe appointments were not always obferved.

SECT. XIX.

The king's title, at firſt, was very ſhort; *The king's title.* but, in time, became fomewhat lengthened. Alphonfo I. ftiled himfelf only king of Portugal, in which he was imitated by his three immediate fucceffors; but Alphonfo III. added Algarva, which he had conquered from the Moors (*h*); and Alphonfo V. the words, *citra et ultra mare*, to denote his conquefts in Africa (*i*). The Portuguefe having, in the reign of king John II. eftablifhed their dominion in Guinea, that prince took the title of Lord of Guinea (*k*); and Emanuel, under whom the Eaſt-Indies

(*g*) Thuan. Tom. II. Lib. LXV.
(*h*) Faria y Soufa, in Epit. Part III. cap. vi. p. 206.
(*i*) Ibid. cap. xiii. p. 260.
(*k*) Ibid. Part III. c. xiv. p. 272.

and

and Brazil were difcovered and fubdued, enlarged his title with many pompous additions, and ftiled himfelf king of Portugal and Algarva, on both fides the ocean in Africa, lord of Guinea and the conquefts, and of the navigation and trade to Ethiopia, Arabia, Perfia, and India (*l*). This title has ever fince been ufed without any alteration.

In the Portuguefe language it runs thus:

Dom — por a Graça de Deos, rey de Portugal e dos Algarves, daquem e dalem mar em Africa, fenhor da Guiné e da Conquifta, Navegacao e Commercio da Etiopia, Arabia, Perfia e da India (*m*).

And in LATIN.

— — — Dei gratia rex Portugaliæ et Algarbiorum citra et ultra mare in Africa, dominus Guineæ, Conquifitionis, Navigationis et Commercii Æthiopiæ, Arabiæ, Perfiæ, Indiæque (*n*).

Orders and letters from the king to his fubjects begin with thefe words: Eu el

(*l*) Faria y Soufa in Europa Portuguefa, Tom. II. Part IV. cap. i. Sect. XXX.
(*m*) See Corps Univerfel. Dipl. de Mr. Du Mont, Tom. VI. Part II. p. 370.
(*n*) Ibid. Tom. VIII. Part I. p. 147.

Rey,

Rey, I the king. And in the subscription, El Rey, The King; without the name *.

The Portuguese monarchs having always deserved well of the papal see, and the church of Rome, pope Benedict XIV. conferred on John V. the honourable appellation of Rex Fideliſſimus †; which some are for rendering, Moſt Faithful, and others as signifying, Moſt Believing ‡.

SECT. XX.

The arms of the kingdom of Portugal, are, five escutcheons, Jupiter, placed cross-

---

* This I have seen in several royal warrants and orders.

† The pope's bull of the 23d Dec. 1748, together with the Speech made by his Holineſs on that occasion, are to be found in Mem. de Montgon, Tom. VIII. Pieces Juſtificatifs, Nº. 19.

‡ Pope Pius V. was even in his time for diſtinguiſhing king Sebaſtian with a new title, ſuitable to his zeal for the Catholic religion, and left it to his own choice. Sebaſtian anſwered, none would pleaſe him better than, *obedientiſſimus eccleſiæ filius*; and a late Portugueſe writer ſays, that the pope did actually confer the ſaid title on that prince and his ſucceſſors, (Diogo Barboza Machado na collecçam dos documentos e Memorias de Academia real da Hiſtoria Portugueſa de 1726. Noticias do 22d Outubro, p. 19, e na Bibliotheca Luſitana, Art. Don Sebaſtian) but that none of them ever bore it. It is farther very probable, from a paſſage in the abovementioned ſpeech of the pope, that Benedict XIV. took notice of this circumſtance, and inſtead of the adjective *obedientiſſimus*, ſo derogatory to majeſty, he conferred on king John V. the ſurname of *fideliſſimus*, as ſomething ſofter. If this conjecture be well grounded, *fideliſſimus* is beſt rendered by Moſt Faithful. Gebauer's Hiſt. of Portugal, written in German.

wiſe,

wife, each charged with a like number of befants, Luna, placed in faltier, and painted, Saturn, for Portugal; the fhield bordered, Mars, charged with feven towers, Sol, with gates, Jupiter, for Algarva. The creft is furmounted with a dragon, Sol; the fupporters are likewife two dragons; the dexter holding a banner, Luna, with five efcutcheons, Jupiter; and the finifter a banner, Mars, with feven towers, Sol.

This coat of arms is differently explained by different writers (o), but to the Portuguefe it is full of miracles and myfteries; for as they believe that at the battle of Ourique Chrift appeared to count Alphonfo I. and enjoined him to bear thefe arms; fo they make the fhields to fignify the five Moorifh kings who were conquered, and the five befants, Luna, Chrift's five wounds *; and all thefe together, with the five fhields, indicate the thirty filver-pieces for which Judas betrayed our Saviour. Farther, the crofs-wife pofition of the five fhields and filver-pieces of money, reprefents Chrift's crofs; and the dragon on the creft,

---

(o) Mariana, Lib. X. cap. 17. et Faria y Soufa, in Epit. P. iii. c. ii. p. 182.

* It is in remembrance of thefe wounds that the kings of Portugal are faid to add to their fignature of their letters patent, and other inftruments, five dots, called quinas.

the brazen serpent set up by Moses, as that represented Christ (*p*).

SECT. XXI.

The Portuguese hold their country to be a kingdom founded by God himself; and this they would prove from a record of their first king Alphonso, where it is affirmed upon oath, that Christ, when he appeared to him before the battle of Ourique, directed him to assume the title of king, at the same time promising to the new kingdom his particular protection and favour (*q*). Thus they account themselves God's particularly beloved people, and his chosen portion, as were formerly the Jews (*r*). And they farther believe, that the fifth monarchy, foretold by the prophet Daniel, is that of Portugal (*s*): likewise, that Isaiah, with other inspired persons, have prophesied, that the Gospel should by them be

Supposititious pre-eminences.

(*p*) See Schmaufs. Part. II. p. 265, 278, where every thing remarkable in the Portuguese arms is described at large.

(*q*) This record, discovered in 1596, in the archives at Alcobara, is to be found in Anton. Brandao, Monarchia Lusitana, Tom. III Lib X. p. 127; and in Antonii de Sousa de Macedo Lusitana Liberata, p. 96, 97.

(*r*) Gregorio de Almeida na restauracon de Portugal prodigiosa, P. I. chap. v. p. 28.

(*s*) Daniel ch. ii. v. 44. Ant. de Sousa Macedo Lusit. p. 709.

preached to the Moors and Pagans (*t*). They can even find in the Scriptures the intire succession of the Portuguese kings (*u*). From these old, and a many more new, miracles and prophecies*, they confidently conclude Portugal to be in a particular manner the care of Divine Providence; and as these imaginations lead them to fancy themselves the principal people in the world, so do they affirm that their kings ought to take place of all others †.

SECT. XXII.

Portugal was a fief and tributary to the see of Rome.

Alphonso having, as is pretended, assumed the title of king by Christ's immediate command, took care to have it immediately confirmed by his vicegerent the pope; and the more easily to obtain this favour, he submitted his kingdom to be a fief of the

---

(*t*) Isaiah, ch. lx. 9. lxvi. 19. Revelations xvi. 12. Vid. Almeida, P. I. c. ii. p. 8, 9, &c.

(*u*) Esd. Lib. IV. cap. xi. 12. Vid. Almeida, P. I. c. iii. & Ant. Sousa de Maced. Lusit. p 117.

* The before quoted work of Almeida is quite full of such chimeras, and the author's particular view there is to give an account of the miracles and prodigies, which accompanied the revolution in Portugal, in the year 1640.

† This is peremptorily affirmed by Anton. de Sousa de Macedo in Lusit. Liber. p. 778, 779, were it on no other account than that Christ himself was the immediate founder of the kingdom.

see of Rome, with a promise of paying a yearly tribute *. At first this acknowledgement was duly paid †; but in process of time, the kings of Portugal came to think that they were not obliged to any such acknowledgment ‡.

SECT. XXIII.

Of all the kings of Portugal, only Alphonso I. (*x*) and Edward were crowned (*y*). The latter obtained from pope Eugenius IV.

---

* Alphonso VIII. king of Castile and Leon, accounted Portugal a fief of Leon ; and so far from acknowledging the royalty which Alphonso had assumed, declared war against him for his presumption. Under these circumstances, the pope's friendship was absolutely necessary to him: accordingly, in 1142, he applied to Innocent II. for the title of king, and offered to pay to St. Peter, and the see of Rome, an annual tribute of four ounces of gold; and in the following year Innocent acknowledged him as king, on his engaging to pay a yearly tribute of two marks of gold. Vid. Anton. de Sousa de Macedo in Lusitan. Liber. p. 109, 110. and Faria y Sousa, in Eur. Port. Tom. II. P. I. c. iii. n. 32, 33. Pope Alexander III. confirmed this royalty by an express bull of the 23d of May, 1179, which is to be seen in Faria y Sousa, Epit. Part IV. p. 355.

† King Sancho I. refused paying it, which brought on no small disturbance from the pope; but Alphonso II. in 1213, discharged twenty-eight years of arrears with fifty-six marks of gold paid down at once. Gebauer's Hist. of Portugal, Part I. p. 51.

‡ So says Mariana, Lib. IX. c. xx. but Schmauss. in his State of Portugal, P II. p. 399. is of opinion that this tribute has not yet been discontinued.

(*x*) Anton Brandao na Monarch. Lusit. Tom. III. Lib. X. c. 14.

(*y*) Faria y Sousa, in Europ. Portug. Tom. II. P. III. c. 2.

that he and his succeffors should be anointed and crowned by the archbishop of Braga (z). But instead of making use of this permission *, they are only proclaimed, and solemnly acknowledged by the states, to whom they take the usual coronation oath, which is returned by doing homage to the sovereign †. These ceremonies are still observed (a).

SECT. XXIV.

Title of the king of Portugal's eldest son. The king of Portugal's children formerly were termed Infants, without any distinction; but under king Edward, the eldest son was, by way of pre-eminence, stiled the Prince (b); and lastly, John IV. added the title of prince of Brazil (c); which is still used.

(z) The pope's brief is in Rouffett's Supplem. au Corps Diplom. Tom. I. P. II. p. 378.
* King John V. on his accession to the crown in 1715, was for being crowned, and many preparations were made, yet the solemnity was never carried into execution.
† The ceremonies and rejoicings on the inauguration of cardinal Henry, are to be found in Heronimo Coneftaggio nell' Istoria dell' Unione del Regno di Portugallo alla Corona di Castiglia, Lib. II. fol. 52, 53; and of the occurrences at the accession of John V. a brief account is given in the Ceremonial de Portugal, ch. ii. §. 2. and in the Ceremonial Diplomat. de Mr. Rouffett, Tom. III. p. 377.
(a) New Historical and Genealogical Accounts, P. VIII. p. 687.
(b) Faria y Sousa, in Epit. P. III. cap. xiii.
(c) Don Lewis de Menezes, Conde de Ericeira na Historia de Portugal restaurado, Part. I. Lib. X. p. 235.

SECT.

PORTUGAL.

SECT. XXV.

Origin of the Royal family.

The royal family of Portugal is a branch of that of France, the stem of all the kings of Portugal. Count Henry of Burgundy, was grandson of Robert I. duke of Burgundy, which Robert was grandson * of Hugh Capet. The throne of Portugal has been twice possessed by illegitimate branches; for king John I. was a natural son of king Peter I. and John IV. grandfather to the present king, was descended from Alphonso I. duke of Braganza, an illegitimate son of the said king John I.

SECT. XXVI.

Lisbon, the capital and royal residence.

The capital of the kingdom of Portugal, which the kings since John I. have made their constant residence, is Lisboa or Lisbon †. It lies on the north bank of the Tagus, and is built on seven hills, the valleys between them forming the streets,

---

* This the Portuguese knew nothing of, till T. Godefroy first laid it open to them in his Traité de l'Origine des Roys de Portugal issus, en lige masculine de la maison de France qui regne aujourd'huy; à Paris 1612. 4.

† Luis de Camoens, the Portuguese Poet, terms Lisbon the princess of all other cities.—" Nobre Lisboa que no mundo, facilmente das outras hẹ Princesa." Vid. Of. Lusiadas, Canto III. Oct. 57.

which are a French league in length, but ill paved and very filthy, being never cleaned but on Corpus-Christi day (*d*). On the first of November 1755, it was almost totally destroyed by an earthquake and fire (*e*), and even now is far from having recovered itself.

The principal royal seats to which the court frequently retire, are Belem*, Alcantara, and Mafra †.

SECT. XXVII.

Officers of state. Portugal had formerly many high officers of state, the principal of whom were the constable (Condestable), the marshal (Marishal), the great standard-bearer, (Alferez Mor) (*f*); but in process of time these of-

---

(*d*) Memoires Instruct. Tom. II. p. 141, &c.
(*e*) Mercure Hist. et Polit. Tom. CCXXXIX. p. 611, &c. Tom. CCXL. p. 24, &c.

* This consists of a village, a fort, and a convent; the last was built by king Emanuel with great magnificence, as the burial-place for the royal family. The Portuguese boast highly of this structure, and say, that Philip II. king of Spain preferred it even to the Escurial. Faria y Sousa, in Eur. Port. Tom. II. Part IV. cap. i. n. 37.

† This most stately structure was erected by king John V. in a wild sandy country, near the small town of Mafra, pursuant to a vow made in a dangerous sickness. The building was carried on with such ardour, that 12,000 workmen were employed in it, and it is said to have cost immense sums. See Memoires Instructifs, Tom. I. p. 183.

(*f*) Concerning these, see Noticias de Portugal de Manoel Severin de Faria, Discurso II. §. 2, 3, 4.

fices were abolished, and only the titles of them made hereditary in some eminent families (g). The like has been done with the titles of admiral of Portugal, and admiral of the Indies (h).

SECT. XXVIII.

The principal court-officers are the lord-steward (Mordomo Mor), the lord chamberlain (Camereiro Mor), the lord chief justice of the court (Merinho Mor, or Alguazil Mor) the grand marshal (Appofentador Mor), the master of the horse (Eftribeiro Mor), the cup-bearer (Copeiro Mor), the great-huntsman (Monteiro Mor), the first chaplain (Capalam Mor *), the lord-almoner (Efmoler Mor (i).

Court-officers.

SECT. XXIX.

The Portuguese, like the Spaniards, believe that the Gospel was made known to them by the Apostle James the elder †;

State of religion in Portugal.

(g) Vid. Faria y Soufa, in Epit. Part IV. cap. x. p. 369.
(h) Ibid.
* This office was united by king John V. to the patriarchate of Lifbon. See Faria y Soufa, Epit. de las Hift. Portug. p. 444.
(i) Faria y Soufa, in Epit. This office, John V. annexed to the Patriarch of Lifbon. See the Bruffels edition of the continuation of Faria y Soufa Epitome de las Hiftorias Portiguefas, p. 444.
† Some members, however, of the Royal Academy of History, called this ancient opinion in queftion, and even

and are no less zealous for the Catholic religion, detesting heretics and all whom they do not look upon as true Catholics. This gave rise to the distinction among them of old Christians (Christams Velhos) and new Christians (Christams Novos). By the latter they mean the descendants of converted Jews, who are, however, very much suspected; and by the former those of a pure untainted Christian lineage, which in Portugal is a high recommendation (*k*). They pay great devotion to the saints, and particularly St. Antony of Padua* and St. Xavier (*l*); in other respects they give themselves little concern about the essentials of religion, the whole of it consisting in external observances (*m*), in which, however, decency is too frequently disregarded; nay, sometimes

---

wrote against it; so that the Academy became divided into two parties, till at length the affair was laid before the king, who ordered, that in any writings of the academy concerning St James's preaching in Spain and Portugal, it should be treated as a doubtful matter, which could neither be well assi med or denied. Colleçcam dos Documentos e Memorias da Acad. Real de Historia Portug. de 1726, nas noticias do 2. Mayo.

(*k*) See Schmaufs. Part II. p. 283.

* This is the patron of the city of Lisbon; but in 1756, both the city and the whole kingdom made choice of St. Francis de Borgia as their particular guardian against earthquakes. Merc. Hist. Polit Dec. 1756. p. 811.

(*l*) See Schmaufs. Part II. p, 303, 304, &c.

(*m*) Memoir. Instruct. Tom. II. p. 146.

they

they are attended with the most offensive extravagancies §.

SECT. XXX.

The church of Portugal was formerly under the administration of the three archbishops of Braga, Lisbon, and Evora. The first, not satisfied with the primacy of Portugal, is likewise for having that of all Spain; and formerly there used to be violent contests between him and the archbishop of Toledo, who makes a like claim (*n*). Under the ecclesiastical jurisdiction of the archbishop of Braga are the dioceses of Porto, Viseu, Coimbra, and Miranda *. The suffragans to the archbishop of Lisbon are, Portalegre, Guarda, Cape de Verd, St. Thomas, and Congo †; and under the archbishop of Evora, are the sees of Elvas and Faro ‡. This establishment was made on the occasion of king John V. erecting Lis-

---

§ See what the author of the Memoires Instructifs says of the processions on Corpus-Christi day, and of the amours in Passion-week, Tom. II. p. 164, 168. Tom. I. p. 135, 136.

(*n*) See Schmaufs. Part. II. p. 284, 285.

* Formerly he had for suffragans the bishops of Porto, Viseu, Guarda, Lamego, Miranda, and Leiria.

† Formerly his diocese comprehended Coimbra, Portalegre, Funchal, on the island of Madera, and Angra in that of Tercera.

‡ This see has been removed hither from Silves.

bon into a patriarchate. For Clement XI. having at the folicitation of that prince, erected the court chapel into an archiepifcopal and metropolitan church in 1716, immediately after conferred on the new archbifhop the title and dignity of a patriarch, together with precedence before all archbifhops in Portugal, and in the Portuguefe Eaft and Weft-Indies; with many other advantages, particularly annexing the cardinalfhip to the patriarchate *. But it being fit that the patriarch fhould have an ecclefiaftical jurifdiction, Lifbon was divided between him and the archbifhop of that city. The latter retained the Old City, as it was called, with its caftle and fuburbs; and the former had the weft fuburbs, or New Lifbon, together with an affignment of twenty thoufand dollars per year from the incomes of the archbifhopric of Lifbon; and laftly, he had given him as fuffragans, Leira, Lamego, Funchal in Madera, and Angra in Tercera, which were taken from the other archbi-

---

* King John V. who from his childhood was very fond of fplendor in divine worfhip, fpent incredible fums on the erection of the patriarchate; and the maintenance of it is faid to have coft him more than all his troops. The pomp with which the patriarch of Lifbon celebrates mafs, far exceeds that of the pope himfelf on the moft folemn occafions. Mem. Inftructifs, Tom. II. p. 163, 165. and Tom. I. p. 213.

shoprics (*o*). The archbishop of Goa, who is likewise stiled primate of East-India, had formerly a very extensive diocese; but the Portuguese having lost most of their conquests in those countries, his only suffragan is the bishop of Macao.

The archbishop of St. Salvador in Brazil, has under him the bishops of Olinda, St. Sebastian in Rio de Janeiro, and St. Lewis de Maranham. Cape de Verd, St. Thomas, and Congo, were taken from that diocese, and transferred to the archbishop of Lisbon, on the erection of the patriarchate.

SECT. XXXI.

The archbishops and bishops nominated by the king, and confirmed by the pope.

The king nominates the archbishops and bishops, and the pope confirms them; and till this confirmation, none can take possession of his diocese, or perform his office. Thence it was, that in the year 1640, Portugal having shaken off the Spanish yoke, and the court of Rome, from a fear of Spain, declining to confirm the bishops nominated by the new king John IV. the far greater part of the sees came to be without bishops.

(*o*) See the Continuation of Faria y Sousa, Epit. de las Historias Portug. p. 444.

One

One fourth part of the incomes of the Portuguese bishops goes to the king, which he at pleasure disposes of in pensions; but in foreign countries this does not take place, the king there levying the ecclesiastical tythes, and the bishops have no other income than what the king pleases to bestow (*p*).

SECT. XXXII.

The great power of the pope in Portugal.

There is no catholic kingdom in Europe, where the pope's power is so great as in Portugal: his bulls, by virtue of an agreement between king John II. and pope Innocent VIII. are of force here, without any examination of the king's council (*q*). The pope's nuncio at Lisbon has his peculiar tribunal, to which all the clergy in Portugal are amenable, and from which there is no appeal, except only to the see of Rome. With this spiritual power and jurisdiction are connected a great many temporal advantages. The pope has his apostolical receiver, as he is called, within the kingdom, who levies imposts on clergy and laity. Bulls and collations, which must be applied for at

---

(*p*) See Schmaufs. Part II. p. 295.
(*q*) Faria y Sousa, in Epit. P. III. cap. xiv. Eman. Telles de Reb. Gest. Joannis II. p. 153.

Rome,

Rome, run away with prodigious fums *; and the monies for appeals and difpenfations, together with thofe which the nuncio draws from the country †, is likewife no inconfiderable matter; fo that, according to fome writers, the fee of Rome has a greater income from Portugal than the king himfelf, deducting the neceffary expences of government (r).

This exceffive power of the pope in Portugal is partly owing to the firft king, Alphonfo Henriquez, having made his kingdom tributary to the fee of Rome, and partly to the difputes which his four firft fucceffors had with the clergy concerning the liberties of the church; in which they were fo firmly fupported by the pope, that king Denis, at laft, was obliged to come to a very difadvantageous agreement, renouncing all jurifdiction over the church (s). Since that time the papal power in Portugal has

---

* The archbifhop of Evora pays to Rome no lefs than 90,000 dollars before he can take poffeffion of his dignity. Relation de la Cour de Portugal fous Don Pedre II. Tom. II. ch. i. p. 265.

† The nuncio in Portugal makes money of every thing, felling fo much as the monk's cells. The nuncio Bicchi, who was afterwards cardinal, made a fortune of 35,000 Roman fcudi before he left Portugal. Mem. Inft. Tom. II. p. 138.

(r) Relation de la Cour de Port. fous D. Pedre II. Tom. II. c. i. p. 26, 268.

* See an Hift. Account of the Difputes between the kings of Portugal and the fee of Rome, in Germ. p. 8, 52.

ftood

stood firm and unshaken, and the kings on all occasions shewed themselves very obedient sons of the holy see. They have, however, of late something departed from their implicit submission; and both Peter II (*t*). and John V. (*u*) and especially his present majesty Joseph, have on several occasions resolutely asserted their rights against the papal encroachments.

SECT. XXXIII.

Inquisition. The pope's refusal, after the famous revolution in Portugal in the year 1640, to confirm the bishops nominated by the new king John IV. gave a fair opportunity for casting off the papal yoke; and things looked as if the opportunity would have been embraced: but the inquisition declared against every thing of such a tendency, and thus secured that authority, which was tottering (*x*). The inquisition had been first introduced by John III *. It has three courts

---

(*t*) Relat. de la Cour de Port. Tom. II. c. i. p. 320.
(*u*) Historic. Account of the Disputes, in Germ. p. 134.
(*x*) Relat. de la Court de Port. Tom. II. c. i. p. 272, 303.
* And this, as some reputable authors relate, through the artifice of a cheat, one Juan de Saavedra, who pretended to be an extraordinary envoy from the pope. See Faria y Sousa in Europa Port. Tom. II. Part. IV. cap. ii. n. 34, 38. and Memoires de Portugal du Chevalier d' Oliveira, Tom. I. ch. xi. p. 301, 302.

in

in Portugal, namely, at Lisbon, Evora, and Coimbra. Under the first is the province of Estremadura, part of Beira, together with the Portuguese foreign possessions on this side the Cape of Good Hope. Within the jurisdiction of the second, are the province of Alen-Tejo and Algarva. The third comprehends the provinces of Entre Douro e Minho, Tras os Montes, and the other part of Beira. There is likewise an inquisition at Goa, to which are subject all the possessions of the Portuguese in Asia and Africa, as far as the Cape of Good Hope*; but Brazil has no inquisition.

The constitution of the Portuguese courts of inquisitions is entirely the same as in Spain. The supreme tribunal of inquisition at Lisbon has the superintendency of them; otherwise, they are all mutually independent (y). Their proceedings against prisoners are kept so close, that not the

* For these particulars, see Colleççam dos Documentos e Memorias da Acad. Real da Hist. Port. l. c. p. 379, 380. In these it farther appears, that the first inquisition was set up at Evora, by John III. with the advice of his confessor the bishop of Ceuta; and those at Lisbon, Coimbra, and Goa, by the king's brother cardinal Henry. Of the impostor Juan de Saavedra, not a word is mentioned.

(y) See Schmaufs. Part. II. p. 310, 311. Memoir. Instruct. Tom. II. p. 143.

least intelligence concerning them transpires (z).

The Portuguese inquisition formerly proceeded not only with extreme rigour, but likewise with the most flagrant injustice against the new Christians, or converted Jews (a). Some kings, and even popes, endeavoured to moderate such abuses, but without effect *; till at length John V. and his son the present king Joseph have so far restrained the excessive power of the inquisition, that it ceases to be such an object of terror as formerly †. Great numbers of

---

(z) Vid Noticias reconditas posthumas del procedimiento de las Inquisitiones de Espanna y Portugal, Parte I. p. 1. e Colleçcam dos Documentos e Memorias da Academia Real da Historia Portugueza de 1723, na Noticia General das Santas Inquisiçoenso do Reino de Portugal, p. 383.

(a) Noticias recondit. Parte II. p. 43, 44.

* King John IV. ordered, that the goods of persons imprisoned by the inquisition should not be liable to confiscation; but on his demise, this order was no longer regarded. (Noticias reconditas, Parte II. p. 44, 47.) Peter II. applied to the pope for his assistance to bring the inquisition into order; but that tribunal found means to set the two courts at variance, and thus totally frustrated the design. Ibid. p. 50, 55. Pope Innocent XI. sent to the inquisition a mandate for abating its severity against the new Christians, but they made light of it. Ib. p. 31—37. And as little obsequiousness did they shew to pope Benedict XIII. when he was prescribing certain forms to be observed in their processes. Account of the Disputes between the king of Portugal and the pope.

† John V. ordered, that the sentences of the inquisition should be laid before the courts of judicature for examination, and that the prisoners should be allowed council for their defence; likewise, that no foreigner should be impri-

PORTUGAL.

English, and other Protestants, live in Portugal in an open profession of their religion, without any molestation on that account (*b*); the objects of the inquisition being only Jews, heretics, blasphemers, sodomites, polygamists, and adulterers (*c*).

An Auto de Fé is a high festival among the Portuguese; and on these occasions it is that their superstition and hatred against other religions appear in all their extravagancy (*d*).

SECT. XXXIV.

The multitude of religious orders with which Portugal swarms, contributes, like the inquisition, to the support and strength of the papal authority. Of these orders, the principal and most opulent were the Jesuits *, whom John III. admitted

Religious orders in Portugal.

---

soned without his permission. (Mem. Instruct. Tom. I. p. 141, 146.) King Joseph went a step farther, and gave orders that no capital sentence should be carried into execution, unless signed by himself. New Genealogical Historical Accounts, Part VIII. p. 692.

(*b*) Memoires Instructifs, Tom. I. p. 146.
(*c*) Ibid. p. 139, 141, 145, 147, 148.
(*d*) Ibid. Tom. I. p. 158, 159.

* Faria y Sousa in Epit. Part. III. c. xvi. Part. IV. c. ix. says, that the Jesuits were in his time possessed of above two hundred thousand ducats a year within Portugal and its dependencies, and this sum must have been considerably increased.

the firſt of all Chriſtian princes, with a view of employing them in miſſions to the Indies (*e*). But theſe fathers having in 1752 inſtigated the Paraguay Indians their converts, to an open inſurrection againſt ſettling the limits in that country between the crowns of Spain and Portugal; and in 1758 being deeply engaged in a plot againſt the king (*f*); they were baniſhed for ever out of Portugal, and all the Portugueſe dominions (*g*).

The number of religious houſes in Portugal, though not eaſy to aſcertain, is very great *. The capital of all is the

---

(*e*) Maffeii Hiſt. Ind. Lib. XII. p. 526, 527. Vaſconcell. Anacephalaeos. Actorum Reg. Luſit. p. 287.

(*f*) See Mr. Harrenberg's Hiſtory of the Order of Jeſuits, written in German.

(*g*) Ibid.

* Some compute them at nine hundred; Schmaufs at eight hundred and ſeventy; but herein he is miſtaken, for want of rightly underſtanding Faria y Souſa, on whom he founds his calculation, and who having (in Epit. p. 364, 365.) given a liſt of the convents of the ſeveral orders, adds, that the Jeſuits, who came laſt to work in the vineyard, had, more houſes than all the other orders put together, and larger incomes, amounting to above 200,000 ducats. Laſtly, he ſays, that this account relates only to the kingdom of Portugal, in which he found 450 convents, excluſive of the conquered countries. The laſt words Mr. Schmaufs applying to the Jeſuits, gives them 450 convents in Portugal only; to which he adds thoſe belonging to the other orders, which makes a total of 870. From this remark it will appear, that in Faria y Souſa's time, which was about the year 1626, the number of convents in all Portugal were no more than 450; ſo that to be raiſed to 900, ſpeaks a prodigious increaſe.

Ciſter-

Cistercian monastery at Alcobaza, which was founded and richly endowed by Alphonso I.

Great number and wealth of the clergy.

Difficult as it is to ascertain the number of religious people, a certain writer takes it for granted that the whole body of the clergy in Portugal, with their dependents, may fairly be reckoned one half of the kingdom, and that they are possessed of more than two thirds of the country (*i*). Both these accounts seem to exceed.

SECT. XXXV.

Religious orders of knighthood.

The religious orders of knighthood in Portugal are three: that of Avis, St. James, and of Christ; and all have large revenues.

The first was founded under king Alphonso I. about the year 1147, and derives its name from the city of Avis, granted to it, as the seat of the order, by Alphonso II. At first it was under the Spanish order of Calatrava, but king John I. raised it from this subjection. It is said to consist of seventy-three commanderies, which bring in annually 67350 Ducados de Plata (*k*).

(*i*) Relation de la Cour de Portugal, sous Don Pedre II. Tom. II. ch. i. p. 265.

(*k*) About 18000 l. T. Roderigo Mendez Sylva, en Catalogo Real y Genealogico de Espanna, fol. 52, 53.

The order of St. James some likewise hold to have been brought from Spain into Portugal under Alphonso I. and that, at first, the grand-master of Castile was its chief, till king Dennis, in the year 1290, detached it from Spain, and gave it a grand-master of its own: its commanderies are sixty, with an annual income of 120,000 ducats.

The order of Christ was instituted by king Dennis in the year 1319*, who obtained the ratification of it from pope John XXII. This order is the principal of the three, and the most opulent, having 454 commanderies; the annual income of which amounts to 250,000 Ducados de Plata, tho' some make it 500,000 (*m*).

The capital vow of all these orders of knighthood was to make war against the Moors, for which they have at present no opportunity. The knights of the first and third made likewise a vow of chastity; but at the solicitation of king Emanuel, this was remitted to them by pope Alexander VI. with permission to marry (*n*).

---

* A Spanish comedy quoted by the countess D'Aunoy, Relation du Voyage d'Esp. Tom. III. Letter XI. gives a very entertaining account of the origin of the Order of Christ.

(*m*) Sylva, fol. 59. b. et 60 a. Schmauss, Part. II. p. 355, &c.

(*n*) See his bull of the 20th of June, 1496. in Leibnitii Cod. J. G. Diplom. p. 475.

The grand-masterships of these three orders were annexed to the crown by John III. who, in 1551, obtained a bull for that purpose from Julius III (*o*). But when the kings of Spain came to be masters of Portugal, they gave each order its respective grand-master (*p*): and this of late has sometimes been done even by the kings of Portugal.

The knights of St. John, or Malta, have likewise several commanderies in Portugal; and their chief is the grand prior of Crato, whom the king nominates (*q*). The commanderies both of this and the three other orders are likewise in the king's gift; and not a few of them have been conferred hereditarily on some families, in reward of eminent services (*r*).

SECT. XXXVI.

State of the sciences, and universities in Portugal.

The spiritual yoke under which the Portuguese continue to groan, has affected the sciences, which, by reason of the too strict restraints laid on freedom of thought, can-

(*o*) Colleçcam dos Docum. e Memor. da Acad. Real da Hist. Port. de 1722. no Catalogo dos Mestres e Administratores da Ordem de Avis.
(*p*) Faria y Sousa, in Epit. Part. IV. c. 9.
(*q*) Ibid. Likewise Relation de la Cour De Port. Tom. I. p. 33.
(*r*) Memoires d'Ablancourt, p. 176, 177. and Relation de la Cour de Port. Tom. I. p. 33.

not thrive; though the nation has both an adequate difpofition and capacity (*s*). In Portugal there are two univerfities, Coimbra and Evora. The former was founded by king Dennis on his obtaining a bull for that purpofe from pope Nicholas IV. in 1290 at Lifbon, but afterwards removed to Coimbra; from which place Alphonfo IV. brought it again to Lifbon; and at length John III. tranflated it a fecond time to Coimbra; inviting the moft learned perfons in Europe thither, which brought it into great reputation. It has fix profefforfhips of divinity, fix of canon law, and eight for the civil Roman law; likewife fix for phyfic, one for the mathematics, and one for mufic, befides feveral others for the languages and philofophy, which was formerly much cultivated here. The fecond, at Evora, was erected in 1558, by cardinal Henry, afterwards king; and teaches only divinity and philofophy, grammar, and rhetoric. The Portuguefe fpeak very highly of thefe univerfities, and particularly of the former (*u*);

(*s*) Preface to the Chevalier d'Oliveira's Memoirs of Portugal.
(*t*) Manoel Severim de Faria nas noticias de Portugal, p. 206.
(*u*) Pedro de Mariz Dialogos de Varia Hiftoria, Dial. V. c. ii, Faria I. c. p. 207.

but

but late accounts reprefent them as in a very indifferent condition (*x*).

SECT. XXXVII.

King John V. was a great patron of the sciences; and in imitation of other European countries, erected several academies in his kingdom for their advancement. The principal is the Academy of Portuguefe hiftory at Lifbon *; and king Jofeph inftituted an Academy of Sciences at Tomar, on the model of that at Paris (*y*). There are, befides, feveral other literary focieties in Portugal; the chief object of whofe ftudies are the improvement of the Portuguefe language, grammar, oratory, and poetry. Among thefe are, Academia dos Singulares, dos Generofos, dos Anonymos; farther,

Academies and literary focieties in Portugal.

(*x*) Mem. Inftruct, Tom. I. p. 195.
* It was founded on the 8th of December 1720, under the title of Academia Real da Hiftoria da Portugueza. Of its foundation and conftitution a full account has been written by its fecretary the marquis of Alegrete, in his Hiftoria da Academia Real da Hiftoria Portugueza, Tom. I. The Academy entered on its labours with great zeal and application, and has publifhed the hiftory of its meetings, and the memoirs read at them, together with feveral hiftorical differtations in a large collection, intitled, Colleçcam dos Documentos in Memorias da Academia Real da Hiftoria Portugueza: Lifboa 1721, and the following years, fol. between which time and 1736, fourteen volumes have appeared.
(*y*) New Genealogical and Hiftorical Accounts, Part XL. p. 325.

Academia Portugueza; dos Inftantaneos, dos Applicados, dos Eftudiofos, dos Canoros; and laftly, the Academia dos Problematicos, which is at St. Ubes (z).

SECT. XXXVIII.

Portuguefe poets. Thefe Societies foment the general love and difpofition of the Portuguefe for poetry, which is fo great, that, as Faria y Soufa fays, every ftream in Portugal was a Hippocrene, and every hill a Parnaffus (a). Among their celebrated poets, and thefe form a large body, is king Dennis (b), and his natural fon Alphonfo Sanchez, with many other eminent perfonages (c). But Luis de Camoens bears the palm from them all, and is accounted the Virgil of Portugal *.

SECT. XXXIX.

Philofophy and divinity. The fchool philofophy has been the more able to maintain its fway in Portugal, as

(z) See Letters from a learned Portuguefe on the State of the Sciences in Portugal, in the Hamburgh Weekly Literary Correfpondent, 1763. N° III. and IV.
(a) Epit. de las Hift. Portug. P. IV. c. xv.
(b) Bern. de Brito nos Elogios dos Reis de Portugal, p. 33.
(c) See the lift of the Portuguefe writers in Faria y Soufa, Epit. P. IV. c. xv.
* It was he who compofed the celebrated Epic poem, Os Lufiadas, on the difcovery of the Eaft-Indies, which to this day is cried up by the Portuguefe as an incomparable mafterpiece. See Voltaire's Effay on Epic poetry.

the frequent and severe censures to which new books and writings are subject, render the propagation of any new or strange doctrines almost impossible. A certain writer says, that the errors which Des Cartes and Newton have driven out of other European countries, have fled for shelter into the Portuguese schools; and that their names, and those of other reformers of the philosophic sciences, are execrated in Portugal, as those of heretics and blasphemers (*d*). If in such circumstances it be so very difficult to introduce any innovations in philosophy, no less difficult and much more dangerous must it be to attack, though indirectly, theological tenets which have received the sanction of councils.

SECT. XL.

The Roman law is the capital study of the Portuguese lawyers; and some have acquired such a reputation therein, as to have been called to teach it in Spanish and French universities. A few, however, have addicted themselves to the common

Jurisprudence.

(*d*) Mr. Busching, in his description of Portugal, cites this from a book written by an Italian capuchin, 1746, and entitled, Verdadeiro Methodo de Estudiar.

laws of the land, and practical jurisprudence *.

SECT. XLI.

Physic. No great medical improvements can be expected in Portugal; the late discoveries in philosophy, physic, anatomy, and chemistry, being for the most part unknown in that kingdom.

Upon the whole, the state of sciences in this part of Europe is, in general, far from being on the same happy footing as in other countries, tho' intire books are filled with only the names of Portuguese writers †.

SECT. XLII.

Laws. Portugal was once a part of Spain, and had the same laws; but since it became a distinct kingdom, the kings have occasionally made laws, which Emanuel caused to be digested and made publick in one col-

---

* Concerning this class of writers, see Buderi Biblioth. Jur. Select. c. vi. §. 4.

† Nic. Antonius's Bibliotheca Hispana likewise gives an account of the celebrated Portuguese literati and their works; but a far more stately monument has been erected to them by their countryman Abbot Diogo Barbosa Machado, in his Bibliotheca Lusitana, printed at Lisbon in the Portuguese language, 1747, 1749, 1752.

lection, with the title of, Ordinanzas de Portugal (*e*). The laws of the succeeding kings were, by order of Philip II. collected and published by the celebrated George Azavedo: but besides these, which are called the royal law, the civil law takes place likewise in Portugal *; and in cases where the royal law is either silent, or does not clearly decide, it directs the sentence, but in all may be introduced as a comment (*f*). In affairs relating to the church or clergy, the pontifical law is the rule of conduct.

SECT. XLIII.

Portugal consists of six provinces; each of them, relatively to the administration of justice, is called a Comarca, and divided into several Corregedorias or Correiçoens. Of these, in the Comarca Entre Douro e Minho, there are four; in that of Tras os Montes, likewise four; in that of Beira,

Inferior courts of justice.

(*e*) Arthur Duck de Usu et Authoritate Juris Civilis, Lib. II. c. vii. §. 9. et Buder. in Biblioth. Jur. Select. c. vi. §. 4.
* King John I. had Justinian's Code translated by his secretary John Das Negras. Faria y Sousa, in Europa Port. Tom. II. P. III. cap. i and the lawyers assembled at Coimbra, even decided by the civil law the disputes concerning the succession on the demise of king Henry. See Duck. l. c. §. 13, 16.
(*f*) Duck, ibid. l. c. §. 10, 11.

six;

six; Estremadura, six; Alen-Tejo, five; and in that of Algarvas, two. The Corregedorias are held in the cities (Cidades); and under each of these are the villas and small towns, with certain districts comprehending a number of villages, and termed Confelhos de Juridiçao. Every Corregedoria has its judge, (Corregedor); and in all places there are many other officers of justice, with various titles, according to their employments; as, Ouvidores, Proveedores, Jezfes de Civel, de Crimen, &c. (g).

<small>Upper courts.</small> These are lower courts, from which an appeal lies to the two upper courts; the first and principal of which is held at Lisbon, with the title of Casa de Supplicaçao; the other, which likewise was set up at Lisbon, was by Philip II. removed to Porto, and is called Confelho de Relaçao. Between these two high courts the whole kingdom is divided; yet with appeal from the latter to the former, in causes exceeding a hundred milrees *. The president of the former is called Regedor, and of the

---

(g) Faria y Soufa, in Epit. P. IV. c. xii.

* According to Faria y Soufa; yet, by an edict of king Peter II. 1696, no appeal is allowed of but when the value of the cause exceeds 250 milrees in immoveables, and 300 in moveables.

latter

latter Governador. Both, befides many affeffors, have a great number of other officers, (*b*); fo many that the multitude of judges and law officers may in general be reckoned a great oppreffion of the people †.

SECT. XLIV.

The Portuguefe in the fixteenth century, *Military force.* made feveral important conquefts in Eaft-India, which at the fame time gained them great reputation, and improved their military knowledge and difcipline: but this was of fhort continuance; for the unfortunate expedition of king Sebaftian to Africa, deftroyed the whole military force of the Portuguefe; and the kingdom foon after falling under the Spanifh dominion, has never yet recovered itfelf. On the revolution in 1640, king John IV. was obliged to raife an intire new army; and this would fcarce have been able to have kept him and his fucceffors on the throne, without the French and Englifh auxiliaries under count

---

(*b*) Faria y Soufa, P. IV. cap. xii.
† Faria y Soufa, l. c. p. 377, fays, that till the time of king John, four Corregedores ferved for the whole kingdom; and that afterwards thefe, with other officers of juftice, increafed to a prodigious number. He adds, that if fix people happened to meet together, one, or fometimes two, or even three, were lawyers.

Schomberg; yet the Portuguese arrogantly attribute the several advantages obtained in this war to their own valour and capacity *.

In the long peace which followed this war, the Portuguese discipline sunk into a total relaxation; so that in the war for the Spanish succession, little or nothing was done by them but in conjunction with the English and Dutch auxiliaries. On the peace of Utrecht, John V. reduced his forces to 13000 men; and towards the conclusion of his reign they did not exceed 8000 (*i*). Besides, many strange abuses had crept in †, and such as must necessarily be of bad consequence. King Joseph on his accession to

---

* The Academia dos Generosos, on occasion of the victory over Don John of Austria at Almeixial in 1663, published at Amsterdam, in 1673, a large quarto of Latin, Spanish, and Portuguese, panegyrics on the Count de Villa Flor, the Portuguese general, with this title; *Applausos Academicos e relaçeon da felice successo da celebre victoria de Almeixial*. Whatever self-love and arrogance could suggest on such an occasion, is here displayed in the most inflated fustian; for instance, p. 110.

    Lysiæ—quondam fama vulgata per orbem.
    Innumeris plena exuviis, onerata triumphis,
    Claraque tot bellis, quot non gens ulla—

And, p. 123.
    Lysiæ gens inclyta, Martis
    Grandis honos, decus Augustum, immortale theatrum
    Bellandi, quoties Mars impius acuit iram.

(*i*) See New Genealogical Historical Accounts.

† Among these abuses it must not be omitted, that lieutenancies and ensigncies were given to the very lackeys of the upper nobility, who yet continued in their services as before. See Mem. Instuct. Tom. p. 45, 46. Tom II. p. 130.

his government made it his first care to restore military discipline, and fill up the complement of his army. In the year 1760 it consisted of twenty-two regiments of foot, six of cuirassiers and four of dragoons, making with the artillery about twenty thousand men. In 1762 a Spanish war caused it to be farther augmented; and even after the peace, it was, according to the public accounts, completed to 40,000 men, who were trained to the Prussian discipline.

Portugal has several fortified places on the Spanish frontiers, but which in the latter years of king John V. were in a ruinous condition. Towards Gallicia are Viana, Valenza, Caminha; towards Leon, Miranda de Douro, Guarda, Castello Branco; and on the borders of Estremadura stand Estremos, Evora, Elvas. *Fortified places.*

SECT. XLV.

The Portuguese were the first Europeans who made discoveries in the Atlantic Ocean; and their possessing themselves of Brazil, together with the extensive conquests in the East-Indies, naturally produced a naval force, which in the sixteenth century became *Marine.*

came confiderably augmented. But falling under the Spanifh dominion, and being thereby intangled in the wars of that crown, and particularly in that againft the United-Netherlands, they loft the beft part of their Eaft-India poffeffions, and likewife of their trade to that continent, to the great weakening of their naval force. Farther, the Spaniards during their fixty years dominion deprived Portugal of almoft all its men of war, and all its cannon *. Thus, till the time of the revolt by which John IV. was raifed to the throne, the Portuguefe marine lay totally neglected, and has never fince rifen to any confideration †. In the laft years of John V. it was in fuch decline, as not to be able to protect the coaft of Portugal againft the depredations of pirates (*k*). This difgrace rouzed king Jofeph immediately to take in hand the augmentation of the navy, and to put the management of it

* Anton. de Soufa de Macedo in Lufitania Liberata, cap. vii. p. 536, fays, that the Spaniards carried away out of Portugal above three hundred large fhips, and two thoufand pieces of cannon.

† See Relation de la Cour de Portugal fous Don Pedre II. p. 59, 60, where we find that at that time, the whole kingdom did not afford above 300 feamen, and that the king's fhips were manned with foldiers.

(*k*) See New Genealogical Hiftorical Accounts, Part I. p. 32. Part. VII. p. 656.

PORTUGAL.

on a better footing (*l*). In the year 1760, the Portuguese navy consisted of fifteen ships, third, fourth, and fifth rates, carrying seven hundred and sixty-four guns, two thousand four hundred and sixteen marines, and three hundred gunners. The usual station of the men of war is Lisbon harbour, the entrance of which is strongly guarded by several forts (*m*).

SECT. XLVI.

The Portuguese reckon by reis *, and millereis, or a thousand reis; though these are only imaginary pieces; and sometimes by crusadoes, which in exchange go for 400 reis.

Coins.

The Real Coins are,

1. GOLD.

		Reis.
Dobras	Value	24,000
Half ditto		12,000
Moedas de Ouro †		4800
Half ditto		2400

(*l*) See New Genealogical Historical Accounts, Part I. p. 691.
(*m*) See Memoires Instruct. Tom. I. p. 44.
* Or properly Reals, the plural of Real.
† Commonly called Moidores, or Lisbonines.

			Reis.
Quarter ditto	—	—	1200
Tenth ditto †	—	—	480

Since the year 1722 have been coined on a lower ſtandard,

				Reis.
Dobras	—	—	Value	12800
Half ditto	—		—	6400
Quarter ditto	—		—	3200
Eighths, likewiſe called Eſcudos				1600
Half Eſcudos	—		—	800
Quartos	—	—	—	400

2. SILVER.

				Reis.
Patacas	—	—	Value	600
Cruſados Novos		—	—	480
Half Ditto	—	—	—	240
Quarter ditto	—		—	120
Teſtoes *	—		—	100
Half ditto	—	—	—	50
Vintes	—	—	—	20

3. COPPER.

Pieces of ten, five, three, one, and ½ reis.

† Theſe are alſo called Cruſados Novos. The firſt cruſados were coined by king Alphonſo V. on his deſign of going a croiſade to Paleſtine; they were of the fineſt gold, and two grains heavier than the ducats of thoſe times. Noticias de Portug. p. 182.

* Theſe are ſo called from the Teſtons, a French coin, and the appellation of which came from the heads in the impreſ-

Mil-

Millereis are in Hamburg bank-money, three marks seven schillings three pfennings: in Saxon money, one dollar seventeen grosses eight pfennings.

The royal mint is at Lisbon, and to it is delivered all the gold coming from Brazil, but under very bad management (*n*).

SECT. XLVII.

The revenues of the crown were at first very small (*o*), till the East-India trade and foreign conquests raised them to a considerable amount; but the greater part of this trade, and of the conquered countries, being lost under the Spanish government, besides the alienation of many of the demesnes, the revenue became very much diminished *. In order to set it on a tolerable footing after the revolution in the year 1640, some additional taxes became necessary, by which, however, every thing was so exhausted, as scarce to leave room for farther imposts on any future exigency †. The

sion of them. Faria nas Noticias de Portug. Disc. IV. §. 31. p. 186.

(*n*) Memoir. Instruct. Tom. II. p, 158, 159.
(*o*) See Faria y Sousa, in Epit. P. IV. c. iv. p. 354.
* Faria y Sousa, in Epit. Part IV. c. iv. p. 354, reckons the revenue of Portugal, under the Spanish government, at above 4,000,000 of ducats.
† King Peter II. in the year 1697, having demanded of the states of the kingdom a tax for the augmentation of the army, they declared to him, and not till after half a year's

amount of the present revenues is computed at nineteen millions of crusados. The sources from which they chiefly arise are these:

1. The hereditary estates of the house of Braganza, which formerly made one third of the whole kingdom.

2. The royal demesnes.

3. Duties, which are very high, being above twenty per cent. on all goods imported.

4. Land-tax.

5. The excise on wine, flesh, and fish, which is considerable, and brings in the more, as the clergy themselves are likewise obliged to pay it.

6. The monopoly of Brazil tobacco.

7. The coinage.

8. The Croisade-bull, by which a very lucrative trade in indulgences is carried on, to the advantage of the crown *.

deliberation, that they could not contrive any other imposts, the people being already so loaded, that nothing more could be laid on them. Relat. de la Cour de Portug. Tom. I. c. i.

* This indulgence-traffic was first introduced by king Philip I. who procured the croisade-bull, which he had obtained from pope Gregory XIV. in the year 1591 for maintaining the Portuguese forts and garrisons on the coasts of Africa, to be renewed every three years; and his successors have not been wanting to do the like. This croisade-bull properly contains three distinct bulls, namely, 1. The bull for the living; by which the purchaser procures the full pardon of sins, with many other spiritual privileges or immunities. Vid.

9. The

9. The grand masterships of the orders of knighthood, which since king John III. have been annexed to the crown.

10. The ecclesiastical tithes in the dependencies of Portugal.

11. The fifth of the Brazil gold, and the farm money paid by the Diamond Company there (*q*).

12. The goods of persons condemned by the inquisition *.

13. The tenth penny paid for all goods and things sold, grain excepted, called Almorifazgo. From this the clergy, the nobility, and the knights of orders are exempt (*r*).

Explication de la Bula de la Santa Crusada por Fra. Manuel Rodriguez, fol. 7. 1601. 2. The bull for the dead, by which the buyer can deliver one or more souls out of purgatory. Rodriguez, fol. 160, 164 ; and 3. The bull of composition, which quieted the conscience of those who had defrauded or robbed others ; at the same time retaining the ill-gotten goods. Rodriguez, fol. 164, 190. The bull is notified from the pulpit, and recommended to the people by the priests. A commissary-general, appointed for that purpose, causes printed copies of the three bulls to be sold by his agents, who are spread all over the kingdom ; and the pope comes in likewise for a share of the produce. See Relation de la Cour de Portugal, Tom. I. ch. ii. p. 54, 57. The bull itself is to be found in Tom. II. p. 521.

(*q*) See above, §. 7.

* Very little of these confiscations coming into the king's treasury, king John IV. put a stop to them by an express ordinance ; but the inquisition opposed it ; and on the king's demise it was no longer observed. Vid. Noticias Reconditas del Procedimiento de las Inquisiciones, p. 44, 45, &c.

(*r*) See Schmauss, Part II. p. 462.

King John V. though in his reign the revenue received a great addition by the Brazil gold and diamonds, left debts to a very confiderable amount.

SECT. XLVIII.

Agriculture.

The Portuguefe are no lefs negligent of agriculture than the Spaniards, as too mean, and not profitable enough for their avidity; on which account they generally betake themfelves to trade or the fea, as offering greater profits; and thus flock to their foreign fettlements to make their fortunes. This paffion for trade is fo univerfal, that all the ordinances made by the government for the increafe of agriculture, have remained without effect, and a great part of the country lies quite uncultivated (*s*).

SECT. XLIX.

Manufactures.

Though the Portuguefe have great quantities of fine wool, filk, and feveral metals, and get many commodities from their dependencies, which might be turned to great advantage in manufactures and fabrics, yet, inftead of working them up, they export

(*r*) See Schmaufs, Part II. p. 462.

every thing raw; for linen and sweetmeats excepted, scarce any thing used to be made in Portugal (*t*). The manufactures lately erected *, and even the fabric of looking-glass, though begun in the king's name, soon dropped for want of support †.

SECT. L.

This deficiency of manufactures hinders the domestic trade of the kingdom from rising to any degree of importance.

<small>Domestic</small>

SECT. LI.

Its foreign trade indeed is very large, comprehending all the four parts of the world. The Portuguese, however, like the Spaniards, instead of being their own carriers to foreign countries, leave other nations to bring their goods to them. These are chiefly grain, cloths, and other woollen and silk manufactures, gold and silver tissues,

<small>and foreign trade</small>

<small>in Europe.</small>

(*t*) See Schmaufs, Part II. p. 425, 426.

* It is said in Memoir. Instruct. Tom. I. p. 207, 208, that the town of Cavilham had above a thousand looms for making woollen stuffs and stockings; but that for reasons of state, they were suffered to go to decay.

† In the said Memoir. Instruct. Tom. II. p. 160, it is said, that the English would not be quiet till they had totally overthrown this fabric, and that they watched all opportunities to defeat every foundation which might hurt their trade.

linens,

linens, laces, and manufactures of every kind, down to trinkets, toys, and things of the lowest value. In return they receive from the Portuguese, salt, wine, oil, and variety of fruits; East and West-India goods, as pearls, diamonds, Brazil-wood, and tobacco, indigo, sugar, spices and drugs (*u*). But all come very short of the foreign manufactures brought into Portugal; so that the balance must be made up with large sums of money, of which the greater part goes to the English *.

The principal trading cities and sea-ports are, Lisbon, Porto, and St. Ubes.

SECT. LII.

Trade to the distant parts of the world.

The Portuguese formerly were in possession of the whole trade to Africa and the East-Indies, which they extended along the west and east coast of Africa, to Arabia and Persia; and from thence along the whole southern coast of Asia to China; and through all the islands of the Indian sea as far as Japan. But this immense trade was in a

(*u*) Memoires et Considerations sur le Commerce et les Finances d'Espagne, Tom. II. ch. xi. p. 261, 262.

* Mr. de Real says in the place above quoted, that no less than twenty-five millions (by which he probably means French livres) go every year out of Portugal to England.

great

great meafure loft whilft Portugal was under the Spanifh dominion; and now is reduced within fuch a narrow compafs, that the Portuguefe trade only to the coaft of Guinea for flaves, gold and ivory, and to what few places remain to them in the Eaft-Indies, but chiefly to Goa and Macao: hence the principal article is the trade to Brazil, which not only fupplies them with many valuable commodities, but likewife takes off great quantities of European merchandize (x).

SECT. LIII.

Feliciano Velho Oldenburg, who held the tobacco farm a long time, obtained in the year 1753, a patent from king Jofeph for an exclufive trade to Macao and Goa, empowering him fucceffively to fend five fhips to the firft place, and to the fecond eleven, within ten years, paying the king a certain fum for each fhip. But fuch an undertaking requiring a great deal of money, Oldenburg divided an adequate capital into fhares, and admitted other merchants into partnerfhip with him; referv-

Trading companies.

(x) M. de Real Science du Gouv. P. I. Tom. XI. p. 119.

ing

ing to himself the conduct and administration of the whole trade in his own name (*y*).

In like manner the king, in 1755, granted to a company of merchants the exclusive trade to Maranham and Great Para for twenty years, with the privilege of being immediately subject to him and no other court, with two men of war to convoy their fleet. The body of Lisbon merchants strongly remonstrated against this company, but without effect (*z*).

SECT. LIV.

Administration of government.

The administration of state affairs is conducted by several councils or boards, of which the following are the principal,

1. Confelho de Eftado, the council of state, instituted by king Sebastian, in imitation of that of Spain. This assembly takes cognizance of all important affairs, domestic and foreign. The king himself is the president, and nominates as many counsellors as he pleases. One of the most considerable persons in the council of state is, the Escrivam da Puridade, or privy secretary of state, yet he has no vote in it. All

---

(*y*) New Genealogical Historical Accounts, Part LIII. p. 471.
(*z*) Ibid. Part LXXIV. p. 135.

peti-

petitions and informations to the king pafs through his hands; and through them likewife return the royal anfwers and determinations. On account of the multiplicity of bufinefs, he has feveral under-fecretaries and clerks.

2. Confelho de Guerra, council of war, which fuperintends the army and marine, and the promotion of the military officers. The board of war owes its inftitution to king John IV.

3. Defembargo do Paco*, the palace council. This is the fupreme tribunal, to which are fubordinate all the other courts of juftice, and perfons belonging to the law; and in which all royal edicts, patents, and grants, are made out. The prefident is always a perfon of great diftinction, befides whom it has five counfellors, called Defembargadores, feven clerks, and feveral other inferior officers.

4. Mefa da Confcientia e Ordens, the court of confcience of the orders †; which was founded by king John III. after the

---

* It is fo called, being always held in the royal refidences, and continually accompanies the king.

† Is fo called, from its being authorized by a royal warrant to reprefent to the king, when any thing is propofed contrary to his confcience. Faria y Soufa, in Europa, Port. Tom. II. Part. IV. ch. ii. n. 86.

grand-

grand-masterships of the three orders were annexed to the crown. It has a superintendency and jurisdiction over the orders of knighthood, universities, hospitals, chapels, and many other spiritualities. It consists of a president, five counsellors, (Deputados) who are all divines and canonists, three judges (Ouvidores), who must be of one of the three orders of knighthood, and three clerks.

5. Conselho da Facenda, the board of treasury, takes cognizance of the royal revenue, and appoints officers for the due management of it. It consists of three departments, each with a counsellor of state as superintendant (Veedor), besides three literary counsellors, (Desembargadores Letrados) together with four clerks (*a*).

SECT. LV.

In the dependencies. The Portuguese dependencies are under viceroys and governors; as the East-Indies under the viceroy of Goa, and Brazil under an officer of the like title at St. Salvador. The other provinces, islands, and forts, have

---

(*a*) Concerning all these councils and boards, see Faria y Sousa in Epit Part. IV. c. xii. p. 376, 377, and Schmaufs, Part XI. p. 202, 203, &c.

PORTUGAL. 333

governors, some of whom receive orders from the said viceroys, and others immediately from the king.

East-India has a court of justice at Goa; and for Brazil there is one at St. Salvador, and a second lately erected at St. Sebastian *.

SECT. LVI.

The internal constitution of the kingdom of Portugal stands in need of many amendments, for the country is very far from being sufficiently cultivated, and there is a total want of manufactures. These defects must be absolutely removed, that the specie which goes to foreigners for necessary goods may remain in the kingdom, the state recover itself from its languor, and set its land and sea force on a footing suitable to the safety of the nation and the dignity of the crown. The next thing is to keep their East and West-India possessions in a good state of defence, as hereon depends the principal branch of the national commerce; and that of the East-Indies being extremely reduced, its restoration should by all means be taken

Domestic state-interest.

---

* This court was erected by king Joseph in 1754, for the inhabitants of Rio de Janeiro, and Minas Geraes. New Genealogical Historical Accounts, Part LIII. p. 475, 476.

in

in hand *, as hereby the Portuguese marine may again become respectable; which is absolutely necessary, for the defence of those remote countries †.

<small>Foreign</small>

Portugal bears so little proportion to most other powers, that it must not think of entering into a war with them, as it can gain but little, and be a considerable loser. This is particularly applicable to Spain, which by its situation and superiority is a very dangerous neighbour to the crown of Portugal. Formerly Portugal could rely on the assistance of France against Spain; but since the latter has been under a king of French extraction, Portugal has the united forces of both to fear, of which the last war has already been one instance.

From this alteration of circumstances, it behoves Portugal to keep itself closely united with Great Britain, being the power which can most readily and effectually assist it, as appeared in the year 1735 and 1762;

---

* The properest time for this would be, according to a remark in Campbell's Present State of Europe, ch. xii. p. 364, when the other European powers who have settlements in the East-Indies, shall be at war with one another. Such an opportunity was the war for the Austrian succession; but the Portuguese court neglected to make use of it.

† M. de Real, Science du Gouvernem. Part. I. Tom. II. p. 119, prophesies from several reasons, that the Portuguese will lose their East-India possessions, and that within no long time.

PORTUGAL.

and such an alliance is the more natural and the more easily maintained, the Portugal trade being of vast advantage to England. While the English can enjoy it undisturbed, their assistance will never be wanting; so that both crowns are in some measure dependent on each other for their mutual emolument; and whilst this situation lasts, the alliance between them will be durable (c).

The very same causes which unite Portugal to Great Britain, require likewise a good understanding with the United-Provinces, as in case of necessity, they likewise can be serviceable to Portugal, and have the same motives for it as Great Britain.

The power of the see of Rome in Portugal is by much too great, and such a pernicious and disgraceful invasion of the sovereign's rights, that to free itself from subjection, would be no less for its advantage than its reputation. Indeed the present administration does not seem to receive the papal mandates with the former implicit obedience.

All the transactions between Portugal and the northern powers, as Denmark and

---

(c) Campbell's Present State of Europe, ch. xii. p. 363.

Sweden, relate only to trade; and the distance between the Portuguese court and Germany, Poland, Prussia, and Russia, does not admit of much correspondence.

SECT. LVII.

Conventions with other powers. The rights and obligations of the crown of Portugal, in respect of other powers, rest chiefly on the following conventions.

I. With SPAIN (*d*).

II. With FRANCE.

1. Alliance of the first of June 1641 (*e*); and of 1701 (*f*); 2. The treaty of peace at Utrecht, the 11th of April 1713 (*g*); and 3. Of Paris, on the 10th of February 1763 (*h*).

III. With GREAT BRITAIN.

1. Treaty of amity and commerce of the 29th of January 1642; and of the 10th of

---

(*d*) These may be seen in the second chapter, §. 67.
(*e*) Du Mont Corps Diplomat. Tom. VI. P. I. p. 214, and Mably, Droit Public de l'Europe, Tom. II. ch. xii. p. 340.
(*f*) Rousset, Supplem. au Corps Diplomat. Tom. II. P. II. p. 1.
(*g*) Du Mont, Tom. VIII. P. I. p. 353, and Mably, Tom. II. p. 136, 340.
(*h*) New Secretary of State for Europe, Part IX. p. 118.

PORTUGAL.

July 1654 (*i*); 2. Alliance of the 16th of May 1703 (*k*).

IV. With the UNITED NETHERLANDS.

1. Armistice and alliance of the 12th of June 1641 (*l*). 2. Treaty of amity and commerce of the 6th of August 1661 (*m*), and of the 30th of July 1669 (*n*).

SECT. LVIII.

Portugal has produced several eminent statesmen and warriors. The most celebrated were the constable Nuño Alvarez Pereira, and the secretary John das Regras, who lived in the time of John I. and were the two chief instruments of raising that prince to the throne. Under Emanuel lived Vasco de Gama, who discovered the East-Indies, and Alphonso de Albuquerque, who conquered a great part of that country; under Alphonso VI. Sancho Manoel, count de Villaflor, Lewis de Vasconcellos e Sousa, count of Castel-Melhor, Anthony de Sousa de Macedo, one of the most learned men that ever appeared in Portugal; under Pe-

Warriors and statesmen.

(*i*) Du Mont, Tom. VI. P. I. p. 238. and P. II. p. 82. Mably, Tom. II. ch. xii. p. 333.
(*k*) Id. Tom. VIII. P. I. p. 127.
(*l*) Id. Tom. VI. P. I. p. 215.
(*m*) Id. Tom. VI. P. II. p. 366. Mably, Tom. I. ch. xii. p. 136, 137. et Tom. II. ch. xii. p. 335. suiv.
(*n*) Ib. Tom. VII. P. I. p. 114.

ter II. Lewis de Menezes count of Ericeyra, Manoel Telles da Silva marquis de Alegrete, both excellent historians.

SECT. LIX.

The principal Portugueze historians are Bernard de Brito (*o*), Antony and Francis Brando, Antony Vasconcellos (*p*), and Manuel de Faria y Sousa (*q*). The chief of the foreign writers are John Baptist Birago (*r*), Lequien de la Neuville (*s*), de la

---

(*o*) Monarchia Lusitana, Tom. I. Alcobæa, 1597, Tom. II. Lisboa, 1609, fol. This work was begun by Brito, and continued in a much better manner by Antonio and Francisco Brandaon, to six volumes. The seventh was published at Lisbon by Raphael de Jesus, in 1683; and the eighth by by Manuel dos Santos, who, as the seventh volume met with a very bad reception, has given it quite a new form; but together with the ninth and tenth, it is not yet come to the press.

(*p*) Anacephalæsis, i. e. summa capita actorum regum Lusitaniæ, Antwerpiæ, 1621, 4to.

(*q*) Epitome de las Historias Portuguesas, en Brusselas, 1677, fol. The author published this work at first in Portuguese rhimes, which is the reason of his being so florid and poetical. A new edition of it was printed at Brussels in 1730, with the following title, Historia del Regno de Portugal; and the history is continued down to 1729. Besides the Epitome, Faria y Sousa has published the History and memorable Actions of the Portuguese in the four parts of the Globe, a voluminous work. The first part is entitled, Europa Portuguesa, Tom. I. Lisboa, 1678. The second Asia Portuguesa, Tom. I. Lisboa, 1666. Tom. II. 1674. Tom. III. 1675. fol. And the third, Africa Portuguesa, Tom. unico, Lisb. 1681. fol. America Portuguesa was never published, and is said to have been lost. Biblioth. Lusit. Art. Manoel de Faria e Sousa.

(*r*) Historia del Regno di Portogallo. Lion, 1644. 4to.

(*s*) Histoire Generale de Portugal, à Paris, 1700. II. Tomes, 4to.

Elede,

PORTUGAL.

Elede (*t*), and Gebauer's (*u*) General History of Portugal; Antony de Herrera (*x*), Jeremy Coneſtaggio (*y*), John Baptiſt Birago II. Fernando Correa de la Cerda (*a*), the count of Ericeyra (*b*), Cajetanus Paſſarellus (*c*), and the abbe Vertot (*d*), who wrote the Revolutions of Portugal.

SECT. LX.

Accounts of the ſtate of Portugal have been publiſhed by Manuel de Faria e Souſa (*e*), Antony Carvalho da Coſta (*f*), John

Authors who have written on the ſtate of Portugal.

(*t*) Hiſt. Gen. de Portugal, à Paris, 1734. 8 Tom. 12mo.
(*u*) A German work, printed at Leipſick, 1756. 4to.
(*x*) Cinco libros de la Hiſtoria de Portugal y Conquiſta de las Iſlas Açores, en los años de 1582, y 1583. Madrid. 1591. 4to.
(*y*) Iſtoria della difunione del regno de Portogallo dalla corona di Caſtiglia. Amſterdam, 1647, 8vo.
(*a*) Cataſtrophe de Portugal na depoſiciao del Rei D. Alphonſo Sexto, e ſubrogacao do prencipe D. Pedro, eſcrita por Leandro Dorea Caceres e Faria, Liſb. 1669. 4to. The author concealed himſelf under this fictitious name; he was preceptor to king Peter II. and afterwards biſhop of Porto. (See Biblioth. Luſit. Art. Fernando Correa de la Cerda.) This work was tranſlated into French under the following title, Relation des Troubles arrivez dans la Cour de Portugal, en 1667 et 1668. Amſterdam, 1674. 12mo.
(*b*) Hiſtoire de Portugal reſtaurado, Liſboa, 1680, 1698. 2 Tomes, fol. et ibid. 1751. 4 Tomes, 4to.
(*c*) Bellum Luſitanum ejuſque regni ſeparatio a regno Caſtellenſi, cum abrogatione ſuper adjecta Alfonſi regis Luſitani. Lugdun. 1684, fol.
(*a*) Hiſtoire des Revolutions de Portugal, à Amſterdam, 1712, 8vo.
(*e*) In his Epitome de las Hiſtorias Portugueſas, Part IV. and in his Europa Portugueſa, Part III. is contained a deſcription of the kingdom of Portugal.
(*f*) Corographia Portugueza e Deſcripção Topographica do famoſo regno de Portugal, com as noticias das fundaçoens

Jacob

Jacob Schmaufen (*g*), and other (*h*) writers.

das cidades, villas, e lugares, que contem varoens illuſtres, genealogias das familias nobres, fundaçoens de conventos, catalogos dos biſpos, antiquitades, maravilhas da natureza, edificios, e outras curioſas obſervaçoens, Liſboa, 1706, 1708, 1712. 3 Tomes, fol.

(*g*) The Modern State of the Kingdom of Portugal, and the Territories thereto belonging, Halle, 1759, two parts, 8vo. a German work.

(*h*) Among theſe we muſt reckon,

Annales d'Eſpagne et de Portugal, par Don Juan Alvarez de Colmenar, Amſterd. 1741, 4 Tomes, 4to.

Noticias de Portugal, por Manoel Severin de Faria. Declaram-ſe as grandes commodidades que tempara creſcer em gente, induſtria, comercio, riquezas e forças militares por mar e terra. Liſboa, 1655, fol.

Relation de la Cour de Portugal ſous D. Pedre II. avec des Remarques ſur les Interêts de cette Couronne, et l'Hiſtoire des plus conſiderables traitez qu'elle ait faits avec eux. Traduit de l'Anglois, Amſterd. 1702, 2 tomes, 12mo.

The Ancient and Preſent State of Portugal, by John Stevens, London, 1705, 8vo.

Henrici de Cocceii Diſſertatio de Juſticia Belli et Pacis in Statu Regni Portugallici fundata; in ejus Exercitation. curioſ. Vol. I. p. 882.

Memoires Inſtructifs pour un Voyageur, Amſterd. 1738. 2 Tomes, 8vo.

Memoires de Portugal, dreſſez par le Chevalier d'Oliveyra, Amſterd. 1741, 2 Tomes, 8vo.

End of the First Volume.

A

TABLE

OF THE

MOST INTERESTING PARTICULARS

Contained in thefe THREE VOLUMES.

A.

ACADEMIES and focieties of fciences, account of, i. 229.
—— and literary focieties in Portugal, account of, i. 311, 312.
—— of fciences and polite literature eftablifhed in France, i. 91, 92.
—— of fciences at Haerlem, ii. 402, 403.
—— founded at Peterfburg in 1732, for training up 240 Ruffian, and 220 German young gentlemen for the army, iii. 420.
—— three, of polite literature and fcience in Spain, i. 216, 217.
Accounts of the ftates of Poland, iii. 321, 322.
Adminiftration of government, and ftate-affairs in Spain, the feveral councils concerned in it, i. 243—247.
—— of government in Portugal, how conducted, i. 330, 331, 332.
—— of the Church of Portugal, formerly under the archbifhops of Braga, Lifbon, and Evora, i. 297.
—— of government, and ftate-affairs of France, ii. 148—151.
—— of ftate-affairs in England, ii. 319—321. Adminiftration of government in the Englifh counties, 321. Adminiftration of government in Scotland, 321, 322. Adminiftration of government in Ireland, 322. Adminiftration in the other dependencies, 323.
Admiral of Portugal and admiral of the Indies, the offices of, fuppreffed, but the titles hereditary in fome families of eminence, i. 295.
Advantages of the fucceffion in the male line, as eftablifhed in France, ii. 47.
—— and defects of the Britifh form of government, ii. 228, 229.

Vol. I.   a   Advantages,

TABLE.

Advantages, whether it can last, ii. 233, 234.
Affection of the French for their monarch censured on account of its excess, ii. 27.
Agriculture totally neglected in Spain, i. 236, 237.
────── state of, in France, ii. 189, 190.
────── state of in Denmark, iii. 78, 79.
────── state of, in Poland, iii. 314, 315.
────── so much neglected by the Portuguese, that they purchase grain from foreigners, i. 263.
Air and temperature of countries, how varied. i. 9.
────── in the northern province, and hills of Spain, exceeding cold, i. 156.
────── and temperature of Portugal more agreeable and moderate than that of Spain, i. 260.
Alguazil Mor, or Merinho Mor, lord chief justice of the court, one of the chief court-officers of Portugal, i. 295.
Alcaldes of Spain, account of, 223, 224.
Alps, the highest mountains in Europe, separated into three chains, i. 721.
Alsace and Suntgau, ceded to Lewis XIV. at the peace of Munster, together with the three dioceses of Metz, Toul, and Verdun, ii. 21.
America, to the extent of above a thousand geographical miles from north to south, possessed by the Spaniards, i. 162.
American trade, confined to those European nations who have colonies in that country, i. 145.
Amsterdam, bank of, ii. 442, 443.
Antient and modern poets of Spain, account of, i. 217, 218.
────── constitution of Sweden, iii. 235—238.
Antipathy between the Spaniards and French exceeding violent, i. 176. ascribed by Garsia, a Spanish author, to the immediate operation of the devil, ibid.
Appenage, the revenue of the younger princes of the blood in France, so called, ii. 59.
Apposentador Mor, or grand marshal, one of the principal court-officers of Portugal, i. 295.
Arabs first introduced Physic into Spain. Blended astrology with it. From Spain it was further propagated over Europe. Its present improvement owing to the many discoveries in natural philosophy, botany, chemistry, and anatomy, i. 227.
Archbishops, and bishops of Spain, account of, i. 206, 207, 208. nominated by the king, 208, 209.
────── of Gnesna appointed to superintend the administration of Poland upon the king's decease, as being primate of the kingdom, i. 108.

Arch-

TABLE.

Archbishops of Spain, eight in number, i. 206.
────── of Goa, stiled primate of the East Indies, his only suffragan at present the bishop of Macao, i. 299.
────── of Rheims invested with the privilege of inaugurating the French king, ii. 56.
Architecture, sculpture and painting, state of, in Holland, ii. 405.
Arianism, the first heresy that arose in the church, in opposition to true believers, i. 117.
Arms and titles of states, account of, i. 36.
────── of Russia, account of, iii. 374, 375, 376.
────── of the king of Spain, account of, i. 194, 195.
Armies of Lewis XIV. far exceeded those before his time, i. 234.
Articles of the peace of Utrecht prescribed by the crown of Great Britain, i. 86.
Arts, state of, in the United Netherlands, ii. 403. 404.
────── knowledge of, introduced into Russia by Peter I. iii. 398. A particular academy for painting, sculpture, and architecture, founded in 1764, by the empress Catharine, i. 398, 399.
────── cultivated with success by the French, ii. 99, 100.
────── of the antients revived by the modern Italians, i. 130.
Arragonians, deprived of all their privileges by Philip V. and subjected to the laws of Castile, i. 187.
Assembly of the French clergy, i. 85, 86.
────── of the states of Spain called Cortes, convened only at certain solemnities, or upon account of settling the succession, i. 187.
────── of the states of the kingdom of France met annually under the Merovingian kings. Their assemblies called Campus Martii. The appellation changed to Campus Maii when they met in May. All the affairs of the kingdom discussed at these assemblies. Resolutions taken by a majority of votes. Clergy present for the first time at the diet held at Soissons in the month of May, 750. ii. 36. States of the kingdom under the Carlovingian princes, called the parliament. Cities summoned to the diet by Philip IV. 37. The states rendered entirely dependant upon the crown by Lewis XI. Last general diet held in France in the year 1614. 38. Assembly of the states retain at present only the right of chusing a king upon the total failure of the royal male line. The right of deciding a contested election, and, according to some, the right of appointing a regency in certain cases, 40. Assemblée des notables, a convention of the clergy, the upper nobi-

TABLE.

lity, and the parliament, i. 41. Was held at Roan in 1617, and at Paris in 1626. ibid. All royal ordinances, edicts, declarations, and letters patent, to be registered in the parliament of Paris. Till so registered, not valid. Parliament has a right to remonstrate against such acts when it judges them to be detrimental to the nation, ii. 426.

Assembly of the great council of Poland, account of, iii. 255.

Asses and mules of more general use in Portugal than horses, i. 262.

Atlantic Ocean, and Bay of Biscay, the Northern limits of Spain, i. 156.

Audiences, Spanish courts of justice, account of, i. 224, 225.

Auvergne, county of, in France, full of high mountains, ii. 3.

Avis, order of knighthood, founded under king Alphonso I. Said to consist of seventy-three commanderies, i. 307.

Azores, or Flemish Islands, in the Atlantic Ocean, belong to the Portuguese i. 265.

B.

Balance of Europe, i. 149. Consequences of it, 150. Alterations in the balance of power, 151, 151. Particular balance in the North, Germany, and Italy, 154.

—— of Italy and the North, preserved upon several occasions by the English, ii. 329.

Banks of Europe, account of, i. 247.

Bank of England, erected in 1694. Owes its existence to the national debts. The government's best support in all pecuniary exigences, ii. 318.

—— of Copenhagen, founded by Frederick IV. in 1736. ii. 88.

Barrier in the Austrian Netherlands, ii. 412, 413.

—— treaty, concluded between the United Provinces, and the emperor Charles VI. in 1715, put the latter in possession of the town of Venlo, and fort Stevens-Waart, ii. 345.

Basil, council of, endeavoured to abolish the annates, expectative, and reservations, but without effect, ii. 79.

Bath, noted for it's mineral waters and warm baths, ii. 175.

Batavia, capital of the Indian possessions, belonging to the United Provinces, ii. 396. Its principal commodities what, ibid.

Batavians in Cæsar's time, inhabited part of Guelderland, Holland, and Utrecht, descended from the Patti, ii. 359.

Bavaria, supported in its claim to the Austrian succession by France, i. 92.

Beaver,

TABLE.

Beaver, plenty of, in North America, ii. 186.

Beef, of Portugal, excellent, i. 261.

Belem Alcantara, and Mafra, the chief royal feats belonging to the king of Portugal, i. 294.

Benefices of Spain, formerly at the difpofal of the pope. The nomination to the archbifhopricks and bifhopricks afterwards yielded up to the king, i. 208.

Bernia, one of ancient names of Ireland, ii. 181.

Bezaay Geld, or fowing-money, a tax upon fowed fields in the United Netherlands, ii. 422.

Bible, tranflated into Englifh in the time of queen Elizabeth, ii. 209.

Bill in parliament, what, ii. 223. Bills, private and public, ibid. A bill muft be read three times in order to be paffed, ibid. Money bills always begin with the houfe of commons, ibid.

Bifcay, remarkable for its excellent fire-arms, i. 237.

Bifcayners, the firft Europeans that failed on the whale fifhery, ii. 430.

Bifhopricks in France, one hundred and nine in number, ii. 75.

Bifhops of Spain, forty-five in number, i. 206.

——— rank next to vifcounts, and precede barons, ii. 260.

Black Prince, fon to Edward III. one of the illuftrious Englifh commanders, ii. 332.

Body guards, at firft the only ftanding troops of the kings of France, ii. 108.

——— of two regiments, raifed by king Charles II. ii. 281. In fubfequent reigns greatly augmented, 282.

Bookfelling, the fciences greatly promoted by it, i. 131.

Bois de Vincennes, remarkable for the porcelain made there, ii. 142.

Boifleduc, diftrict of, in the United Provinces, remarkable for its linen manufactures, ii. 426.

Bologna, the Concordat concluded there in 1515, between Francis I. and Leo X. The king's nomination of bifhops and archbifhops confirmed by it, and the annates recovered by the pope, ii. 80.

Bofworth field, battle of, Richard III. flain at it, and the crown of England won by the earl of Richmond, afterwards Henry VII. ii. 194.

Botany, anatomy, chemiftry, and all other branches of phyfick, cultivated with fuccefs in the Netherlands, ii. 404, 405.

Boundary of Europe, extended by modern geographers to the Volga, and by others ftill farther, even to the Oby, i. 71.

TABLE.

Brazil, in America, possessed by the Portuguese. Part of Guiana and Paraguay comprised under it, i. 262.

Braga, archbishop of, primate of Portugal. Contest between him and the archbishop of Toledo for the primacy of Spain; has under his jurisdiction the dioceses of Porto, Viseu, Coimbra, and Miranda, i. 297.

Brigadiers, immediately under the marshals de camp, ii. 113. first brigadiers made by Lewis XIV. in 1667. ibid.

Briare, canal of, one of the principal in France. Undertaken by the duke of Sully, in the reign of Henry IV. Continued by James Guyon and William Bouteroue. Emoluments of it greatly decreased since the making of the Orleans canal, ii. 242, 243.

Britons, descended from the Gomerians. Called Britons by foreigners. They call themselves Cumri, or Gomri, ii. 188.

—— subject to no laws but of their own making, ii. 225.

British form of government, advantages and disadvantages of, ii. 228. Prophecied by an eminent French author to draw near its period, ii. 233.

—— dominions in America, exceed the mother-country in extent, ii. 284.

—— antiquities, chief object of the attention of the Society of Antiquaries, at London, ii. 267.

—— subjects, obtained at the peace of Versailles the liberty of cutting logwood in the Bay of Honduras, ii. 312.

Brittany, nobility of, drop their nobility upon engaging in trade. On retiring, may resume it with all its privileges, ii. 35.

Brothers of the sword, or sword-bearers, spiritual knights, who made themselves masters of Livonia and Courland, and established Christianity there. Since lost those countries, i. 122.

Broils, occasioned by the religious disputes between the Gomarists and Arminians, caused M. Barneveldt, advocate of Holland, to be beheaded, ii. 399.

Buen-Retiro, Aranjuez, Casa del Campo, La Florida, El Pardo, Villa Viciosa, St. Iidefonso, and the Escurial, are the principal royal seats of Spain, i. 200, 201.

Buildings of note in London, account of, ii. 249, 250.

Bull-fights, principal diversions of the Spaniards, i. 176. The first public and solemn bull-fights exhibited in the year 1100, ibid.

—— Unigenitus, introduced in France as a law both of church and state, in the reign of Lewis XIV. ii. 88.

Burgesses, the members of parliament for towns and boroughs so called, ii. 221.

Bye-

Bye-laws, what, ii. 275.
Bynkershook and Grotius, the only two Netherland civilians that have written concerning the law of their own country, or the law of nations, ii. 401.

C.

Calvinism, established in the United Netherlands, Scotland, part of Germany, Swisserland, and Transilvania. Tolerated in England, Denmark, Sweden, Russia, Poland, and Hungary. In the two last countries very much oppressed. Persecuted in France, but has a great number of secret votaries in that kingdom, i. 123.

Canary-Islands in the Ocean, belonging to Spain, i. 262.

Canon law, and Roman law, have both been introduced into Poland, iii. 295.

Cardinal Alberoni, his plan for procuring the East and West-India trade, and the dominion of the sea to the house of Bourbon, i. 146.

Carthaginians and Phœnicians, established colonies on the south and west coasts of Spain. The former in the second Punic war, totally driven out by the Romans, i. 165.

Castellans of Poland, governors of the fortified places, iii. 240, 241.

Castile and Arragon, formerly the two capital kingdoms of Spain. Now incorporated, i. 161.

Catalonia and Galicia, air of, remarkably damp, i. 156.

Celtic language, supposed to be the origin of the Irish and Welch, i. 94.

Chelsea hospital, old and disabled soldiers provided for in it, ii. 284.

Chinese, arrogant boast of, i. 92.

——— require always to be paid in silver in their commerce with the Europeans, i. 145.

Chivalry, had its rise in the middle ages. Chief duty of, to defend religion, widows, orphans, and the fair-sex. Kings members of that glorious body, i. 101.

Ceuta, Oran, and Mafalquiver, on the coast of Barbary in Africa, belong to Spain, i. 162.

Christina, queen of Sweden, set up for the crown of Poland, in violation of the laws of that kingdom, i. 108.

Christianity, the prevalent religion in Europe, i. 117. Christiany in Europe divided into three religious sects, the Roman, the Greek, and the Protestant, 118.

Church, its dependance upon and connection with the state, i. 42, 43.

TABLE.

Church of Rome, according to the principles of the pope's politicks, constitutes one large general state, of which the temporal states are but parts, and subject to his supremacy, i. 119.

—— of England, established in England and Ireland, and tolerated in Scotland, i. 123.

Civilians formerly made the explanation of the Roman and papal laws, their chief business. Of late have applied themselves to the law of nations, and the nobler parts of jurisprudence, i. 126.

Cities of Spain, divided into ciudades and villas, i. 162.

Clergy, secular and regular, their great number in Spain, i. 214.

—— of England, account of, ii. 259—261. Convocation of the clergy, account of, 261, 262.

—— constitute the first order of the state in Roman Catholic countries, i. 97.

Climate, its influence upon the body, i. 17, 18. Its influence upon the mental qualities, 19, 20, 21.

Coinage, different standards of in Europe inconvenient, i. 138, 139.

Coins of Spain, account of, i. 228—250.

—— of England, account of, ii. 289—291.

—— of Sweden, iii. 182—186. Coinage, antiently the privilege of the kings of Sweden only. By Magnus Ladulas granted to the bishops and counsellors of state. Totally annexed to the crown by king Gustavus, 186, 187.

—— of Poland, account of, iii. 307—310.

College of cardinals, superintend the affairs both of church and state in Rome upon the demise of a pope, i. 108.

Commerce, carried on in the Mediterranean, and the Archipelago, between the Roman provinces, totally destroyed by the overthrow of the western Roman empire. Restored by the republicks of Venice and Genoa. Again brought to an end by the irruptions of the Tartars and Turks, i. 140.

Commercial treaties entered into by several European powers, whereby one state agrees to allow certain advantages to the subjects of another, particularly in tolls and duties, i. 143.

Conflans, Roussillon, and several considerable parts of the Netherlands, ceded to France, by Philip IV. at the peace of the Pyrenees, i. 169.

Connections between the several states of Europe, formerly much more confined than at present, i. 249.

Constantinople, patriarch of, the spiritual head of the Greek church, i. 118.

TABLE.

Constitution of the church of Scotland, ii. 262, 263.

——— of banks different. Those of Venice, Amsterdam, Nuremberg, and Hamburg banks of exchange. Those of London, Genoa, Stockholm, Copenhagen, and Dantzick, loan banks, i. 147.

Contest between the emperor Charles VI. and king Philip V. not totally extinguished by the peace of Utrecht, i. 88.

Conventions, remarkable ones, between Spain and other powers, i. 251—254. Principal ones between Portugal and other powers, 239.

——— between European powers, i. 152, 153.

Convocation diet, the first held after the king of Poland's death, account of. Forms of proceedings the same in this as in ordinary diets, ii. 261, 262.

Coronation, account of, i. 37.

Coronations, laid aside in Spain, i. 197, 198.

——— and coronation-diet in Poland, account of. Cracow formerly the place for this election. Coronation diet opens on the third day after the coronation. Coronation diet when succeeded by a pacification and exorbitantia diet, iii. 266, 267.

Country messengers of Poland, account of, number of, amounts to, iii. 243.

Counts and barons, first introduced into Sweden by Eric XIV. and into Denmark by Christian V. i. 100.

Courland, became an immediate fief of the crown of Poland, in 1659, iii. 216.

Court of justice and police in the king of Spain's palace, i. 223.

Courts of king's bench, common-pleas, exchequer, and chancery, account of, ii. 278, 279. High court of admiralty, and earl marshal's court, 280. The house of lords the supreme court of judicature of the kingdom, ibid.

——— of justice of Sweden. Eighty-two village-courts. The towns have their peculiar courts. Appeals lie from these to the provincial courts, which are twenty-one in number, and from these to the high tribunal. Three high tribunals in Sweden, the first at Stockholm, the second at Jonkoping, and the third at Abo. How these tribunals are governed. Those who think themselves wronged by any of these tribunals, may apply to the council of state for a revision, and from thence make an appeal to the states assembled in diet, iii. 175, 176, 177.

——— of justice of Poland, divided into lower and upper. Principal lower courts of Poland, are, 1. the country-courts. 2. The starosts-courts. 3. The country receiver's courts. 4. The town-courts. 5. The justices court. 6. The deputy waywode court. 7. Mixed courts. 8. The bishop's bishop's court, iii. 196, 197. Upper courts, are, 1. The chancery, or assessorial courts. 2. The relation-court. 3. The diet-court. 4. The upper-country courts. 6. The marshal's court. 7. The referendary-court. 8. The courts martial. 9. The capture court, ibid.

Court of the former czars. pretty much in the Asiatic taste. New modelled by Peter I. Court of Russia equal to any in Europe for magnificence. Its officers very numerous, iii. 382, 383, 389.

—— spiritual, archbishop's courts, court of delegates, ii. 262. Courts of law, 227.

Croisades, a consequence of the papal ambition, i. 80.

Crown of Prussia, of considerable weight, not only in the affairs of the North, but likewise in the general concerns of Europe, i. 88.

D.

DAILY lectures, held by sixty divinity professors at the Sorbonne, ii. 95, 96.

Danish, Norwegian, Swedish, Dutch, and English languages, in some measure a kin to the German, i. 94.

Daughters of the king of France, have a pecuniary portion on their marriage. Whilst they remain single, supported by the income of certain estates, ii. 60.

Dauphiné, province of, annexed to the crown of France under Philip VI. ii. 58.

Debts of all the kings of Spain in arrear as far back as Charles V. i. 236

—— of some European states occasioned by standing armies, i. 139.

Declarations of war, treaties of peace, and marriage contracts of the king of France, and royal children registered in the chamber of accounts at Paris, ii. 108.

Decretales Gregorii IX. Clementiræ, Extravagantes Johannis XX. & Extravagantes communes, the only books of the papal, or canon law, received in France. Decretum Gratiani considered only as the work of a private person, ii. 103.

Defenders of the church, a title formerly conferred upon the Swiss by the pope, but now obsolete, i. 115.

Denmark; account of the name of, iii. 1, 2. Situation, boundaries, and extent of, 2. Air and weather, 2, 3. Mountains, fields, and rivers of, 3. Fertility of, in the animal kingdom, 3, 4. In the vegetable kingdom, 4. In the mineral kingdom, 4, 5. In the fossile kingdom, 5.

Divi-

TABLE.

Division of, 5. Dependencies of Denmark, in Europe the duchy of Holstein, and the counties of Oldenburg and Delmenhorst, 19. Dependencies of in Asia, the town of Tranquebar, with its precinct, containing fifteen villages, 14. Dependencies of, in Africa, Fort Christianburg, on the coast of Guinea, 15. Dependencies of, in America, the islands of St. Thomas, St. John, and some other small islands of the Caribbes, transferred to them by the English, and the island of St. Croix which they purchased from the French, ibid. Sketch of the history of, 15—27. Character of the Danes, 27, 28. Number of inhabitants in Denmark much less considerable than formerly, 30. Danish nobility, account of, 31, 32. Danish burghers, account of, 33. Danish peasants, ibid. Danish kings, their power, formerly under limitations, 33, 34. States of Denmark, 34, 35. Danish form of government rendered absolute in the reign of Frederick III. 35, 36. Danish king's code, 36, 37. Danish king's obligations, 37. Danish kings have made the best use of their unlimited authority. Danish coronation, account of, 43, 44. Danish title, 44. Arms of Denmark, account of, 45, 46, 47. Titles, privileges, and obligations of the king of Denmark's children, and the princes of the blood, 47, 48, Origin, and singular good fortune of the royal family of Denmark, 48, 49. Capital and royal residence of the king of Denmark, 49, 50. Danish great officers of state, 50, 51. Danish court, of what officers composed, 51, 52. Flourishing state of the sciences in Denmark, 63, 69. And of the fine arts, ibid. Danish laws, 64, 65. Danish courts of justice, account of, 66, 67. Danish land-forces, state of, 68—71. Fortified places of Denmark, 71. Danish navy, account of. First improved by Christian IV. 71, 72. Danish coins, account of, 63—76. Revenue of Denmark, chief branches of, 76, 77, 78. Danish manufactures, account of, 79—81. Danish maritime commerce, now the most considerable in the North, 81, 82. Domestic trade in Denmark, 82. Danish trading companies; East-India-company, 83, 84. Guinea and West-India company, 85. African company, 85, 86. General trading companies, 86, 87. Levant company, 87. Danish trading towns and sea-ports, 88. Administration of state-affairs in Denmark, 89, 90. Interest of Denmark, 91, 92. Remarkable treaties between Denmark and other powers, 92, 93, 94. Danish statesmen, and warriors of eminence, 84, 85. Danish historians of reputation, 95. Remarkable accounts of the state of, 96.

TABLE.

Departments of the several state-officers, and the various particulars belonging to them, i. 39.

Dependencies of Spain, under the care of viceroys and governors, i. 247, 248.

Deposition of a king, its consequences, i. 36.

―――― of monarchs, several examples of, i. 111, 112.

―――― nineteen examples of, amongst the kings of Europe. That of Charles I. of England, the most remarkable, i. 111, 112.

Descent of the royal family, i. 199.

Descartes, Gassendi and Malebranche, the most eminent of the French philosophers. Preferred to all the antients and moderns, by the author of Lettres Germaniques et Françoises, ii. 94.

Despotic government, account of, i. 31.

Diets, or states, account of, i. 29, 30.

―――― held at certain times in Burgundy, Brittany, Languedoc, Provence, Lower Navarre, and Artois. The only business of these diets to regulate the assessments for the taxes, demanded by the king, ii. 41.

Diet of Lamego, resolutions of, contain the first and capital laws of the kingdom of Portugal, i. 282.

Dignity of admiral of France suppressed by Lewis XIII. Replaced by that of grand maitre, chef et surintendant geral de la navigation et commerce de France. Dignity of admiral restored by Lewis XIV. in 1669, in favour of his natural son the duke of Vermandois, ii. 121.

―――― of the patriarch of Constantinople, depends intirely on the sultan, or grand vizir's pleasure, i. 118.

Dioceses of Metz, Toul, Verdun, and Strasburg, under the sovereignty of France, ii. 77.

Disputes about the limits of North America, between the French and English, gave rise to the war in 1755. Alliance between France and Austria occasioned thereby. France obliged to purchase peace with the loss of its North American possessions, ii. 23.

Distempers, different ones peculiar to different nations, i. 19.

Divinity, Sorbonne, the nursery of, at Paris, ii. 95, 96. Too much neglected in the English universities, 270, 271.

―――― the faculty of, at Paris, especially the Sorbonne, the nursery of French divines, ii. 95.

Division of the Christian church into the Greek and Latin, occasioned in the VIIth century, by the jealousy of the bishops of Constantinople and Rome, i. 118.

Doctors of Sorbonne, thirty-six in number, ii. 95.

Domat, Montesquieu, and De Real, the most eminent of the French civilians, ii. 97.

Do-

Domestick and foreign state-interest of Portugal, account of, i. 332—336.

Dominion of the Franks greatly enlarged by Charlemagne, ii. 14.

Don Gratuit, or free-gift, an extraordinary contribution exacted by the kings of France from the clergy, ii. 84.

Dragoons of France have a colonel-general, and a maître de camp general, ii. 119.

Drente, province of, has no vote in the assembly of the United Netherlands, ii. 376.

Duelling, practice of, put a stop to by Lewis XIV. ii. 27.

Duke of Riperda, some manufactories set up by him in Spain, and workmen invited over from Holland and other countries. These promising beginnings dropped at his fall, i. 238

Dunkirk, a sea-port of great importance till the peace of Utrecht, ii. 122.

—— and Marseilles, made free-ports by Lewis XIV. ii. 144.

Dutch navy, came near the English in the last century, i. 137.

—— possessed themselves of the spice-trade, by seizing upon the best Portuguese settlements in the East-Indies, i. 142.

—— East-India company, the most considerable and wealthy of all, i 146.

—— the best spoken in the province of Holland; varies in the several provinces, ii. 363.

E.

Eastern empire, at last reduced to the capital Constantinople alone, i. 81.

East-India and China trade, highly detrimental to Europe. The vast gain of this trade continues enlarging prodigiously. Europe threatened hereby to be impoverished, i. 145.

—— company of France, erected in 1664. stood its ground, but made no figure. Mississippi-company united to it with the Chinese and African companies, by Mr. Law, under the title of The Perpetual Company, ii. 147.

Ecclesiastics of all denominations, exempt from every jurisdiction but the pope's, i. 119.

—— of France, in much greater subjection to the king, than the ecclesiastics of other countries, i. 82.

Ecclesiastical jurisdiction, acquired such extent from the emperor Lewis the Pious, and his successors, that the temporal became of little consideration, i. 81. Reduced within narrow limits by the edicts of Francis I. 82.

—— exchequers, established at Paris, Rouen, Lyons, Toulouse, Bourdeaux, Aix, and Pau, on account of the con-

contributions payable by the clergy of France, and the disputes which they occasion, ii. 84.

Ecclesiastical causes, part of the canon law used in, ii. 103.

——— and religious concerns, as far as they come within the prerogative, fall under the cognizance of the conscience-council. The king's confessor present when he holds this council, ii. 150.

Edict of Nantz, revoked by Lewis XIV. in 1685. Half a million of the inhabitants of France withdrew thereupon to protestant countries. Number of concealed protestants in France, computed at two millions, ii. 73, 74.

Efforts made to limit the Prussian monarch's prerogative, i. 355, 356, &c.

El consejo de estado, the Spanish council of state, its president always the senior counsellor, i. 244.

El ordinamiento real, a digest of all the royal ordinances of Spain, published by Ferdinand the Catholic, i. 222.

Election-diet in Poland, account of, at first fixed to six weeks, iii. 262.

——— compact, and other laws observed by the Poles, iii. 267, 268.

——— supplanted out of all European states, except Germany and Poland, i. 107.

Elector of Saxony, elector of Bavaria, and elector Palatine, alternately guardians of the administration of government in Germany upon the demise of the emperor, i. 108.

Eleven chambers of accounts in France, that of Paris the principal, ii. 108.

Eminent poets at present scarce in France, ii. 93.

Emperor of Germany, of age upon entering into his 18th year. The electors at age upon completing that year. The dukes of Saxony, and princes of Anhalt in their 21st. Most other princes of the Roman empire of age at their 25th year. Kings of France enter on their majority in their 14th year. Those of Great Britain at the end of their 18th. Those of Denmark at the beginning of the 18th. Those of Sweden at the conclusion of their 21st year, i. 109.

——— of France, a title assumed by the king of France in treaties with the grand signor, and other princes of Asia and Africa, ii. 52.

——— of the West, a title acquired by Charlemain for himself and his successors, ii. 14.

Engineers of France, subordinate to the surveyor of the fortifications, ii. 114. Divided into four classes, ibid.

England, thought to have been formerly joined to France by an isthmus, and separated from it by some violent convulsions in nature, ii. 170.

TABLE.

England division of, ii. 178, 179. Islands of, 179, 180. English, origin of, 199, 200. Character of 201—207. English language, account of, 208, 209. Nobility and gentry of, 212—215. Form of government of, 216, 217. Union of with the kingdom of Scotland, 218, 219. State of parties in, 229—233. Fortresses of, 284, 285. Crown revenues of, ordinary and extraordinary, 295, 296. Manufactures of, 305, 306, 307. Great trade of, 307, 308. Its foreign trade in Europe, 309. To the Levant, 309, 310. To Africa, ibid. To the East-Indies, 310, 311. To America, 311, 312. Bank of, 317, 318. Sea ports and trading towns of, 318, 319. Collections of public records and historians relative to, 333. Complete histories of, 334, 335.

English East-India company, next to the Dutch in wealth, i. 146.

—— conquest, all recovered by Charles VII. of France, except Calais, ii. 17, 18.

—— lost Calais, their last French conquest, in 1558, ii. 19.

—— charged by certain French writers, with affecting the dominion of the sea, and an universal exclusive trade, i. 147.

—— have the free exercise of their religion in many foreign parts where they are settled on account of trade, i. 125.

Engravers of reputation, admitted into the academy of sculpture and painting at Paris, ii. 100.

Engraving, state of, in the Netherlands, ii. 406.

Envoys in ordinary, the custom of keeping them at foreign courts, introduced in order to preserve the balance of power in Europe, i. 150.

Esmoler mor, or lord-almoner, one of the principal court-officers of Portugal, i. 195.

Estribeiro mor, or master of the horse, one of the chief court-officers of Portugal, ibid.

Equity of the Roman laws, caused it to be used through the whole kingdom of France, ii. 102.

Europe, its name, from whence derived, i. 70. Extent and limits of, 70, 71. Mountains of, 72. Waters of, 72, 73, 74. Fertility of, in the animal, the vegetable, and the fossile kingdoms, 74, 75, 76. Division of its countries, 76, 77. Dependencies, 77. Revolutions of, 78—91. Character of, 91, 92. Various languages of, 92, 93, 94, 95. Number of its inhabitants. Causes why so inconsiderable, 95, 96, 97. Difference of ranks in the states of, 97—100. Forms of government in the states of, 102, 103. European elective kingdoms by whom governed upon the demise of a king, 108. European

states

TABLE.

states with regard to their strength divided into four classes, i. 136.

Europe lies within the temperate zone, a small part excepted, i. 70.

—— extensive enough to contain five hundred and fifty millions of inhabitants, i. 95.

European states, most of, maritime powers, on account of the great foreign trade carried on by means of the waters which separate it, i. 74. European Christendom, according to the opinion of some made but one political body, with the pope for its spiritual, and the emperor for its temporal head. i. 113.

—— nations of various origin, i. 91.

Excellent marble, and quarries of very good stone found in Scotland, ii. 177.

Exports of the French to foreign nations exceed their imports. The surplus made up in specie. Advantage in this trade wholly on the side of the French, ii. 144.

Expulsion of the Moors, a work of near 800 years. Occasioned 3,700 combats, or engagements, i. 167.

Extent of a country, how determined, i. 8.

F.

FAmiliars of the Spanish inquisition, two thousand in number. Their business to apprehend those against whom there is an information, i. 218.

Faro islands, twenty-five in number, iii. 10. Their situation with respect to Iceland, 11. Belong to Norway, ibid. Produce plenty of grain, with great numbers of sheep. How governed, ibid.

Females excluded from the succession in elective governments, i. 107, 108. Absolutely excluded from succeeding to the crown of France, 46. Not excluded the regency, ibid. Instances of kings of France who have committed the regency to their consorts or mothers, 49.

Fertility of a country, the several productions included in it, i. 11.

Festival of St. Anthony of Padua, tutelary saint of Lisbon, celebrated by a bull-fight, i. 276.

Finances of a state, account of, i. 52.

Fine arts, painting, sculpture, engraving, and architecture, cultivated with less success by the English than the French, ii. 173, 174.

Fifteen millions of people, or thereabouts, said to have been killed or put to death in the new world by the Spaniards, i. 163.

TABLE.

Fifteen capitanias, or governments, in the Portuguese dominion in Brasil, i. 266.

Fifth monarchy, foretold by the prophet Daniel, thought by the Portuguese to be Portugal, i. 289.

First chaplain, capalam mor, one of the principal court-officers of Portugal, i. 295.

Foreign affairs, the several particulars comprehended by them, i. 60.

—— laws prejudicial, i. 133.

—— commerce, first taken in hand by the English, in the reign of queen Elizabeth. Their example herein followed by the French. The northern states have engaged in foreign commerce with great industry in the present century, i. 142.

—— commerce, of Spain, account of, i. 239—242. Foreign interests of, 249—251.

—— concerns of the Spanish monarchy, greatly altered since Spain has been under a king of the house of Bourbon, i. 249.

Fortifications of Sweden, account of, iii. 180.

Fortified places belonging to Spain, account of, i. 227. Fortified places of Portugal, account of, 319. Fortified places of Poland, account of, iii. 307. Fortified places belonging to Russia, account of, said to have twenty-four on the Baltic, nineteen towards Poland, Crim Tartary, and Turkey; Fifteen in Siberia; Nine on the Wolga. Large arsenals at Petersburgh, Moscow, Novogrod, and Riga, 410, 411.

Foundation of nobility, twofold, i. 97.

—— of unlimited monarchy in France, laid by Lewis XI. ii. 18.

Foundlings, particularly respected in Spain, where they are honoured with the title of hidalgos, i. 181.

France, account of, the name of, ii. 1. Its situation, limits, and extent. Air and temperature, 2, 3. Remarkable mountains of, 3. Its fertility in the animal, vegetable, and fossile kingdoms, 4—8. Division of its monarchy, 8, 9. Independent principalities of, 9, 10, 11. Dependencies of it in Asia, Africa, and America, 11, 12, 13. Revolutions of, 13—23. The French, a mixture of several nations, 23, 24. Character of the French, 24—28. Language of, 29, 30. Number of its inhabitants, 30, 31. Nobility of, 31—36. Form of government, 36—41. Fundamental laws of, 43, 44. Succession to the throne of, 44—47. French king's majority, how settled. Guardianship

dianſhip, and regency of, 48—51. Title of, 51, 52. Arms of, 52, 53, 54. Pre-eminence of, 55, 56. Coronation of, 56, 57, 58. Title of the heir to the crown of, 58, 59. Revenues of the younger princes and princeſſes of, 59, 60. Origin of the royal family of, 60, 61. Capital of, 61. Royal ſeats of, 61, 62. Great ſtate-officers of, 62—65. Great court-officers of, 65—68. Upper clergy of, 75—78.

France, the firſt European power in the XVIIth century, i. 91.

Franco-Gallia, France ſo called in the middle ages, ii. 1.

Franks, under their king Clovis, by one ſignal victory, put an end to the Roman government in Gaul, and erected a powerful monarchy, ii. 13.

Francis I. taken priſoner at the battle of Pavia. Compelled to renounce Flanders and Artois, together with his claim to the Milaneſe and Naples, ii. 19.

French and Daniſh royal families particularly fortunate, i. 112.

——— clergy, not exempt from taxes, ii. 83, 84. French poets, account of, 92, 93. French hiſtorians, great number of, 93, 94. French lawyers have cultivated the Roman law with ſucceſs, 96, 97. French phyſicians and ſurgeons, moſt in repute of any in Europe, 97, 98. French mathematicians countenanced by the government, 98. French laws, account of, 101—104. French courts of juſtice, account of, 104, 105. French parliaments, 105, 106. French great council, 107. French fortifications ſuperior to thoſe of other European ſtates, 115. French military inſtitutions ſuperior to thoſe of the reſt of the Europeans, 215, 216. French marine, account of, 116—122. French coins, 123, 124, 125. French finances, account of, 125—128. French manufactures, account of, 140—142. French inland trade, account of, 142, 143. French foreign trade, 143—146. French trading companies, 146—148. French provinces, how governed, 151, 152. French domeſtic intereſt, 152, 153. Foreign intereſt, 153—156. French claims upon other kingdoms, 156, 157. French treaties with other powers, 151—163. French ſtateſmen and warriors, account of, 163, 164. French hiſtorians, account of, 165, 166. Political writers, 166, 167.

——— language, at preſent uſed in the ſeveral courts of Germany, and all over the North. Has ſupplanted the Latin tongue, as the ſtate language of Europe, i. 93. Cultivated and brought to its preſent perfection by the academy inſtituted by cardinal Richelieu, ii. 29, 30.

French

TABLE.

French thought to be the inventors of posts. Soon brought into use all over Europe, i. 198.
―――― fashions, constantly varying. Copied all over Europe except by the Spaniards, ii. 38.
Free, what state properly so called, i. 4. Take their rise from the abuse of monarchies, ibid.
Free ports, account of, i. p. 147, 148.
Free states of Europe, seven in number, Venice, Genoa, Lucca, Ragusa, St. Marino, the United Netherlands, and the Swiss cantons, four of these aristocratical, i. 103.
Fuero juzgo, or the forum judicum of the Spaniards, composed of the written laws of king Eric, the edicts of succeeding princes, and the decrees of councils, i. 221.
Fundamental laws of France, which the king of his own prerogative cannot alter, three in number; 1. that he shall profess and defend the Roman Catholic religion; 2. that he shall not divide or dismember the kingdom, nor alienate any of the demesne, or property of the crown; 3. that he shall not alter the established succession to the throne, ii. 43, 44.
―――― law of Russia, iii. 70, 71.
Fursts, a class of German nobility, which ranks between the duke, the marquis, and the count.

G.

Gallican church, liberties of, always strenuously asserted by the Sorbonne, ii. 96. Contained in these two propositions; 1. the pope has no authority in temporal matters within the dominion of France; nor are the clergy to obey him on his assuming that power. 2. In ecclesiastical causes his power is circumscribed by the decrees of the antient councils, 87. Liberties of the Gallican church, little regarded by Lewis XIV. in the controversy of the Jansenists, 88.
Gallies of France, in the Mediterranean, formerly thirty in number, since reduced to ten, ii. 119.
Gardes de la marine, three companies of, belonging to the navy of France. Gardes de pavillon amiral, one company of, in the navy of France, ii. 119.
Gascons, witty and courageous, but too much given to boasting, i. 23.
Gaulish Celts, the first inhabitants of Spain, i. 165.
General customs in the provinces and cities of France, sixty in number. Particular customs, one hundred and twenty-three, ii. 101.
Germany, has remained an elective monarchy ever since the extinction of the Carlovingian male line, i. 110. A particular balance-power requisite in Germany, on account

TABLE.

of the rivalſhip of the houſes of Auſtria and Brandenburg, i. 152.

Germans, founders of moſt of the European ſtates, i. 93, 94.

German language, beſides Germany, ſpoken in part of Swifferland and Lorrain, in Royal and Ducal Pruſſia, in the towns and among the gentry in Courland, Livonia, and Eſthonia, in ſome particular parts of Poland, Hungary, and Tranſylvania. Often uſed by the northern powers in ſtate inſtruments, i. 93, 94.

Gibraltar, and the iſland of Minorca, ceded to Great Britain in the year 1717, ii. 197, 198.

Goa, capital of the Portugueſe Eaſt-India poſſeſſions, i. 266.

Golden-fleece, order of, inſtituted in the year 1431, by Philip the Good, duke of Burgundy, i, 202, 203.

Gold medals, the prizes beſtowed by the French academies upon the beſt anſwers to their queſtions, ii. 92.

Gold, and jewels, leſs plenty in Europe, than in the eaſt, i. 76.

Government, the different forms of, i. 3. Which the moſt ancient form, 4. Different forms of government known by different fundamental laws, 26, 27. Different departments of, to whom entruſted, 60, 61.

——— of Ruſſia, extremely ſevere, iii. 354, 355.

Governors in thoſe Spaniſh provinces which are kingdoms, have the title of viceroy. In others ſtiled captain-general. Moſt Spaniſh governors make fortunes, eſpecially in America, i. 147, 148.

Granada, and Andaluſia, remarkable for damaſks, ſattins, and other ſilks, i. 237.

Grandees of Spain, the title of, introduced under king John. Their greateſt privilege that of being covered before the king. Formerly divided into three claſſes. Take place of all officers of ſtate. Put themſelves upon a footing with the electors of the empire, and the princes of Italy. Captain and lieutenant-general made their equals in reſpect of precedence at court, by Lewis I. i. 183.

Grand-maſter of the artillery, commander in chief of the artillery men, ii. 114.

Grant of pope Alexander, Spaniards ground their right of conquering the new world upon it, i. 163.

Great almoner, one of the court officers in Roman Catholic countries, i. 116. Title of, firſt uſed in France under Charles VIII. The zenith of eccleſiaſtical dignities, ii. 65.

Great Britain, name of, by whom introduced, ii. 169. Situation of, 170. Extent of, 170, 171. Mountains of, 171, 172. Rivers of, 174. Fertility of, in the animal, vegetable

table, and foffile kingdoms, 173—176. Dependencies of, 181—188. Revolutions of, 188—199. Number of inhabitants of, 210, 211, 212. Parliament of, 219—225. Fundamental laws and privileges of, 234, 235, 236. Succeffion to the throne of, 236, 237, 238. Privileges of the crown of. Its dominion over the Britifh feas, 244, 245. Capital of, London. Account of that city, 248, 249, 250. State and crown officers of, 250, 251, 252. Officers, and fervants of the court of, 252, 253. Learned focieties, Royal Society; Society of Antiquarians, &c. account, 266, 268. National debt of, 300, 301, 302. Domeftic intereft of, 323, 324. Foreign intereft of, 324—327. Treaties between Great Britain and other powers, 327—331. Eminent ftatefmen and warriors of, 331, 332. Moft accurate writers on the ftate of, 336.

Great Britain, the chief object of Spain's jealoufy, on account of its being in poffeffion of Gibraltar and Portmahon, i. 250. The firft European power in the prefent century, 91.

Great council of war of Spain, divided into two chambers, one takes cognizance of military affairs, the other of law cafes. Counfellors of ftate, by their office, counfellors of war, i. 244.

—— council, principal high court of France, next to the parliaments, and has nine prefidents, fifty-four counfellors, and feveral other members. Its jurifdiction extends over the whole kingdom. Frequently oppofed by the parliaments, particularly that of Paris, ii. 108.

—— feal of the kingdom of France, kept by the lord chancellor, ii. 63.

—— huntfman, monteiro mor, one of the principal court-officers of Portugal, i. 295.

—— officers of the kingdom of Caftile, were the chancellor, the conftable, and the admiral, fuppreffed by the kings of Spain, all but their titles, i. 101.

Greeks and Romans, the moft celebrated of the antient inhabitants of Europe, i. 78.

Greek, the ftrongeft of all European wines, i. 75.

—— language, divided into the old and the new, the old ufed only by the learned. The corruption of it occafioned by the Turks fubduing the eaftern empire.

—— the eftablifhed religion in Ruffia, and tolerated in Turkey, Hungary, Poland, and Tranfylvania, i. 118.

—— Chriftians, at prefent the only Chriftians, who acknowledge the patriarch of Conftantinople, i. 118.

Greenland, when, and by whom difcovered, iii. 11. Chriftianity planted there by Olof Triggefon, king of Norway, ibid.

ibid. Became, in procefs of time, fubject to Norway, ibid. A Greenland company formed at Copenhagen, 12. New Greenland, what part fo called, ibid. Another Greenland company created at Bergen, in Norway, ibid. Twice dropped, and renewed again, 12, 13. An exclufive Greenland trade and fifhery, carried on by the Danifh company of general trade, 13. Where new Greenland begins, ib. Doubtful whether it be an ifland or a peninfula, ibid. Doubtful whether it belongs to Europe or America, ibid. Products of, ibid.

Grenadiers, firft introduced by Lewis XIV. ii. 109.

Guardians appointed to conduct the adminiftration in elective kingdoms, on the demife of a monarch, i. 108.

Guardianfhip and regency, during the minority of an emperor of Ruffia, iii. 370.

——— and regency, during the king of Denmark's minority, iii. 42, 43.

——— and regency of France, generally held by the queen-mother, ii. 49.

Guife, princes of the houfe of, authors of the religious wars, the maffacre of Paris, and the holy league. Duke, and cardinal of, put to death by order of Henry III. ii. 20.

Gunnery and military architecture, taught at feveral fchools in France, ii. 16.

H.

Habeas corpus act, petition of right, declaration of rights, and the fucceffion bill, are acts explaining, inforcing, and enlarging king John's Magna Charta, ii. 235.

Haerlem, academy of fciences, has acquired great reputation by its tranfactions, ii. 403.

Hague, the place where the ftates-general hold their affemblies, ii. 368.

Hand of righteoufnefs, one of the infignia delivered to the king of France at his coronation, ii. 56.

Hans Towns, account of, traded not only in the Baltic, but to the Low-Countries, England, France, and Spain. This confederacy for fome time accounted one of the greateft maritime powers, i. 141.

Harbours for the Englifh men of war, account of, ii. 289. The beft harbours in Scotland and Ireland, 319.

Harveft, a common one in France. Furnifhes grain only for eighteen months, ii. 139.

Haftings, battle of. Harold, king of England, killed at. The Englifh in confequence of it received the yoke of William the Conqueror, ii. 191.

TABLE.

Head of the church, a title assumed by Henry VIII. ii. 241.

Head of the Teutonic order, called the Teutonic grand master. Has a seat and vote at the German diets among the ecclesiastical princes, i. 122.

Heila, a volcano of Iceland, account of, iii. 9.

Heir to the crown of France, stiled the dauphin ever since the reign of Philip VI. ii. 58.

Hengist and Horsa, leaders of the Saxons, called in by the Britons against the Scots and Picts, ii. 189. Turned their arms against the Britons themselves, and drove them into Wales, 190.

Henry V. king of England, conquered the greatest part of France. On marrying the princess Catharine, acquired a right to the succession, ii. 17.

Heptarchy, seven kingdoms, gradually erected by the Saxons and Angles. United under Egbert king of the West Saxons, ii. 190.

Hereditary stadtholder, captain-general and admiral of the generality lands, dignities conferred upon William IV. by the states-general, ii. 392.

Herencia, Segovia, and some other towns of Castile, noted for their cloth manufactures, i. 237.

Heresy of the Albigenses, appeared so dangerous to the see of Rome, that it undertook to extirpate them by arms and the inquisition, ii. 73.

Herrings, swarm upon the coast of Scotland in spring and summer, ii. 176.

Hetman, the commander of the Ukraine Cossacks, so called. Chosen by themselves. Must be confirmed by the czar. Post of, sometimes continues vacant, iii. 407.

Hibernia and Ierna, antient names of Ireland, ii. 181.

High courts of justice in France, next to the parliaments, and the great council, are the chamber of accounts, and the courts of aids and coinage, ii. 108.

────── court of admiralty at Paris, held in the name of the admiral of France. Fines in the high court of admiralty, divided between the admiral of France and the king, ii. 121.

────── offices of the crown, the court, and the law, still remain in Scotland, a privy-council and parliament superseded by the union, ii. 321.

────── steward, a post of the highest consideration and power under the Carlovingian race, ii. 62. Suppressed by Philip II. 63. His functions divided between the constable and the grand maître de France, ibid.

High and mighty lords, a title given to the states-general

of the United Provinces by all the European powers, except Spain, ii. 380.

Highlands of Scotland, abound with timber and fuel-wood, ii 177.

Highlanders of Irish extraction, ii. 200.

Highness, title of, given to Frederick Henry, prince of Orange, by Lewis XII. king of France, ii. 397.

Hills, the advantages and disadvantages of, i. 10.

Hispania, an antient name of Spain, derived from Hispanus, a grandson of Hercules, i. 156.

History, at present more cultivated in England than it was formerly, ii. 269, 270.

Histories of Poland, account of, the most remarkable, iii. 321.

History of France, what the sources of. Complete histories of France, by whom published, ii. 165, 166.

Historians, very numerous among the French. Partial and unexact, ii. 93.

Holland, the most monied country in Europe. Gives law to other nations in the business of exchange, i. 138. Famous for its eminent painters, 405. The country low and swampy. Like the Zealand islands intirely level, ii. 339. Greatly improved by the industry of the inhabitants, 344. Province of Holland alone contains a million of inhabitants, 364.

Holy Ghost, order of, instituted by Henry III. of France. Number of the knights belonging to it one hundred, ensign of, ii 69, 70.

Holy Island, Cocket and Farn, belong to Northumberland, ii. 179.

Homage to a sovereign, in what it consists, i. 10.

——— of the king's vassals for the great fiefs, received by the chamber of accounts at Paris, ii. 108.

Home trade of Spain, account of, i. 239.

Honour of the salute, acquired to the English by Oliver Cromwell in his wars with the Dutch, ii. 196.

Horned cattle, very uncommon in Spain, i. 159.

——— cattle of Scotland, somewhat small, ii. 176.

Horses of Spain, highly valued, i. 158.

——— of Scotland, somewhat small, ii. 176.

Horse and foot militia of England, formerly amounted to 200,000. A new militia formed in 1757, ii. 283, 284.

——— posts, first instituted by an edict of Lewis XI. in 1464, i. 148.

House of Austria, alliance between it and France, formed in 1756. The branches of the house of Bourbon in Spain and Italy included in this alliance, i. 152.

Houses

TABLE.

Houses in London, reckoned at 150,000, ii. 148.

House of lords, the supreme court of judicature in England, to which appeals lie from all the other courts, ii. 180.

—— of commons, is more numerous than the house of lords, ii. 225.

Household of emperors and kings, account of, i. 116.

—— of the king of Spain, exceeds most European courts in the number of officers, i. 202.

—— troops of the king of England amount to 7383, ii. 283.

Hugh Capet, founder of the royal family of France. French authors not agreed with regard to his extraction. Originally had no right to the crown, ii. 60.

Huguenots, a nick-name given to the French protestants. Henry IV. of France granted them the free exercise of their religion by the edict of Nantz, ii. 73.

I.

JAMES the Elder, the apostle, supposed by the Spaniards to have first preached Christianity amongst them, i. 203.

Jansenist party causes violent disturbances in France, ii. 74.

Iceland, island of, when peopled, iii. 8, 9. Came under the Danish dominion at the same time with Norway, 9. Extent of, ibid. Its name, whence derived, ibid. Consists of a heap of rocks and mountains, ibid. Principal vegetables of, ibid. Supplied with flour by Denmark, 10. The poor at Iceland, how supported, ibid. Horned cattle and sheep tolerably plenty in Iceland, ibid. Horses at Iceland, very small, ibid. Foxes commoner than other beasts of prey in Iceland, ibid. Wild fowl, and birds of prey, plenty in Iceland, ibid. Supplied with plenty of fish by its bays and the ocean, ib. How governed, 11. The Icelanders originally a Norwegian colony, 29. Alone acquainted with the ancient Norwegian language, ibid. Reformation opposed in Iceland, 57, 58. Two sees in Iceland, Scalhold and Holum, 59. Most of the ancient written monuments of Northern history owing to the Icelanders, 63. Laws of Iceland, account of, 66. Iceland trade, account of, 87, 88.

Jesuits banished for ever out of the dominions of Portugal, for being concerned in a plot against the king in 1758. i. 306.

—— devoted by a particular vow to the see of Rome. Have done the pope more service than any other order of monks. Lately suppressed in France, Spain, and Portugal, i. 120, 121.

Jews,

Jews, tolerated in some cities of France, ii. 74.
Judaism, tolerated in some countries, i. 117.
Importations of the Spaniards, far exceed their exports. Consequently they are losers by the foreign trade, i. 240.
Imposts on the subject, highest in France, Spain, and Holland, i. 139. So grievous in France, that they damp the industry of the people, ii. 139.
Income, derived by the see of Rome, from the kingdom of Portugal, more considerable than that of the king himself, i. 301.
Indolence of the Spaniards, has its source in pride, all pretending to be descended from the Visigoths, i. 175.
Independent and free countries in France, two in number, the counties of Avignon and Venaissin, and the principality of Dombes. The former belong to the see of Rome, the latter to the duke de Maine, ii. 10.
Infantado, the estate assigned for the maintenance of the royal children of Spain so called, i. 199.
Inferior courts of France, distinguished by the appellation of prevôtés, mairies, chatellanies, and judicatures, depend upon particular dukes and counts. From these an appeal lies to the district of provincial courts. From these to the upper-provincial courts and the parliaments, ii. 105.
Influence of French politics, greater in Sweden than in Denmark. The two last wars against Russia and Prussia owing to this, ii. 155.
Inhabitants of a country, different sorts of, i. 15. Number of, in different countries, 23, 24.
────── of Europe, computed at only an hundred and fifty millions, i. 95. Inhabitants of the European states, divided into four principal classes, the nobility, the clergy, the citizens, and the peasantry, i. 97.
────── of Spain, computed at seven millions and a half, i. 179.
────── of Portugal, computed at eighteen hundred thousand, or two millions of souls, i. 178.
────── of France, said to have amounted to twenty-five millions in the year 1621. To twenty-two millions in 1733. In other years seldom exceeded nineteen millions. Computed at present by some at twenty, by others at eighteen, and by others at only seventeen millions. Causes of this population. Causes that obstruct a farther increase, ii. 30, 31.
Inland tolls upon commodities, suppressed by Philip V. of Spain, in order to promote commerce, i. 139.
────── trade of France, greatly facilitated by the rivers and canals. Promoted by the yearly marts and fairs of the principal towns, ii. 143.

TABLE.

Inquifition, a great reftraint to philofophy and divinity in Spain, i. 218, 219. One of the main pillars of the fpiritual authority of Rome. At firft only a temporary tribunal for fuppreffing the Waldenfes and other heretics. Since made conftant and perpetual in Spain, Portugal, Rome, &c. 120. Firft court of, held at Seville in 1480. Eighteen courts of, in the Spanifh monarchy. Supreme court, held at Madrid, 211. Inquifitor-general, prefident of, ib. Supreme court of inquifition, how compofed, 211, 212. Other courts of inquifition, how compofed. Proceedings of the court of, 212, 213. Jews refufing to embrace Chriftianity, condemned by it to be burned alive. Thofe convicted of herefy condemned by it to be ftrangled. The poffeffions of the perfons condemned, confifcated. Their defcendants branded with indelible ignominy, 213.

—— three courts of, in Portugal, at Lifbon, Evora, and Coimbra. A fourth court of inquifition at Goa. Conftitution of the Portuguefe courts of inquifition, intirely the fame as in Spain, i. 303, 304.

Infurance-company, inftituted by Frederic IV. at Copenhagen, in 1727, iii. 88.

Intendants, infpectors, and treforiers generaux, belonging to the naval eftablifhment of France, ii. 121, 122.

Introduction of the fciences in moft countries in Europe, particularly the northern, owing to Chriftianity, i. 120.

—— of unlimited monarchy into Sweden, iii. 138—140.

Ireland, account of, ii. 181, 182. Irifh, origin of, 200. Character of, 208. Language of, 209, 210. Nobility of, 216. Archbifhops and bifhops of, 263. Standard of money in, 293.

Iron and copper produced in England, but in fmall quantities, ii. 175.

Iflands feated about England, account of, 179, 180.

—— of Cape Verde, poffeffed by the Portuguefe. Seafalt, the only product of, i. 265.

Ifland of Bombay, one of the principal fettlements of the Englifh Eaft-India company, ii. 184.

—— of Jamaica, abounds in fugar. Its number of fugar-mills in the year 1670, no lefs than fixty. Two millions of pounds of fugar made there every year. At prefent ten times the quantity, ii. 187.

—— of Madeira, famous for its wine, fugar, and other products, poffeffed by the Portuguefe, i. 165.

Italian language, the fpeech of European mufic, i. 93.

Junction de Meux mers, otherwife call'd the canal of Languedoc, the moft aftonifhing work of the kind in Europe,

rope, begun in 1666, and finished in 1680, under the inspection of Paul Riquet. Issues out of the Garonne to Besiers, and from thence to Cette, a sea port on the Mediterranean, length of forty French leagues. Construction of, cost thirteen millions of money. Carried on one hundred and twenty fathom under ground. Kept in repair by Riquet's heirs, who receive the profits of it, ii. 143.

Jura, or Ila, one of the largest of the western islands belonging to Scotland, ii. 181.

Justices of peace in England, appointed by the king, ii. 277—294.

Juverna and Iris, ancient names of Ireland, ii. 181.

K.

Keeper of the great seal, a new office, created by Henry II. of France, in 1551. That office has subsisted in France at the same time with that of lord chancellor, ii. 69.

Kent, county of, includes the islands of Thanet and Sheepy, ii. 179.

King of England's majority, how settled, ii. 239. Guardianship and regency appointed during the minority of, ibid. Regency, during the absence of, and in other cases, 240. Titles of, 240—243. Arms of, 243, 244. Coronation of, 245, 246. King's eldest daughter, title of, 246, 247. His supremacy over the church of England, 263, 264.

——— Charles II. of Spain, constrained by the peace of Munster to renounce all claim to Portugal. At his death did not leave ready money enough to defray the charges of his funeral, i. 170.

——— Recared I. first king of Spain that embraced the Roman Catholic religion, i. 184.

——— of Spain, subscribes his name only to letters to foreign princes, i. 193.

——— of Portugal's power, absolutely unlimited, except in settling the succession and the arbitrary imposition of new taxes, i. 282.

——— Dennis, one of the celebrated poets of Portugal, i. 312.

——— of France's prerogative, anciently under restraints from the states of the kingdom, ii. 36.

——— of France, when said to hold his lit de justice, ii. 42, 43.

——— of France, accounted the greatest king in Christendom. Kings of France, in virtue of certain bulls exempt from excommunication, ii. 54, 55.

King

TABLE.

King Pepin, the first French monarch that caused himself to be inaugurated and crowned with religious ceremonies. Imitated herein by all his successors, ii. 56.

―――― of France, has the regale, or right of levying the incomes of the vacant dioceses, and disposing of all ecclesiastical employments belonging to them, till the new prelate has taken the oath of allegiance to the king. Regale extended to all countries subject to the crown of France, ii. 18.

―――― of France's ordinances, edicts, and declarations, obligatory throughout the whole kingdom. Must be previously registered in all the high courts of justice, ii. 104.

―――― of France, took upon himself the guaranty of the emperor's pragmatic sanction, for securing the succession to his dominions, i. 89.

―――― of France, became sovereign justiciary of that kingdom, upon the successive union of the dukedoms and counties to the crown, ii. 104.

―――― of France's houshold troops, the principal and best part of his forces. Established by Lewis XIV. Whole body consists of 12,000 men, ii. 110.

―――― in Europe, allow emperors no superiority over them, i. 113.

Kings of Arragon, in any disputes with their subjects, obliged to submit to a judge called El Justicia, i. 185.

―――― of Portugal, have of late too resolutely asserted their rights against the papal encroachments, i. 302.

―――― of France, formerly resided at Paris at the Louvre, ii. 61.

―――― of Sardinia, formerly held the scale between the houses of Austria and Bourbon. The union of those powers unfavourable both to him and the balance of Italy, i. 152.

King's-evil, ceremony of touching for, when performed by by the king of France, ii. 57. This ceremony performed every week by Lewis XI. upon a certain occasion. King of France touch for other diseases besides the evil, ib.

―――― library at Paris, exceeds all the libraries of Europe in manuscripts. Charles V. the first founder of this library, ii. 98.

―――― printing house at Paris, built by cardinal Richelieu. Cost 360,000 livres, ii. 100.

Kingdoms, hereditary or elective, i. 32.

―――― of France, surrounded with one hundred and twenty strong fortifications, ii. 115. By some eminent writers termed the first kingdom in the universe, 54.

TABLE.

Kingdom of France, has fifty courts of admiralty. From all these an appeal lies to the high court of admiralty, ii. 121.

——— of Portugal, maintained by the inhabitants to be founded by God himself, i. 289.

——— of Pruffia, had its rife in 1701, i. 87.

——— of Spain, contains 1500 cities or walled towns, i. 161.

——— of Naples and Sicily, Ifland of Sardinia, Dutchy of Milan and Auftrian Netherlands, formerly belonged to Spain. All difmembered from it by the peace of Utrecht, in the year 1713. Spanifh nobility fufferers by this change. Some years after Naples and Sicily fell to one Spanifh prince, Parma and Placentia to another, i. 164.

Knere, in Ruffia, on a footing with princes, i. 100.

Knights, all the celebrated orders of, whether temporal or fpiritual, owe their origin to chivalry, i. 100, 101. Some account of them, 116, 117. Farther account of them, 14, 15, 16.

——— of Malta, have 250 commanderies in France, ii. 78.

Knighthcod, three remarkable orders of in Ruffia. Order of St. Andrew inftituted in 1698, by Peter I. Enfign of the order, iii. 384.

——— order of Catharine, inftituted likewife by Peter I. in honour of his queen. Enfign of. This order conferred only on princeffes and other perfonages of high birth, i. 385. Order of St. Alexander Newfkoi, inftituted by the fame prince, but not confirmed till after his deceafe. Enfign of this order, ibid.

——— remarkable orders of in Spain, are thofe of St. James, Calatrava, Alcantara, and Montefa. The grand mafters of thefe orders formidable, even to kings. Ferdinand the Catholic prevailed with pope Innocent VIII. to inveft him with the grand mafterfhip of thofe three orders during life. The three grand mafterfhips annexed to the throne by pope Adrian VI. knights of Malta, poffeffed of eftates in Spain to the amount of 60,000 l. fterling per annum, i. 214.

——— three religious orders of in Portugal. Several temporal orders of knighthood in France, ii. 68—72. Three orders of, in Great Britain, ii. 253, 254, 255.

——— two celebrated orders of, in Denmark, viz. the order of the Elephant, and the order of Danebroge. The order of the Elephant, inftituted by Chriftian I. Received its prefent form from Chriftian V. Number of the knights belonging to it fixed at thirty. Enfign of the order, account of, iii. 53. Order of Danebroge, its inftitution attributed

tributed to king Waldemar II. Number of knights belonging to it fifty, exclusive of the sovereign and his sons. Ensign of the order, 44, 45. The order of Fidelity added to the former two by queen Magdalena Sophia. Ensign of, 55. Three remarkable orders of knighthood in Sweden, viz. the order of the Seraphim, the order of the Sword, and the order of the North-star. The two former of great antiquity. Both in time became obsolete. A new order similar to that of the Seraphim, instituted by king Eric XIV. at his coronation. The order of the Agnus Dei, instituted by king John III. The order of Jehovah, instituted by Charles XI. The order of the Amaranthus, instituted by queen Christina. All these orders afterwards become extinct, and Sweden remained without any order of knighthood, till Frederic I. renewed the Seraphim and the Sword in 1748. Ensign of the former, what, iii. 163—166. The Swedish princes of the blood, knights of this order, 167. Twenty-four the number of the knights of the order of the Cherubim, 167. The order of the Sword limited to military officers. Has twenty-four commanderies. The companions little short of six hundred. Ensign of this order. Order of the North-star, instituted by Frederick I. Ensign of, 167. Knights of the order of the Seraphim, commanders of the two others. Remarkable orders of knighthood in Poland. First, that of the White Eagle, instituted by Augustus II. ensign of this order. Second order, that of Stanislaus, 282.

L.

LAdrones and Philippine Islands in Asia, belong to Spain, i. 148.

La Junta del despacho Universal, the cabinet-council of Spain. The secretary to this council accounted the most considerable of the king's ministers, i. 244.

Land-forces of Spain, account of, i. 225, 226.

——— of the English, account of, ii. 280, 281, 282. Household troops, their amount, 283. Gentlemen pensioners and yeomen of the guards, ibid.

——— of Poland, account of. Polish infantry, very bad. Hussars of Poland, account of. Polish crown-army consists of four pulks of national troops. Foreign troops of Poland, account of. Total of the crown-army. Total of the Lithuanian army, i. 300—305.

——— of Russia, account of. First step towards the improvement of Russian military discipline made by John Basilowitz. Strelitzes, the principal part of the Ruſſian forces. Diſbanded by Peter I. Military eſtabliſhment of the Ruſſian empire. The irregular troops all ſerve on horſeback, with officers of their own nation. The chief poſts in the Ruſſian army, what, iii. 403—408. Pay of the ſeveral officers from the field-marſhal general to an enſign, 408. Pay of a private man, 409. Pay of the officers and private men in the guards, ibid. Care and recruiting of the Ruſſian army belongs to the war-office, 410.

Languages, variety, i. 22. Latin language originally ſpread itſelf through all the Roman conqueſts. Confounded amidſt national emigrations. Still the peculiar language of the learned in every part of Europe. Uſed in the Romiſh church for divine worſhip, in the pope's ſecretary's office, and was formerly the European ſtate-language. From the Latin language are derived the French, the Valachian, Spaniſh, Portugueſe, and Italian, i. 92, 93.

—— of Denmark, Sweden, and Norway, the ſame, iii. 29. Learned languages, very much neglected in Spain, i. 219.

Latent Jews, common amongſt people of all ranks in Portugal, i. 274.

Law, imperfectly taught in the Engliſh univerſities, ii. 271. Studied in London at fourteen colleges, called the Inns of Court. No leſs than 40,000 perſons live by it, 271, 272. The ſeveral different laws obſerved in England. 1. Common law, 274. 2. Statute-law, 275. 3. Municipal laws, ibid. 4. Foreſt laws, ibid. 5. Martial law, ib. 6. The Roman law, ibid. 7. The canon law. Statute law of England, obſerved in Scotland ſince the Union, 276. Laws of England received in Ireland under Henry II. ibid. Laws of England defective, ibid. Greateſt part of the French laws conſiſt of the royal ordinances, capitularies of Charles the Great, and Lewis the Gracious, the moſt antient of theſe, ii. 103. Moſt law employments in France bought and ſold, ii. 106.

—— of nations in Europe, but little cultivated, i. 133.

Laws, obſervations upon. Laws civil and penal. Laws, who the guardians of, i. 47. 48. Laws, fundamental ones, in limited monarchies, 104, 105. Particular fundamental ones in limited monarchies, 105, 106.

—— of Spain, the revolutions which they have undergone, i. 221, 222.

—— of Sweden, iii. 173. The Upland law reckoned preferable to the other Swediſh provinces, 174. A general code of laws compoſed for the whole kingdom of Sweden

den, under king Magnus Smeck, 174. A new book of statutes, drawn up and adapted to the new limited form of the Swedish government upon the death of Charles XII. 175. Land forces of Sweden, account of. King Gustavus Vasa, author of the first military establishment in Sweden. Gustavus Adolphus, the first who formed a considerable regular army in Sweden, and improved military discipline, 177, 178. Present military establishment of Sweden, founded by Charles XI. 178. The horse maintained by the nobility, the foot by the farmers, ibid. The soldiery exercised every week, and once a year embodied into companies, 178, 179. The troops of Sweden maintained by the crown upon taking the field, 179.

Law, silent as to the time of the king's majority in Spain and Portugal. The kings of those nations generally appear to assume the sovereignty at the beginning of their fourteenth year, i. 170.

Laws of Russia, formerly there were very few written ones, iii. 399. A body of Russian laws, compiled in the year 1647, by order of the czar Alexis Michaelowitz, which with the ordinances of his successors, particularly Peter I. are rules for the courts of justice. A new code of laws drawing up by order of the present czarina Catharine II. Livonia, Esthonia, and Finland, retain their former laws. The Magdeburg law obtains in the Ukraine, 399, 400, 401.

Las siete parditas, a new code of Spanish laws, published by king Alphonso XI. of Castile, in the year 1343, i. 222.

Leyes de Toro, Spanish laws so called, from their being passed at the diet of Toro, published under Ferdinand the Catholic, in the year 1505, i. 222.

Leghorn, Trieste, Ancona, and Embden, the most remarkable free ports of Europe, i. 148.

Letter-founding, bookselling, and printing, flourishing state of, in Holland, ii. 196.

Lewdness, one of the capital vices of the Spaniards, i. 174.

Lewis de Camoens, accounted the Virgil of Portugal, i. 312.

—— XIV. acquired at the treaty of the Pyrenees great part of the Spanish Netherlands, with the county of Roussillon, ii. 21. Accused of aiming at the universal monarchy of Europe, i. 89.

—— XV. received the crown of France, encumbered with a most enormous debt, ii. 22.

Liberty, considered as the supreme good by the antient European nations. By their attachment to it they distinguished themselves from the Asiatics, i. 102.

Libraries, which the moſt valuable in Europe, i. 131, 132.
Literary journals, invention beneficial to literature, ibid.
―――― in Paris, twenty in number, iii. 98, 99.
Limitation of the ancient prerogatives of Poland, iii. 238, 239. Laws and conſtitutions of Lithuania, 295.
Limited, a limited monarch, what, i. 27.
Lineage of the royal family of Great Britain, ii. 247, 248.
Liſbon, ſtreets of, never cleaned but upon Corpus Chriſti day, i. 244.
―――― a great part of, laid in ruins by an earthquake and conflagration in 1755, i. 173.
―――― wine, and that of the province of Alentejo preferred to the other Portugueſe wines, i. 262.
―――― erected into a patriarchate by John V. king of Portugal, i. 297, 298.
Literary ſocieties in Denmark, account of, iii. 62.
―――― ſocieties in Sweden, account of, iii. 171, 172.
Literature and the ſciences, firſt introduced into Ruſſia by Peter the Great, iii. 396. Academy of ſciences, inſtituted by him at Peterſburg, but not opened till after his death. Learned ſeminaries very much wanting in Ruſſia, 396, 397, 398.
Livonia, Eſthonia, and Courland, formerly belonged to the order of the Enſiferi. The two former given up by the laſt grand-maſter Gottard Kettler, to Sigiſmund Auguſtus king of Poland. Livonia and Eſthonia, given up by Poland at the treaty of Oliva in 1660, iii. 215, 216.
Lord chamberlain, or camereiro mor, one of the chief officers at the court of Portugal, i. 295.
Lorrain, acquiſition of, compaſſed by Lewis XV. by engaging to maintain the pragmatic ſanction of the emperor Charles VI. ii. 22.
Loſſes of the pope in Europe, occaſioned by the reformation, abundantly compenſated by the Spaniſh and Portugueſe arms and miſſionaries in the Eaſt and Weſt-Indies, i. 120.
Lower courts of Spain, account of, i. 223.
―――― and upper courts of juſtice in Portugal, account of, i. 315, 316, 317.
Luſitania fell under the dominion of the Romans in the ſecond Punic war, and remained ſo till the beginning of the fifth century. Alani, the firſt who ſeated themſelves in Luſitania Next the Suevi, then the Moors. Alphonſo I. aſſumed the title of king of Portugal. The kingdom united to that of Spain by Philip II. Duke of Braganza proclaimed king by the Portugueſe, who univerſally revolted from Spain, i. 268, & ſeq.

Lu-

TABLE.

Lutheranism prevails in Denmark, Norway, Sweden, Prussia, Livonia, Courland, part of Germany, Transilvania, is tolerated in England, the United Netherlands, and Russia, Poland, and Hungary. Under great restraints in the two last countries; i. 123.

M.

MACAO, city of, in a small island on the coast of China, possessed by the Portuguese, i. 266.

Madrid, the residence of the king's of Spain, i. 198, 199, 200.

Magazines of England kept at the Tower of London, Portsmouth, Plymouth, Woolwich, Hull, and Berwick, ii. 284.

Mahomet II. possessed himself of Constantinople, in the year 1443. i. 81.

Mahometan religion, professed in no part of Europe, except Turkey in Europe, i. 117.

Majority of the king of Spain, not determined by any law. Term of a king of Spain's minority does not seem to exceed fourteen years of age. Regency and guardianship of a minor appointed by the king. Where no such provision has been made, the right belongs to the states of the kingdom, i. 191.

―――― of a king of France under the Merovingians, began at the age of fifteen. Under the Carlovingians was deferred till twenty-one. King of France's majority settled by a perpetual edict at his entrance upon the fourteenth year. This afterwards made one of the fundamental laws of the kingdom, ii. 48.

Majores domus, or mayors of the palace, chief officers of state under the Merovingian race. Took the whole administration into their hands, and left the kings only an empty title, ii. 62.

Malta, knights of, so called from the island of Malta, which Charles V. gave them for their residence. Possessed of large estates in Spain, Portugal, France, and Germany. Their grand-master considered as an independant prince by the European potentates. Only religious order in Europe, which continues to act up to its capital vow, to carry on a constant war with the Turks and African pirates, i. 121.

Manuscripts, at the king's library at Paris, amounted many years ago to sixteen thousand, ii. 98.

Manufacture of paper, Cuenca, and other towns of Spain, remarkable for, i 237.

―――― state of, in Spain, i. 237, 238.

TABLE.

Manufactures of Scotland, ii. 307. Of Ireland, ibid.
——— of Poland, account of, iii. 315.
Maranes, the most laborious of the subjects of Spain, expelled by Philip III. i. 169.
Marble of Portugal, exquisite both in grain and colour, i. 263.
Mariani & Cruciferi, appellations at first given to the Teutonic knights, i. 122.
Marine, to what states necessary. Expence of. Several branches of, i. 50, 51, 52. Marine of Spain, account of, i. 227, 228. Marine of Sweden owes its origin to king Gustavus. Greatly improved by Gustavus Adolphus, and brought to its height by Charles XI. iii. 181. Swedish fleet consists of three squadrons, one at Carlscroon, one at Gottenburg, and one at Stockholm, 182.
Marshals of France, the highest officers in the French king's armies. Are likewise great officers of the crown. Their authority greatly increased since the post of high constable was abolished. Military courts of the constable continued to the marshals of France, with the title of Connestablie and Marechaussée. Eldest marshal holds a court for taking cognizance of disputes upon the point of honour, without appeal. From the marechaussée an appeal lies to the parliament of Paris, ii. 113.
Mathematicks, favourite study of the English, ii. 273.
——— at present cultivated in France with great success, ii. 98.
Mazagan, a fort in the kingdom of Morocco, possessed by the Portuguese, i. 265.
Means for making a state populous, powerful, and respectable, now known and cultivated by all the princes and statesmen in Europe, i. 149.
Meetings of the academy of painting and sculpture, and of architecture, held at the Louvre, ii. 99.
Mexico and Peru, very rich in gold and silver, i. 163.
Middle ages, a remarkable vicious taste in printing, sculpture, and architecture, prevailed in them, i. 130.
Military establishments necessary to a state, i. 49, 50. Greatly encreased in Europe, 234.
——— schools, two large ones for officers, founded by Lewis XV. ii. 116.
——— force and discipline of the Portuguese, account of, iii. 317, 318, 319. Military nobility in France held in much greater esteem than those that belong to the law, ii. 98. Military state of France, 108 – 115.
Militia of England, account of, ii. 283, 284.
Mill-stones of Portugal, of such goodness, that they are carried to Spain and the Indies, i. 264.

Mines

TABLE.

Mines of Norway, great profits that accrue from, iii. 8. magnets and gems sometimes found in Norway, ib.

Ministers of state of Poland, have sometimes risen to be senators, iii. 241.

Minority of a king, its term varies in the several states of Europe, i. 109.

────── of a king of Spain does not seem to exceed fourteen years of age, i. 110.

────── of a king of Portugal, time of, uncertain. Thought to cease upon the king's entering his fourteenth year, ii. 285.

Modern French lawyers study the law of nature, that of nations, the government of France in church and state, and the common law, ii. 97.

Monarchy of the united kingdoms of Denmark, Norway and Sweden, quickly dissolved, i. 81.

────── compounded with aristocracy and democracy in the middle ages, almost the universal form of government in Europe. In the sixteenth and seventeenth centuries it became in most states purely monarchical, i. 103.

Money and coins, account of, i. 53.

────── trade, one of the chief European inventions for the improvement of commerce. Carried on by bills of exchange and banks i. 147.

────── of Russia, account of. The oldest pieces coined in Russia called copecks. A hundred copecks called by the Russians a ruble. Gold pieces struck only upon solemn occasions amongst the Russians. Mints established by the czar at Moscow, Novogrod, Tweer, and Plescow, iii. 415, 416.

Monks, the various orders of, greatly instrumental in supporting the pope, i. 120.

Montpellier, physick publickly taught at the university of, about the close of the twelfth century, ii. 97.

Moors dispossessed of the whole country of Spain as far as the Pyrenean mountains, by Charles the Great, i. 166.

Mordomo mor, the lord steward, one of the principal officers at the court of Portugal, i. 295.

Moscow, capital of the Russian empire. Made the sovereign's residence in the XIVth century. Divided into four circles. Has suffered terribly by the inroads of the Tartars, 377—379. A patriarch of, instituted by czar Teodor Ivanowitz, in the year 1587, i. 118.

Mother-country and dependencies, how distinguished, i. 14, 15.

Mozambique, island of, and many small islands, which go by the name of Quirimba, possessed by the Portuguese in Africa, i. 265, 266.

Mul-

TABLE.

Mulberry-trees, the great number of, in Andalusia and Granada. A nursery for silk-worms, i. 259.

Mules, at present in great vogue in Spain, i. 158.

Multitudes of judges and law-officers in Portugal, a great oppression of the people, i. 317.

Music, Italian system of, adopted by most countries in Europe, i. 128.

N.

NAMES, mutations undergone by those of kingdoms, i. 16.

────── of sovereigns, observations on, i. 38.

────── of Newton and Descartes, execrated in Portugal, as those of hereticks and blasphemers, i. 313.

Name of Spanija, given by the Phœnicians to that part of Spain that was known to them, i. 155.

Nantwich in Cheshire, has the best salt springs in England, ii. 175, 176.

Naples, the Milanese, and Sardinia, with the Spanish Netherlands, ceded by the peace of Utrecht to the emperor Charles VI. who made over Sicily to Victor Amadeus, duke of Savoy, i. 86, 87.

────── Sicily, and the dutchy of Milan, claimed by France. These claims renounced by Francis I. at the treaty of Madrid, and by other conventions, i. 156.

National debt of Sweden, account of, iii. 190.

────── bank of Sweden, account of. Managed by nine directors. The situation of, critical and suspicious, iii. 197, 198, 199.

Natural children, excluded from the succession all over Europe, i. 107.

────── philosophy, enriched by the French, with several useful discoveries, ii. 95.

────── sons of the king of France, declared incapable of succeeding to the throne by a new law, ii. 46, 47.

────── undauntedness of the English, cause why suicide is so frequent among them, ii. 205.

Naval force of Great Britain gave rise to the alliance between France and Austria, ii. 143.

Navy of England, its commencement, ii. 285. increased by queen Elizabeth, 285, 286. Its increase from the reign of queen Elizabeth to that of George III. 286. Divided into three squadrons, 287. In the hands of seven commissioners, ibid.

────── of France, the work of Lewis XIV. A great part of it taken and destroyed by the English in the war for the Auftrian fucceffion. Computed at a hundred fail at the breaking out of the war with England in 1755. Repairs carried on at prefent more vigoroufly than ever, ii. 119.

Navy of Ruffia, the work of Peter the Great, iii. 411. Ruffian marine totally quafhed in the Black and Cafpian feas, by the lofs of Afoph, and the Perfian provinces. In the Baltic has always maintained its reputation. Upon the deceafe of Peter I. the number of Ruffian gallies amounted to an hundred and fixty. Great officers of the Ruffian navy, account of, 412. Officers and private men of the Ruffian navy, how paid. Annual charge of the Ruffian navy computed at one million two hundred thoufand rubles. Whole marine under the infpection of the admiralty, 413, 414. Ports for the Ruffian men of war and gallies, 414.

Netherlands much infefted by inundations of the fea, ii. 341.
────── called United, from the union concluded between them at Utrecht, in the year 1759. Confift of feven provinces, ii. 338. Branches of literature cultivated in the Netherlands, 422.

Neutrality obferved by the ftates-general in the laft war between France and Great Britain, ii. 359.

New code, publifhed under the name of Code Louis, in twelve volumes in 4to. in the reign of Lewis XIV. ii. 104.

New Jerfeys, Pennfylvania, and Maryland, the only parts of Britifh America, that do not immediately depend upon the crown, ii. 186.

News-papers, a French invention, i. 148.

Newton, at the head of the Englifh mathematicians, ii. 273.

New World, thought to be difpofed to fhake off the yoke of the old world, ii. 188.

Nimeguen, peace of, advantageous to the United Provinces, i. 357.

Nine chambers compofe the parliament of Paris. The firft of thefe is called La grande Chambre. Five called Chambres des Enquêtes. Two Des Requêtes. One La Tournelle, ii. 106.

────── cours des aids in France, that of Paris the principal, ii. 108.

────── commiffioners fuperintend the excife in England. Inferior officers of the excife amount to fix or feven hundred, ii. 297.

Nobility, different degrees of, amongft the inhabitants of different kingdoms, i. 24, 25.

────── of Europe, divided into fuperior and inferior, i. 24, 25.

TABLE.

Nobility in Poland, but one species of, i. 100.
────── the first order of the state in protestant countries, i. 24, 25.
────── of Spain, divided into upper and lower. The former stiled titulados, with the word don before their names. The lower nobility and gentry stiled hidalgos. The cavalleros and escuderos amongst these. Noblemen of Spain solemnly renounce their allegiance upon receiving any affront, i. 181.
────── of Portugal, why so much declined, i. 279. Divided into high and low, ibid. Lower nobility in general called fida.gos, 280. Such Portuguese noblemen as held employments at court formerly, received a salary from the king. Noblemen of Portugal accustomed, like those of Spain, to renounce their country upon any discontent, 281.
────── of France divided into four classes, 1. princes of the blood; 2. upper nobility; 3. common ancient nobility; 4. new nobility. Such of the king's natural sons as have been declared legitimate, next in rank to the princes of the blood, ii. 31. Dukes and peers of France at the head of the upper nobility, 32. Common nobility divided into nobles by descent and nobles by birth, 33. New nobility, of whom composed, 33, 34. This kind of nobility hereditary. Nobility, how forfeited in France, 35. Nobility exempt from taxes, and the quartering of soldiers, ibid. Noble families in France reckoned at 40,000, ib.
────── of England, divided into higher and lower. Ranks and titles of the higher nobility, ii. 212, 213. Nobility made saleable under James I. 214. Titles of the lower noblesse in England, 215. Rank of the English nobility and gentry determined by acts of parliament and decrees of the crown, ibid.

Normans, noted for craftiness, ii. 23.

North Laplanders and Samojedes, the only two European nations among whom there are any remains of paganism, i. 117.

Northern nations, with the Germans, Dutch, and English, their own carriers for Dutch goods, ii. 144.

North, Russian power so formidable there, as to make a particular balance necessary in the affairs of Europe, i. 196.

Norway, kingdom of, differently named by the Danes and Swedes, iii. 6. Subject to the government of Denmark almost four hundred years, ib. Extent of, 6, 7. Climate of, 7. Mountains and rivers of, ib. Horned cattle, plenty in Norway, ib. Norway horses, well-shaped, strong,

strong, and swift, ib. Game of all sorts plenty in Norway, ib. Abundantly supplied with fish, 7, 8. It's forests abound with oaks and firs, 8. Grain, scarce in Norway, ibid. Its greatest wealth consists in its metals, ibid. Division of Norway, ib. Norwegia, character of, 28, 29. Norway, constitution of, 38. Reformation, when introduced into, 57. Has four sees, 59. Laws of Norway, 65. Courts of justice of, 67. Skaiters of, 69.

Nueva recompilacion de las leyes de essos regnos, a new code of Spanish laws, compiled by order of Philip II. augmented by several of his successors, i. 122.

Number of lawyers in France, a detriment to the state, ii. 106.

――――― of colleges at the university of Paris, ii. 45. Ten of these for the lower classes, 89.

O.

OATHS taken by the king of France at his coronation, account of, ii. 56, 57.

――――― taken by the members of the English house of commons on the meeting of the parliament, ii. 222.

――――― of fealty, taken by the French archbishops, bishops, and abbots, registered in the chamber of accounts at Paris, ii. 108.

Oats, almost the only grain in the highlands of Scotland, ii. 177.

Odensee, a collegiate school in Denmark, with six professors, iii. 62.

Officers belonging to the king of Spain's houshold, i. 201, 202.

――――― of the crown of France, next in dignity to the lord chancellor, are, the lord steward of the houshold: the lord high admiral: marshals of France: grand-master of the ordnance: to these some add the lord chamberlain: the great huntsman: the master of the horse, and lord almoner, ii. 65.

――――― relating to the king of France's table, kitchen, and cellar, under the lord steward of the houshold. Most of them appointed by him, ii. 66.

――――― of all ranks in France, rewarded according to their merit. The worn-out and disabled, maintained at the Invalids and other hospitals, ii. 116.

――――― of the fleet, and other naval placemen, formerly nominated by the admiral of France. That privilege retained for the crown by Lewis XIV. ii. 121.

TABLE.

Officers of state at the court of England, account of. The most remarkable, ii. 250, 251, 252.

——— and servants belonging to the court of England, account of, ii. 252, 253.

Offices of constable, marshal, and great standard-bearer, formerly subsisted in Portugal, but were afterwards abolished, and the titles of them alone are hereditary in some eminent families, i. 295.

Oil, art of painting in, invented by John Von Eyck. English lay claim to this honour, i. 131.

Old and disabled soldiers, comfortably provided for in Chelsea-hospital, ii. 284.

Orange, formerly a free principality, now annexed to the government of Dauphiné, ii. 10.

Oratory and poetry of the English, account of, ii. 268, 269.

——— and poetry flourished in Gaul, under the Roman dominion, ii. 92.

——— state of, in England, by no means flourishing, ii. 268.

Opposition and corruption, the names substituted in the room of those of Whig and Tory, ii. 232.

Order of St. Michael, the most antient temporal order of knighthood in France. Instituted by Lewis XI. Number of the knights of, ii. 36. Sign of the order. Fell in the reign of Henry II. Restored by Lewis XIV. ii. 68.

——— of St. Lewis. Founded by Lewis XIV. Knights of, sometimes amount to three or four thousand. Ensign of, ii. 69, 70.

——— of Jesuits, expelled France, in 1762, ii. 77.

——— of Lazarus, introduced by Lewis IX. United with the order of our Lady of mount Carmel. Considerable revenues bestowed upon it by Lewis XIV. in 1680, ii. 78.

——— of knighthood, instituted by Lewis XV. for Protestant officers. Entitled Ordre du Merite militaire. Ensign of the order, ii 71.

——— of the Holy Ghost in France, the only order of knighthood in Europe, that has a salary annext to it, i. 117.

——— of St. James, supposed to have been brought out of Spain into Portugal under Alphonso I. Has sixty commanderies, i. 308.

——— of Christ. Chief religious order in Portugal. Instituted by king Dennis, in the year 1319. Has 454 commanderies, i. 308.

——— and ceremonies to be observed at the coronation of a king of France, settled by Lewis VI. on occasion of crowning his son Philip II. ii. 56.

——— of the Golden Fleece, account of, i. 202, 203.

Order

TABLE.

Order of the Garter, the principal order of knighthood amongst the English. Instituted by Edward III. Number of knights belonging to it twenty-five, exclusive of the king. Ensign of, ii. 253.

—— of the Bath, instituted by Henry IV. Number of knights belonging to it fixed at thirty-seven by George I. Ensign of. Motto of, ii. 254.

—— of the Thistle, or St. Andrew, instituted by James V. king of Scotland. Number of knights belonging to it twelve, besides the king. Revived by queen Anne. Ensign of, ii. 254.

Orders of St. Jago, Calatrava, Alcantara, & Montesa, still subsist in Spain, i. 214.

—— and letters from the king of Portugal to his subjects, how begun and ended, i. 286, 287.

—— for every thing relative to the revenue, taxes, contributions, &c. issued in France by the council of finances, ii 148.

Ordinances of Lewis XIV. have been collected and published, ii. 104.

—— mandates, commissions, and letters during a regency in France, run in the king's name, ii. 54.

Ordinary and extraordinary assemblies, held by the clergy of France. Ordinary assemblies of the clergy, either great or small. Former meet every ten years, the latter every five years after the former. Extraordinary assemblies convened only upon an emergency. Assemblies of the clergy convened only by order of the king, ii. 86.

Ores of copper, iron, white and black lead, and, according to some, of gold and silver, found in the large mountains of Scotland, ii. 177.

Origin and increase of the British colonies in America, owing to the intestine troubles in England, ii. 187.

—— of the English, account of. The old Britons intermixed with their conquerors the Romans. Both driven out and extirpated by the Saxons and Angles. Angles and Saxons succeeded by the Danes. Normans brought over by William I. Protestants fled over to England during the oppressions in the Spanish Netherlands, and after the revocation of the edict of Nantz. The English, a conflux of several nations, ii. 200

—— of the antient European nobility in general owing to war, i. 98.

—— of the states of Poland, iii. 239. States of Poland composed of the senators and the nobility, ibid.

Original languages of Europe, divided into the greater and lesser. The greater, three in number, the Latin, German,

and

and Sclavonian, i. 92. The lesser, eight in number, 1. The Greek. 2. The Cantabrian, used in Biscay and part of Navarre. 3. The Cambrian, used in the principality of Wales and Lower Brittany. 4. The Irish, used in Ireland and the Highlands of Scotland. 5. The Islandic, used in Iceland, and some parishes of Dalecarlia. 6. The Finnish, used in Finland, Esthonia, and Lapland. 7. The Lithuanian used in Livonia, Courland, part of Lithuania, and Prussian Lithuania. 8. The Turkish, in Turkey and Crim Tartary, 94, 95.

Orkney islands, belonging to Scotland, twenty-eight in number. That of Pomona the largest. These islands formerly fiefs under the kings of Norway. Annexed to the crown of Scotland in the reign of James III. ii. 181.

Orleans, canal of, takes its beginning from the Loing, and at Port Morant, two miles above Orleans, runs into the Loire. The house of Orleans by an agreement with the undertakers, has the profits of it, ii. 143.

Orthodox, a title formerly bestowed on Casimir king of Poland, by the pope, now grown obsolete, iii. p. 275.

Overnia, an ancient name of Ireland, ii. 181.

Oxford, university of, said to be founded by king Alfred the Great, ii. 264.

—— earl of, founder of the South-sea-company, ii. 316.

Oysters, plenty of, the best supplied by the English sea and rivers, ii. 174.

P.

Painting, three schools of, Italian, Flemish, and French, i. 130.

Paris, has two colleges, besides the university. College-Royal, and that of Louis the Grand, ii. 205.

Parliament of Great Britain, account of, ii 219—229.

Parliaments, twelve in France, of which that of Paris is the principal, ii. 205.

Parties, and their ill effects, i. 25, 26.

Peace of Aix la Chapelle, put an end to the war of 1740, i. 90.

Peter the Great, assumed the title of Emperor of Russia, in the year 1700, iii. 572.

Petersburg, reckoned to consist of 80,000 houses, most of them of wood. Contains 150,000 inhabitants. An hundred thousand men perished at laying its foundations, iii. 381, 382.

Philip

TABLE.

Philip II. of Spain, possessed of dominions more extensive than any of his predecessors, i. 84. This prince's reign the period of Spanish grandeur, i. 84.

Philosophy, little cultivated in the English universities, ii. 270. State of in France, ii. 94, 95.

Poland, derivation of the name of, iii. 209. Situation and confines of, 210. Air and weather of, ib. Mountains of. The Carpathian mountains the principal, 211. Rivers of, the most remarkable are the Vistula, Warta, Niester, Bogg, Nieper, Dwina, Memel, ib. Lakes of, the most extensive, Goplor, ibid. Fertility of, in the animal kingdom, 211. In the vegetable kingdom, 212. In the mineral kingdom, ib. Divided into three chief provinces, Little Poland, Great Poland, and the Great dutchy of Lithuania, ib. Little Poland, contains eleven palatinates, 212, 213. Great Poland and Lithuania contain nine palatinates each. Each palatinate is divided into circles, 213. Polish Prussia ceded by the treaty of Thorn to Poland, by the Teutonic knights in 1466, 214. Polish Prussia contains three palatinates. Retains its liberties, though incorporated into the kingdom of Poland, 215.

——— domestic concerns of the kingdom of, 316, 317. Foreign concerns of the kingdom of, 316, 317. Foreign concerns of, 317, 318. Principal treaties between Poland and other powers, 319—321.

Poles, origin and short history of. The Poles, a branch of the Sclavi. According to the most probable conjecture, descended from the Larzi, iii. 219. Christianity settled in Poland as the established religion by Micislaus I. His son Boleslaus I. who assumed the title of king of Poland, 220. The present inhabitants of Poland, a mixture of several nations, 231. Polish language, derived from the Sclavonian, 233. Number of the inhabitants of Poland, 235. The inhabitants of Poland divided into three classes, nobility, burghers, and peasants, ibid.

Polish diet, consists of 330 persons. Polish diet threefold, ordinary, extraordinary, and occasional. Ordinary diet, how summoned. Its continuance fixed to six weeks. Method of transacting business in the diet, regulated by sixteen laws, 243—250. Extraordinary diets, what. Generally last only a fortnight, or three weeks. Never to be held but upon the most urgent occasions, 250. Country diets, 250, 251. Report diet, account of, 251. Other provincial diets held annually, ibid.

——— assembly of the council of state, account of, 252, 253. Public associations of Poland, account of, 253, 254, 255.

TABLE.

Polish king's prerogative, account of, 255, 256, 257. Obligations which the king of Poland lies under, 257, 258. Poland, an elective kingdom, 258, 259, 260. Polish king's death always occasions an interregnum, 260. Polish king's title, 273, 274, 275. Polish arms; account of, 275, 276. Polish queen, obligations imposed upon, 276, 277. Polish king's sons have no right to the crown. Are to be employed in publick affairs only by consent of the states. Are stiled most illustrious, and bear the arms of Poland and Lithuania, 277. Polish crown, and court; great officers, 278, 279, 280. Polish great military officers, 280, 281. Polish land employments, 281. Polish land dignitaries, 281, 282. Poland, ecclesiastical state of. Archbishops of, two in number. Bishops of, fifteen in number. Archbishop of Gnesna, principal ecclesiastic and primate of Poland and Lithuania. The lower clergy in Poland and Lithuania, very numerous. Above two thirds of the lands of the kingdom of Poland possessed by the clergy, 283—286. Pope's power in Poland, 286, 287. Tolerated religions in Poland, 287, 288, 289. Religious peace, account of, 288, 289. Dissidents, account of, 289, 290. Socinians, Mennonists, Quakers, and Anabaptists, punished with death in Poland. Dissidents allowed the free exercise of their religion in Poland, 290, 291.

Political nature of a country, particulars to be considered in it, i. 13, 14.

Politics, what, i. 6.

Pope and his legates, very powerful in Spain, i. 209, 210. Inquisition, the basis of their power, 210—214. His power inconsiderable in France, 86, 87, 88.

——— titles conferred by him on kings, on account of services done to religion, five in number. 1. Most Christian, on the king of France. 2. Catholic, on the king of Spain. 3. Defender of the Faith, on the king of England. 4. Most Faithful, on the king of Portugal. 5. Apostolic, on the king of Hungary, i. 114.

——— the head of the Roman Catholic church, has usurped the dignity of a divine vicegerent. Sole and supreme judge in matters of faith, i. 119.

Portugal, name of, whence derived, i. 159, 160. Situation and bounds of, ib. Air and temperature of, ibid. Hills of, 261. Rivers of, ib. Products of in the animal kingdom, 261, 262. Products of in the vegetable kingdom, 262. Products of in the mineral kingdom, 263. Division of the kingdom of, 264. Dependencies of, In the Atlantic ocean. In Africa. In Asia. In America, 265—268. Origin, and revolutions of, 268—274.

TABLE.

The Portuguese a mixed people, 274. Character of, 274—277. Antipathy between them and the Spaniards, 277. Portuguese language, very different from the Spanish, 278. Best Portuguese spoken in Entre Minho & Douro; worst in Tra os Montes. Number of the inhabitants of Portugal. Causes of its diminution, 278, 279. Portuguese nobility, divided into high and low, 179, 180, 181. Portuguese form of government, 281, 282. Portuguese fancy themselves the principal people in the world, 289, 290. Portugal, a fief and tributary to the see of Rome, 290, 291. Portuguese royal family, a branch of that of France, 293. Portuguese state and court-officers, 294, 295. State of religion in Portugal, 295, 296, 297. Pope, his great power in Portugal, 300, 301, 302. Portuguese inquisition, account of, 302, 305. Portuguese clergy, great number and wealth of, 307. Portuguese poets, account of, 312. Philosophy obstructed in Portugal by the inquisition, 312, 313. Portuguese laws, account of, 314, 315. Portuguese marine, account of, 319, 320, 321. Portuguese coins, account of, 321—323. Revenues of the crown of, their sources, 323—326. Portuguese, neglect agriculture for trade, 326. Neglect their manufactories, 326, 327. Account of their domestick and foreign trade, 327—329. Portuguese trading companies, account of, 330. Portuguese dependencies, how governed, 332, 333.

Posts, advantageous to commerce, i. 148.

Precedency, amongst Christian potentates, allowed to the emperor of Germany, i. 113.

Prince, title of, granted in England and France only to the males of the royal family. This title very uncommon in Spain and Portugal, but common in Italy, i. 100.

Principal officers belonging to the courts of emperors and kings, five in number, 1. The high steward. 2. The grand marshal. 3. The great chamberlain. 4. The great cup-bearer. 5. The master of the horse, i. 116.

Printing, literature, and science, how promoted by it, i. 46, 47.

——— academy, founded at Madrid, by Charles III. i. 221.

——— present state of in France, ii. 100. Greatly improved in England and Scotland, 274.

Protestant religion, subdivided into three principal branches, Lutheranism, Calvinism, and the church of England, i. 123.

Provinces of Sweden, governed by four and twenty land captains. Finland and Pomerania have each their governor-generals, i. 200.

Prussia,

TABLE.

Pruſſia, the towns and nobility of, governed by two different laws, iii. 295.

───── Eaſtern, retained by the Teutonic knights as a fief under the ſovereignty of Poland. Granted as a ducal fief to the grand-maſter Albert, margrave of Brandenburg. Devolved afterwards to the electoral houſe of Brandenburg. Erected into a kingdom by Frederick III. elector of Brandenburg, in 1701, 214, 215.

Q.

Qualities attributed to the king of England, ii. 227, 228.

Quarter of the national debt in England, the whole ſhare of foreigners, ii. 301.

Quarter-ſeſſions in England, account of, ii, 278.

Queen-dowager, appointed both curatrix and regent by the will of the ſovereign in unlimited monarchies, i. 109.

Queen Elizabeth in the war between her and Philip II. maintained a greater fleet than any of her predeceſſors, ii. 285. Naval force, and trade of the Engliſh greatly encreaſed in her reign, ib. Ready money in England computed at four millions towards the end of her reign, 293. Manufactures greatly encouraged by her, 305.

───── Anne, had the ſum of 700,000 l. aſſigned her for her civil liſt, ii. 299

Queens of Spain, who have ſons buried in the Pantheon, or royal vault at the Eſcurial. Other queens, and the infants or infantas, interred in two vaults under the church, i. 201.

Queſtion whether Catholiciſm or Proteſtantiſm be the ſtronger party debated. i. 124, 125.

───── whether the Proteſtant or Roman Catholic religion be moſt beneficial to a ſtate decided, i. 125, 126.

Queſtions of a country gentleman, Bayle's anſwers to, applicable to the French and Spaniards, i. 177.

───── annually propoſed to all the learned in Europe, by the French academies, thoſe of Peterſburg, and Berlin, and the Royal Society at Gottingen. A medal the prize of the beſt anſwer, i. 229.

Quevedo, Don Franciſco, one of the eminent Spaniſh poets, i. 218.

Quimper Corentin, a ſuffragan biſhop in Bretagne, ii. 75.

Quirquina, one of the commodities with which Europe is ſupplied by America, ii. 144.

Quota, furniſhed by each of the five boards of admiralty in the United Provinces, upon a reſolution of the ſtates to ſend a fleet to ſea, ii. 414.

R.

TABLE.

R.

Raising of the nobility in Poland, account of, iii. 205, 206, 207.

Reformation divided Europe into two religious parties, one adhering to the pope, the other separating from him, i. 83.

Reflections on the Polish form of government, iii. 267—272.

Regency, in what cases appointed, i. 35.

Regents, appointed in a minority, i. 108, 109.

Religion, the several different ones that prevail in different parts of the world. Difference between established and tolerated religions. Advantages of the Christian religion, i. 40, 41, 42.

———— state of, in Spain, i. 203, 204, 205.

———— state of, in France, iii. 72, 73, 74.

———— state of, in Sweden, iii. 168, 169. The Swedes always exceeding zealous for Lutheranism, i. 168, 169, 170.

———— state of, in Great Britain, ii. 255—259.

———— state of, in Denmark, iii. 55—57. Reformation, when introduced in, 57, 58. Rules of faith in the Danish church, 58, 59.

———— Roman Catholic, which, that or the Protestant party the strongest, i. 123. Which, that or the Protestant religion, most conducive to the national good, 155, 156.

———— state of, in Russia, iii. 385. Christianity first introduced in that kingdom by Uladimir I. who was baptised in the year 989. Greek church established in Russia. Public service performed in the Sclavonian language. Extravagant devotion paid by the Russians to St. Nicholas. Fasts observed by them much more strictly than in the Romish church, 386. A schism arose in the Russian church in the XVIIth century. The schismaticks double taxed, and distinguished by a bit of square red cloth on the back of their coats. Endeavours used to effect an union between the Russian and Romish churches, 387, 388. Russian church, under the inspection of the patriarch of Constantinople. Metropolitan of Russia, at first appointed by the patriarch of Constantinople. Afterwards chosen by the Russian clergy themselves, 389. An ecclesiastical commission for the administration of church-affairs, appointed by Peter I. in 1719. Called the sacred synod. Russian clergy at present under two metropolitans, the metropolitan of Kiow, and metropolitan of Tobolski. Archbishops and bishops of Russia twenty-seven in number. Called by the common name of Archirei. These no way subor-

TABLE.

subordinate to each other, 391. Number of monasteries for both sexes very numerous in Russia. Lower clergy of Russia are the protopen, or archpriests, the popes or priests, and the deacons, 392, 393. Russians formerly of opinion that orthodoxy was to be found in their church alone, 393. Both the Lutherans and Reformed tolerated in Russia. The Catholics, Armenian Christians, and Moravian brethren likewise allowed freedom of conscience. Mahometans and pagans very numerous in Russia. A society instituted there for propagating Christianity, 394, 395.

Religious orders of knighthood, bound by their institution to defend and propagate the Christian religion by the sword, i. 121.

Republic of St. Marino, the most inconsiderable in Europe, i. 77.

Residence of a sovereign, where, i. 37.

Resignation, twelve remarkable examples of, amongst the European monarchs, i. 111.

Revenues of a state, whence they arise, and means of increasing them, i. 53—60.

—— of France, exceed those of the rest of Europe, i. 139.

—— of the European nations, very different, i. 139.

—— of the republic of Poland, iii. 312—314.

—— of the crown of Spain, account of, i. 231—236.

—— state of, in Scotland, ii. 296. In Ireland, ib.

—— national of Great Britain, greatly increased by the commodities imported from the East-Indies, Africa, and America, ii. 197. Revenue, how levied in England, 297, 298. Some branches of, farmed in Scotland, 298. Revenue, levied in Ireland in the same manner as in England, ib. King's particular revenue, account of, 310, 311, 312.

Revolt of the Catalonians, occasioned by Philip III. engaging in a war against the Protestants of Germany. Revolt of the kingdom of Portugal owing to this, i. 169.

Right of the states of a realm at the extinction of the royal family, i. 110.

Riphean mountains, form the most natural boundary between Europe and Asia, according to Strahlenberg, i. 71.

Rivers and waters, the advantages resulting from them to a kingdom, i. 11.

—— of Spain, not navigable, on account of the many rocks, sand banks, and water-falls, i. 158.

Roman Catholic religion prevails in Portugal, Spain, Italy, France, Hungary, Poland, the Austrian Netherlands, part of Germany, Swisserland, and Transilvania. Tolerated in the United Provinces, Denmark, Prussia, Russia, and Turkey.

TABLE.

Turkey. Likewife in England and Ireland, but not with the exercife of public worfhip, i. 119.

Roman Catholic religion, ftate of, more profperous than that of the Proteftants, as it is more united, i. 122.

——— Catholics, much fuperior to the Proteftants in number. Superior likewife in the article of having a general head to keep them united. The Proteftants notwithftanding this, a match for their adverfaries, i. 125.

——— Catholic and Proteftant univerfities, differ greatly in their conftitution. Science, more improved by the latter than the former, on account of their greater freedom of fpeaking and writing, i. 129.

——— Catholic countries, ftill cultivate fcholaftic philofophy and divinity. Both thefe ftudies neglected by Proteftants, i. 126.

Romances, origin of, i. 127. 128.

Romance, or Spanifh language, a compound of the languages of the Vandals, Suevi, Vifigoths, and Moors. The Roman predominant in it, i. 178.

Romans, drove the Carthaginians out of Spain, i. 172.

——— kept poffeffion of Spain above four hundred years, i. 165.

Royal prerogative of the king of England, ii. 226—228.

——— family of France, the moft antient in Europe, i. 112.

——— family of Spain, a branch of that of Bourbon, i. 199.

Runic characters made ufe of by the Swedes, iii. 132.

Ruffia, account of the name, iii. 123, 124. Situation, extent, and limits of, 325, 326. Climate, and weather of, 326. Mountains of, 327. Remarkable rivers of, 327, 328. Fertility of, in the animal, in the vegetable, in the mineral kingdom, 328—331. Ruffia, the empire of, divided into European and Afiatic. Divided likewife into Proper Ruffia, and the conquered countries. The former divided into Great, Small, and White Ruffia, 331, 332. Origin and Revolutions of, 333—344. Character of, 344. 345. Peter the Great, very much perplexed to bring about the alterations he had planned, 345. Defcription of the Ruffian's perfons, 346. The Ruffians very fond of external fhew. Ruffians of the lower fort lead a wretched life, 346. Ruffians breed up their children very hard, 346, 347. Ruffians greatly addicted to drunkennefs, 347. Ruffian language derived from the Sclavonian, 348. Has forty-two letters, ib. Ruffian empire as large as France and Germany. ibid. Number of the inhabitants computed at 12,000,000. Including the Finlanders, Livonians, Efthonians, Coffacks, Kalmucks, Tartars, Samoeides, and Laplanders, they are computed at 15,000,000.

TABLE.

Russian nobility, formerly divided into kniases, i. e. princes or dioorenins, or common noblemen. Russian princes, divided into three classes, 351, 352. Russian nation consists of three classes, nobility, burghers, and peasants, 354. Russian monarchs always the most arbitrary of all Europe, ib. Russian empire, chiefly destined for the fair sex, 369. Russian coronation, ceremonies attending it, 376, 377.

S.

Sciences and arts, the several sorts of, i. 43, 44, 45. State of the sciences in Europe, i. 126.

Sclavonian language, comprehends the third part of Europe. Spoken by sixty different nations according to some. The Russian, Bohemian, and Moravian, derived from it. Used with different dialects in Hungary, Stiria, the Ukraine, and Lusatia, i. 94.

Scotland, fertility of, ii. 176. Blue amethists, agates, pebbles, of an exquisite lustre when polished. Magnets and crystals found in some parts of Scotland, 177. Division of, 180. Scots, origin of, 200. Language in the Lowlands and Highlands, 209. Nobility of, 216. Form of government of, 217, 218. Has its own laws and customs, 276. Standard of money in, 293.

Seamen in England, better paid than in other countries, ii. 288. When worn out or disabled, plentifully provided for in Greenwich hospital, ib.

Seminaries of learning, different sorts of, and their advantages, i. 46.

Senators of Poland, one hundred forty-six in number, iii. 242.

Silesia belonged formerly to Poland, granted to king John of Bohemia by Casimir the Great, in 1335, iii. 217.

Silk-worms, now bred in most European countries, i. 75.

Sinking fund, account of, ii. 302—304.

Situation of a country, to what relative, i. 7, 8.

Skaldrers, or poets of the North, account of, iii. 63.

Sleswick, dutchy of, how governed, iii. 6.

Soap, best, that of Marseilles and Toulon, ii. 142.

Society, the end of, i. 2.

Solemnities on a prince's accession to the throne, i. 115, 116.

Soroe, an academy of gentlemen in Denmark, with seven professors, iii. 62.

Sovereignty, definition of, i. 2.

Spain, derivation of the name of, i. 155, 156. Situation and limits of. Temperature and air of, ib. Hills of. Rivers

vers of, 157, 158. Fruitfulfulness of, in the animal, vegetable, and fossile kingdoms, 158, 159, 160. Division of, 161. Dependencies of, 162, 163. Its former dependencies in Europe, 164. Peopled by the Gaulish Celts, 164—170. Spaniards, a mixt people, 171, 172. Character of, 172—176. Antipathy between them and the French, 176, 177. Language of, 177, 178, 179. Number of inhabitants of, 179, 180. Spanish nobility, divided into upper and lower, 180, 181, 182. Spanish form of government, the several revolutions it has undergone, 183—187. Spanish fundamental laws, 187—191. Spanish kings, their title, &c. 191—194. Their arms, 194—196. Precedency claimed by them before all Christian kings, 196, 197. Spanish lawyers, very numerous, and in great esteem amongst foreigners, 219. Spaniards, inferior to the rest of the Europeans in physick and surgery, 220. The most celebrated warriors and statesmen of, 254, 255. Historical accounts of, 255—257.

Spain, the first European power in the XVIth century, i. 91. Spanish territories, united under one sovereignty by the marriage of Ferdinand of Arragon with Isabella of Castile, i. 82. Devolved to the house of Austria, between the archduke Philip and the infanta Joan, ib. Charles V. the fruit of this marriage, united in his person the dignities of Roman emperor and king of Spain, ib.

Stadtholdership, brief account of, ii. 382—389. Stadtholder's prerogative, 389—392. Stadtholdership, whether essential and necessary to the fundamental constitution of the state, and whether of advantage to it, 392—395. Parties relating to the stadtholder, 395, 396. Stadtholder's title, 397.

States, at first not so perfect as at present, i. 1.

——— of the realm, empowered to elect a new king, upon the failure of the reigning family, i. 110.

State, territory of, i. 2. United states, definition of, 5. Essential objects of. Contingencies of, 5, 6. How to be considered with regard to state-interest. State-interest, foreign and domestic, 62. How domestic state-interest varies in the several different forms of government, 63, 64. Foreign state-interest, variable and uncertain, 64, 65. False state-interest, what, 65.

——— four classes of European states, relative to their actual force, according to baron Bielfeld ; 1. Those which, besides a large land and naval force, have also a sufficiency of money. 2. Those which in themselves are strong, but stand in need of alliances and pecuniary assistance. 3. Such as are unable to engage in war, except as parties. 4. Such as have no immediate share in the great transactions of Europe,

TABLE.

Stifsampfters of Denmark, account of, iii. 6.
Stuart-line, being extinct in the person of queen Anne, it was provided by the parliament, that the electoral house of Brunswick Luneburg, should sit upon the throne, i. 111.
Subjects, definition of, i. 3.
Succession, male and female, and mixt, i. 33. Election compact, what, ibid.
——— to the throne, the nature of, 106, 107. Succession in the European hereditary families, either male or mixed, ibid.
——— to the empire of Russia, how settled, iii. 359—361. Law concerning the succession to the empire of Russia, cause of most of the commotions which have arisen in that country, 361—369.
——— to the crown of Denmark, how settled, iii. 39, 40, 41, 42.
Sweden, derivation of the name of, iii. 107, 108. Situation, limits, and extent of, 108. Air, and weather of, 109. Mountains, lakes, and rivers of, ibid. Fertility of, 110—112. Division of, 112—114. Dependencies of, 114. Summary of the history of, 114—131. Swedish language, account of, 131. Number of the inhabitants of, 132, 133. Swedish nobility, account of, 133, 134. Swedish burghers and peasants, account of, 134, 135. New and present government of Sweden, 140, 141. Fundamental laws of Sweden, 141. States of the kingdom and diet of Sweden, 141—144. Privileges and obligations of the states of Sweden, 144—146. Council of state of Sweden, 146—148. Rights of the crown of Sweden, 148—150. King of Sweden's obligations, 149, 150. Absolute sovereignty abhorred in Sweden, 150—152. Judgment on the form of government of Sweden, 152—154. Overthrow of the Swedish government foretold by a modern author, 154, 155. The Swedish and English constitutions compared, 155—157. Parties in Sweden, account of, 157, 158. Succession to the crown of Sweden, how settled, 158—160. Regency and guardianship of Sweden, account of, 160, 161. King of Sweden's majority not precisely determined, 161. King of Sweden's accession and coronation, account of, 161, 162. Title of the Swedish king, 162, 163. Arms of, 163, 164. Swedish king's children, their titles, rights, and obligations, 164. Swedish king's residence, 164, 165. Swedish king's household, account of, 165. Flourishing state of the sciences in Sweden, 172, 173. Swedes, their great application in improving their country, 191. Swedish manufactures, account of, 191—193.

Sweden,

TABLE.

Sweden, state affairs of, conduct both foreign and domestic lodged in the council of state. Consists of two departments. Other high offices relative to it, are, the three court tribunals, the war-office, the admiralty, the chancery, the treasury, the exchequer, the mine-office, iii. 200.
—— domestic interest of. Foreign interest of. Treaties of with other powers, iii. 201—235. Remarkable warriors and statesmen of, 205, 206. Remarkable historians of, 206. Accounts of, 207. Sweden in the war of 1700, lost the greatest part of its dependencies, i. 87.

Swifs cantons, owe their rise to the treaties of Munster and Osnabrug, i. 85.

System of laws, varies according to the different form of government, i. 32.

T.

TAgus, much celebrated by the Romans on account of its gold, i. 263.

Tanais, or Don, the river of, considered as the boundary of Europe and Asia, iii. 377.

Tanners: Normandy, Vendome, Limousin, and Tourraine in France, noted for, ii. 142.

Taxes, exceeding grievous in France, ii. 126.

—— paid by the French clergy, ever since the commencement of the monarchy, ii. 83. Taxes paid by the clergy, called tenths, and granted by them to the king every tenth year, ibid.

Templars, knights so called, owed their destruction, and the cruel persecution they underwent, to their prodigious wealth and licentiousness, i. 121, 122.

Teutonic knighthood, either military or honorary. First given as a reward to land or sea-officers. Secondly conferred as marks of particular honour on officers civil and military.

Thames, one of the principal rivers of England. Formed from the conflux of the rivers Thame and Isis. Discharges itself into the North-sea, about sixty miles below London, ii. 172.

Theophrastus Renaudot, a physician of Paris, the first inventor of News-papers, i. 148.

Thirty-one presidents, and two hundred and fourteen counsellors, compose the parliament of Paris, ii. 105, 106.

—— cities in France, have the privilege of a mint. These known by certain marks on the coins, ii. 125.

TABLE.

Thomas de Torquemada, the first inquisitor-general. Caused two hundred persons to be burned during the time of his office, i. 111.

Three courts of coinage in France, Paris, Lyons, and Pau, ii. 108.

—— hundred and twelve millions of livres, the sum at which the revenues of the collective body of France were formerly computed. Four hundred millions, the sum at which they are computed at present, ii. 78.

—— Roman emperors born in Spain, i. 165.

Timber and wood for fuel, scarce in England, on account of the small number of forests, ii. 174.

Titles, conferred on princes by the pope, account of, i. 114, 115.

——— of the hereditary prince, and other royal children of Spain, i. 198, 199.

——— of the superior nobility in German, Latin, French, Italian, Spanish, English. Titles of the inferior, i. 98, 99.

——— of the European monarchs, very prolix, not only with respect to countries which they possess, but likewise with respect to such as do not belong to them, upon three occasions; 1. when they have a right to the reversion or succession of certain lands. 2. When they lay claim to certain states, as France to Navarre. 3. In remembrance of former rights and claims, i. 114.

Title and arms of the king of Portugal, i. 285—289.

——— of the states general, ii. 380, 381. Arms of, 381.

——— of the emperor of Russia. Altered in the year 1721. Whole tenour of the title since this alteration, iii. 371—374.

——— of the presumptive heir to the empire of Russia, iii. 377.

——— of the king of Spain, exceeding prolix, i. 193.

——— of first-born son of the church, given by the pope in his bulls and briefs, to the king of France, ii. 52.

——— of apocrisiarius, given to the head of the court clergy of France, before he had that of lord-almoner, ii. 65.

——— of marshal general, sometimes conferred by the king of France upon one of the marshals of France, as a reward of some extraordinary merit. Gives precedence over all the rest, ii. 113.

Tobacco, Europe indebted for it to the new world, i. 76.

Tobacco and snuff, immense quantities of, exported from Dunkirk, St. Omers, and Strasburg, ii. 142.

Toledo, formerly the residence of the Visigoth kings, and afterwards of those of Castile, i. 199, 200.

TABLE.

Torture, ufed in England in one cafe only, ii. 277.

Toulon, Breft, Port Louis, Rochfort, Havre de Grace, harbours for the king of France's men of war, ii. 122.

Trade, prefent ftate of, in Europe, i. 140, 141, 142. Home trade of Europe, 143. Its trade to other parts of the world, 143, 144. American trade, account of, 145. Eaft-India, detrimental to Europe, 145, 146.

——— carried on between Manilla and Acapulco by the Spaniards, i. 142, 143. Trading companies eftablifhed in Spain, ib.

——— of France, extends to all the four parts of the world. In Europe carried on both by fea and land. Greatly promoted by the feveral fea-ports of that kingdom, ii. 143.

——— to the Levant, chiefly carried on by the French. Favoured by their fituation on the Mediterranean, ii. 144.

——— of France to the Eaft-Indies, formerly very confiderable, in the laft war with Great Britain met with a fenfible fhock. French carry on the greateft part of their Indian trade with filver, and the returns are the fame, ii. 145.

——— French council of, of whom compofed. Deputies of the twelve largeft commercial cities fummoned to it, ii. 151.

——— of Sweden, inland and foreign. Inland trade, account of, i. 193, 194. Foreign trade of, in Europe. To China, 194, 195. Their imports exceed their exports, 195, 196. Trading companies, account of. Company for the Guinea trade. Company of trade and navigation to Afia, Africa, America, and the South countries. Eaft-India-company, 196, 197. Trading, or ftaple-towns of Sweden, four and twenty in number. Stockholm and Gottenburg, the chief of, 199, 200.

——— of Poland, account of, ii. 315, 316.

——— and navigation, make a part of the king of Portugal's title, i. 114.

——— in home manufactures, the moft beneficial of all others. Great numbers at prefent erected in all countries, i. 142.

——— to the Eaft-Indies and China, requires ready money, i. 145.

——— of Scotland, ii. 312. Of Ireland, 312, 313.

Trading companies in England, account of, 1. The Ruffian, i. 313. 2. The Turkey company, 314, 315. 3. The African company, 314, 315. 4. The Eaft-India company, 315, 316. 5. The South-fea company, 316, 317.

Treafon, two-fold, high and petty, ii. 276.

TABLE.

Treaties of peace between France and other powers of Europe, ii. 157.

Treaty of Hanover, between France, Great Britain, and Prussia, occasioned by the treaty of Vienna, i. 88, 89.

Tribunals at Arras, Colmar, and Perpignan, added to the parliaments of France, ii. 206.

Troops, belonging to the marine of France, account of, i. 119.

Turkish, the only despotic government in Europe, i. 103.

Turks, often set on the house of Austria by France, ii. 156.

Tutors, or curators, appointed to take care of the person of a minor king, and regents for the administration. These high offices more frequently united, i. 108.

U.

UBiquists, certain doctors of the faculty of divinity at Paris, so called, ii. 95.

Ulster, one of the four provinces of Ireland, ii. 115.

Unction of the king of France, how performed, ii. 56.

Uniform of regiments, and use of the bayonet, introduced by Lewis XIV. ii. 109.

Union between England and Scotland, effected in the reign of queen Anne, ii. 197. By the earl of Godolphin, 219.

―――― of Utrecht, between the seven United Provinces, effected by the prince of Orange in 1579. Chief contents of, ii. 366–368.

―――― between the provinces of the United Netherlands, strengthened by the stadtholdership, ii. 394.

United Netherlands, derivation of the name of, ii. 337, 338. Situation, limits, and extent of, 338. Air and weather of, 338, 339. Hills of, 339. Rivers of, 339, 340, 341. Fertility of, 342, 343, 344. Counties which compose the state of, 344, 345. Dependencies of, in Europe, 345, 346. In the East-Indies, 346, 347. In Africa, 347, 348. In America, 348. Short history of, 348—358. Language of, 363. Number of inhabitants of, 363, 364. Nobility of, 364, 365, 366. Form of government of, 366, 367, 368. Assembly of the states-general of, 368—371. Extraordinary, or great convention of the states-general of, 372. The supreme power of the state lodged in the particular states of, 373. States of Guelderland, account of. States of Holland, account of, 373, 374. States of Zealand, account of. States of Utrecht, account of, 374, 375. States of Friezland, account of, 375. States of Overyssel, account of, ibid. States of Groningen, account of, 375, 376. Real and singular constitu-

TABLE.

tion of the United Netherlands, 376. Defects of the constitution of the United Netherlands, 377—380. State of religion in the United Netherlands, 398—401. Schools and univerſities in the United Netherlands, 401, 402. State of the ſciences in, 404, 405. Laws of the United Netherlands, 407. Courts of juſtice of the United Netherlands 407, 408. Land-forces of the United Netherlands, 409, 410, 411. Fortified places of, 411. Navy of the United Netherlands, account of, 413, 414. Naval conſtitution of, 414, 415, 416. Coins of, 416. Revenues of the whole ſtate of, 420, 421, 422. And of the particular provinces, 422, 423, 424. State debt of, 424, 425. Manufactures of, 425, 426, 427. Fiſhery of, 427, 428. Herring fiſhery of, 428, 429, 430. Whale fiſhery of, 430, 431. Trade, 431. Home-trade, ibid. Foreign trad, 431—435. Trading companies, 435—439. Weſt-India company, 439, 440. African company, 440. Surinam company, 440, 441. Berbice company, 441. Trading towns of the United Netherlands, 441, 442. Council of ſtate of the United Netherlands, 443—445. General accomptant's office of the United Netherlands, 445. Treaſury office of the United Netherlands, 445, 446. Domeſtic intereſt of the United Netherlands, 446, 447. Foreign intereſt of the United Netherlands, 447, 448. Origin of the inhabitants of the United Netherlands, 359, 360. Character of, 360—362.

United Netherlands, acknowledged as a free ſtate by Philip IV. at the peace of Munſter, i. 169.

——— Netherlands, in a great meaſure owe their exiſtence to the Proteſtant religion, ii. 398.

——— Netherlands, account of the coins of, ii. 418, 419.

——— provinces, at preſent better diſpoſed towards France than Great Britain, on account of the ſuperior naval force of the latter, ii. 154.

——— provinces, thrown into great trouble and perplexity by the prince of Orange's being murdered at Delft. Offer the ſovereignty over them to Henry III. king of France, and afterwards to Elizabeth queen of England, ii. 354.

——— Eaſt-India company, eſtabliſhed in 1701, ii. 315.

Univerſities, number of, amounts to one hundred and thirty in Europe, i. 129. In Spain alone to twenty-two, 216. Two univerſities in Portugal, 309.

——— of Sweden, three in number, Upſal, Abo, and Lund, iii. 170, 171.

——— of Poland, three in number, Cracow, Vilna, and Zamoſcia, iii. 19. State of the ſciences in Poland. Poliſh

lish historians remarkable for their elegant Latin. Poles allowed to be bad orators by an author of their own country, 242. Polish laws, account of, 294.

Universities, all the sciences, both the liberal and the higher taught in, i. 44.

—— in France, besides that of Paris, eighteen in number, ii. 90.

University of Paris, account of, ii. 88—90. Universities in England, account of, 264—266. Universities in Scotland, 266. In Ireland, ib.

—— of Copenhagen, account of, burnt down by the fire in 1728, iii. 60, 61. Rebuilt by king Christian VI. 61. Professors ordinary and extraordinary, amount to fifty, 62.

—— of Oxford, founded by king Alfred, ii. 264.

—— of Utrecht, inaugurated in 1636, and the revenues of a nunnery assigned for its support, ii. 402.

Unlimited monarchies, account of. Tacit fundamental laws, which the prince is bound to observe, i. 30.

—— monarchies in Europe, ten in number, Portugal, Spain, France, Denmark, Russia, Prussia, Sardinia, the Two Sicilies, the pope in the ecclesiastical state, and the grand-master of the order of St. John, in the island of Malta, i. 103.

Upper courts of Spain, account of, i. 225.

Ur-appa, white-face, in the Phœnician language, thought to be the origin of the name of Europe, ii. 70.

Use of fortresses well understood by the French, ii. 115.

—— of Latin, in the law-courts of France, prohibited by Francis I. in the year 1589, ii. 29.

Usury, the prevalence of in Portugal, ascribed to the mixture of Jewish blood, i. 275.

Utrecht, city of, sends two members to the admiralty boards of Holland, ii. 414.

—— peace of, deprived Spain of all its European dependencies, ii. 164.

—— peace of, equally glorious and advantageous to Lewis XIV. i. 86.

V.

Vacancies in the nobility of the seven United Provinces, not yet filled up, ii. 364.

Vacant bishoprics and abbies, revenues of, made part of the royal revenues under the Norman and Plantagenet kings, ii. 294.

TABLE.

Vaderland's history of the United Netherlands, a paper war concerning the De Wit party, occasioned by it, ii. 397.

Valencia, a province belonging to the kingdom of Arragon in Spain, i. 161.

——— Arragon, and Catalonia, incorporated together, with their privileges and incomes, by the decree of a diet held at Terragona in 1319, i. 189.

——— archbishops of, has three suffragans, i. 207.

Value of foreign money, the proportion between that and the money of Holland, variable, ii. 418, 419.

——— of money, formerly the same in Scotland as in England. Afterwards greatly diminished. English standard to take place in Scotland by the treaty of union, ii. 293.

——— of money, the same in Ireland as in England till the time of Edward IV. Then coined one fourth worse than that of England, ii. 293, 294.

——— of the several kinds of grain exported from fifty-seven English harbours, amounted in 1746, and 1750, to 7,405,786 l. ii. 304.

Vamba, a Visigoth king and his successors, down to king Roderigo, both anointed and crowned, i. 197.

Vanhoven, one of the most noted writers against the stadtholdership, ii. 396.

Vanillas, Vigogna wool, timber, cotton, cacao, coffee, cochineal, gems, iron, logwood, fish, gold, hides, indigo, ginger, copper, firs, pearls, pimento, quinquana, rice, sarsaparilla, silver, tobacco, wool, wax, and sugar, commodities with which Europe is supplied by America, i. 144. Vast quantities of silver yielded by the mountains of Potosi in Peru, 163.

Velasco, family of, possessed of the hereditary title of constable of Spain, i. 199.

Velaw and Holland, several parts of, excel in the paper manufacture, ii. 422.

Velvet, gold and silver stuffs, damasks and silks, woollens and cottons of all sorts, manufactured at Amsterdam, ii. 426.

Venereal disease, the commonest disorder in persons of both sexes in Spain, i. 173.

——— disease, said to have been brought from the new world into Europe by the Spaniards, i. 19.

Venetians and Hans-towns, possessed of the best part of the trade of Europe, till the close of the fifteenth century, i. 141.

Venice, bank of, one of the chief banks of exchange in Europe, i. 147.

TABLE.

Venice and Genoa, reftorers of the commerce carried on in the Mediterranean and the Archipelago, i. 140.

Venloo, the Hague, and Middleburg, the places of the three high courts of juftice of the generality-lands in the United Provinces, ii. 408.

Vent of the knives, rafors, and fciffars, made in Auvergne, exceeding great. Five thoufand families faid to live by thefe manufactures, ii. 142.

Verdegreafe, the town of Montpellier, deals greatly in that commodity, ii. 142.

Verponding, a tax laid upon houfes and other immoveables in the United Provinces, ii. 422.

Verfailles, the ufual refidence of the kings of France, fince it was built by Lewis XIV. ii. 62.

Verfes and fongs of the Spanifh rhymers upon religious fubjects, exceeding ludicrous and prophane, i. 205.

Vervins, peace of, concluded between France and Spain in 1598, i. 251.

Viceroys, governors, and even miffionaries of Spain, extremely expert in the art of enriching themfelves, i. 174.

Viceroy, or lord lieutenant of Ireland, at the head of the adminiftration of that kingdom, ii. 322.

Villancios, little copies of verfes, fung in the churches of Spain at the feftivals, i. 205.

Villas, towns of Spain, of a clafs inferior to the ciudades, i. 162.

Villiers, George, duke of Buckingham, an eminent Englifh ftatefman in the reigns of James and Charles I. ii. 331.

Vincennes, Madrid, Meudon, Trianon, Marly, St. Germain en Laye, and Fontainebleau, royal feats belonging to the king of France, ii. 62.

Vinegar, wine, oil, and flefh, taxed at twelve millions in Spain, i. 235.

Vintage not impeded in France by impofts, or other obftructions, ii. 140.

Vifcount, count, duke, marquis, and baron, titles fubftituted in the room of that of ricos hombres amongft the Spanifh nobility, i. 180, 181.

Violent ferments, occafioned by the different opinions of the Leyden profeffors of divinity. Their parties diftinguifhed by the titles of Arminians and Gomarifts. Thefe names afterwards changed to thofe of Remonftrants and Contra-Remonftrants, ii. 298.

Vifigoth kings, their prerogative limited, i. 181.

Vifigoths, kingdom of, brought to a period by the lofs of one decifive battle againft the Moors, i. 166. Vifigoths, the main ftock of the Spanifh nation, 172. Vandals, Suevi,

TABLE.

Suevi, and Alani, after difpoffeffing the Romans of Spain with great flaughter, met with the like treatment from the Vifigoths, ib.

Vifigoths, firft received written laws from their king Eric, i. 221.

——— Burgundians, and Franks, after feating themfelves in Gaul, retained their own laws, but left the Roman law to the old inhabitants, i. 101. Various cuftoms that obtain in the provinces and cities of France, arife from the mixture of laws, ibid.

Vlardingen, a village of the United Provinces, oppofite to which the Old and New Maefe unite, ii. 340.

Volcanos, terrible ravages occafioned by them, i. 10.

Volmachten, the plenipotentiaries fent by the thirty jurifdictions of the three diftricts of Friezland to the general diet, ii. 375.

Vollenhofen, Twenthe, and Salland, the three claffes into which the nobility of Overyffel is divided, ii. 375.

Vondel, author of a tragedy upon the execution of M. Barnevelt, called Palamedes, or Injured Innocence, ii. 399.

——— Vander Gofe, Feitama, Stanwyck, Dutch poets, highly efteemed by their countrymen, ii. 401.

Votes of the deputies of the feven United Provinces, amount to a hundred. All of thefe have an influence on the general affairs, ii. 377.

W.

WAdftena, a houfe for invalids in Sweden, iii. 180.

Walachia and Moldavia, remained under the fovereignty of Poland, till ceded by Sigifmund III. to the Turks in 1621, iii. 218.

Waldenfes, gave the papacy feveral confiderable fhocks in Gaul, towards the clofe of the VIIIth century, ii. 72.

Wales, divifion of, ii. 179. Welfh, origin of, 200. Wales, brought under the dominion of England by Edward I. Incorporated with England by Henry VIII. Divided into twelve counties, ii. 178, 179. Every where mountainous, 171.

Wars, their frequency in France deprives agriculture of hands, ii. 139.

War, art of, greatly improved by the French. ii. 135.

Warriors of France, account of the moft celebrated, ii. 164.

Water colours alone ufed in painting by the antients, i. 131.

Waywodes, account of, iii. 239.

Wealth of the Englifh, ill confequences of, ii. 203.

Weather

TABLE.

Weather, extremely variable in England, ii. 171. Exceeding temperate in Ireland, both in summer and winter, ib.

West-India trade, the most beneficial branch of the French foreign trade, ii. 145, 146.

Western islands, belonging to Scotland, called in Latin Hebrides. Which the largest among these, ii. 181.

——— or Eren, the name given to Ireland by the inhabitants, ii. 182.

Whales, of the lesser species, freequently seen upon the coasts of Scotland. Large ones sometimes stranded there, ii. 182.

Wheat, rice, tobacco, silk, timber and other requisites for ship-building, iron, &c. the products of British America, ii. 187.

Wight, isle of, included in Hampshire, ii. 179.

Wild-fowl, plenty of, in Scotland, ii. 176.

——— and poultry, plenty in Portugal, i. 261.

William III. prince of Orange, raised to the throne of England upon the abdication of James II. ii. 197.

Wills of the king of France, sometimes declared invalid in their most important articles by the parliament of Paris during the time of a minority, ii. 43.

Wines of Spain, formerly disagreeable both in smell and taste. Improved by Charles V. who caused some German wines to be transplanted into Spain, i. 159.

Winter season, rendered extremely disagreeable in Portugal, by the violent rains, i. 260.

Wittena-gemot, name of a parliament in the times of the Anglo-Saxons, ii. 216.

Wolves, Ireland infested by, ii. 182.

Women of England, character of. Greatly indulged by their husbands. Laws of the land in some cases very severe, in others equally favourable to them, ii. 207.

Wool of the Spanish sheep, the finest in Europe, i. 159.

——— of the Portuguese sheep, little inferior to that of the Spanish, i. 161.

Woollen cloths, fine and coarse linens, laces, paper, parchment, tanned leather, porcelain, hardware, verdegrease, salt-petre, soap, bleached wax, snuff, and tobacco, made in such quantities in France, as to afford large exportations, ii. 142.

Writings of Cujas, Hottoman, Duaren, Baudoin, Brison, Donelle, Geoffroy, and other French civilians, much esteemed, ii. 96.

Written law countries in France, those where the Roman law is considered as the law of the land, ii. 102.

TABLE.

X.

XACA, a bishopric within the diocese of Sarragossa, i. 207.

Xamora, a strong fortification of Spain upon the frontiers of Portugal, i. 227.

Xebeques, a sort of small vessels now used by the French, instead of gallies, ii. 119.

Ximenes, Francis de Cisneros, cardinal of Spain, and archbishop of Toledo, one of the most eminent Spanish statesmen, i. 254.

Y.

YAchts, sloops, fire-ships, bomb-ketches, and other vessels belonging to the crown, included in every account of the British navy, ii. 286.

Yarmouth, a remarkable English harbour upon the North-sea, ii. 318.

Yearly marts and fairs of France, greatly promote its inland trade. Those of Beaucaire, Lyons, and Bourdeaux, the most noted, ii. 143.

Yearly income of the states-general, computed at twenty-one millions of guilders. In war-time raised to above double that sum, ii 421.

────── farms of counties and towns, made part of the royal revenues under the Norman and Plantagenet races, ii. 294.

────── rents of all the lands in England computed at ten millions of pounds sterling at the time of the Revolution, ii. 294.

────── produce of the duties on beer, spirituous liquors, malt, hops, paper, coffee, tea, chocolate, and other commodities, computed at a million and a half, ii. 295.

────── national income of England, computed at a hundred millions, ii. 301.

────── prizes, distributed by the Dublin society for the encouragement of manufactures, trade, and agriculture, ii. 307.

────── tax of hereditary posts, one of the king of France's extraordinary revenues, ii. 130.

────── interest of the national debt as it stood in 1764, amounted to 4,688,177 l. 11s. ii. 301.

────── augmentation of the national capital of England, estimated by a modern author at eleven millions and a half, ii. 301.

ERRATA.

VOL. I.

P. 33. l. 15. *for* is, *read* are.
   37.   2. *for* memorial, *r.* memory.
  141.   3. *from the bottom, for* Afiatic, *r.* Anfeatic.
  189.   *ult. for* country, *r.* county.

VOL. II.

P. 149. l. 9. *from the bottom, for* being, *r.* been.
  156.   10. *from the bottom, for* con, *r.* countries.
  218.   12. *for* for, *r.* firft.
  307.   2. *for* inconfiderable, *r.* confiderable.
  382.   7. *for* ftate, *r.* of the republic.
  398.   18. *for* election, *r.* elect.
  420.   1. *for* have, *r.* has.
  431.   1. *after* train, *infert* oil.

VOL. III.

P.   2. l. 1. *for* his, *r.* this.
   12.   9. *for* who, *r.* which.
  264.   *penult. for* waiting, *r.* wait.
  283.   8. *for* late, *r.* prefent.
  325.   3 and 4. *for* 10 to 25 deg. north lat. *r.* 15, 20 to 25 deg. in breadth.
  371.   9. *d.le* a *lefore* fubject.

www.ingramcontent.com/pod-product-compliance
Lightning Source LLC
Chambersburg PA
CBHW022108290426
44112CB00008B/597